GROWING OLD The Social Problems of Aging

ELIZABETH S. JOHNSON
Boston University

John B. Williamson
Boston College

HOLT, RINEHART AND WINSTON
New York Chicago San Francisco Dallas
Montreal Toronto London Sydney

To
Anna Libera and Margaret Butler

The authors would like to express their appreciation to the following authors and publishers for permission to reprint their work:

Table 3–1, "Sources of Aged's Personal Income, 1972." Reprinted from Marilyn Moon, *The Measurement of Economic Welfare.* New York: Academic Press, 1977.

Excerpts from "The Elderly Easy Targets for Teenagers," by Mike Barnacle. Reprinted courtesy of The Boston Globe.

Excerpts from *Working: People Talk about What They Do All Day and How They Feel About What They Do,* by Studs Terkel. Copyright © 1975 Pantheon Books, A Division of Random House, Inc.

Library of Congress Cataloging in Publication Data

Johnson, Elizabeth S
  Growing old.

  Includes bibliographies and index.
    1. Aged—United States—Social conditions.
2. Aging. 3. Age discrimination—United States.
4. Aged—Psychology. I. Williamson, John B.,
joint author. II. Title.
HQ1064.U5J64 301.43'5'0973   78-67459

ISBN 0-03-040316-2

PREFACE

Growing old is a universal experience which can be made more difficult for an individual because of societal attitudes and values, and the practices which exist because of them. Throughout this book we ask which sub-groups of the aging are especially vulnerable to the negative aspects of growing old. Do victimization, exploitation, discrimination, oppression, and other such injustices affect some of the aging more than others? Why do these injustices persist? These questions provide a framework around which our discussion of the social problems of aging is organized.

The need for consciousness raising on issues related to racism and sexism has come to be taken for granted by many. The terms "racism" and "sexism" have been used in referring to the various stereotypes and forms of institutional discrimination perpetrated against women and racial minorities. In recent years it has become increasingly evident that there is a parallel need with respect to the injustices experienced by people because of the fact that they are aging or aged. "Ageism" has been used to refer to institutional forms of discrimination of the aged. In the chapters that follow we will expand on the concept of ageism. We will define and then extensively use four categories of injustice—victimization, exploitation, discrimination, and oppression—which are aimed at aging and aged individuals.

In our analysis of the injustices directed at people because of their advancing age, we have attempted to be analytical and base our conclusions as much as possible on empirical research evidence. Our goal is to present a balanced, rather than a polemic, analysis of the various forms of victimization, discrimination, exploitation, and oppression that confront the aging and the aged.

This is no easy task given that such terms are typically used in the context of a polemic analysis. How is it possible to organize a discussion around these concepts and, at the same time, purport to offer a balanced analysis? Our strategy has been to ask whether or not the aging and the aged are in fact being victimized; that is, we ask whether the popular conception has a basis in reality. In some cases we find that it does not. We also find it useful to distinguish among different subgroups of the elderly. We often find that some subgroups of the aged population are being oppressed or exploited, but that other groups are quite insulated from the experience.

Some popular conceptions about the injustices experienced by older people are not always consistent with the evidence when the issues are examined systematically. Instead we sometimes find more subtle forms of victimization, discrimination, exploitation, and oppression, forms which are different from popular conceptions but equally oppressive. The prevalent belief that the elderly are more likely to be victims of crime is one such stereotype. In reality, it turns out that the elderly are less likely to be victimized by most forms of crime than are other age groups. However, when we take a closer look, we find that certain subgroups of the elderly, such as the elderly poor living in the inner city, are more likely to be victimized than other elderly groups. Furthermore, many of the elderly restrict their life styles in order to avoid dangerous situations. The fear of crime affects many more people than does the actual experience of being victimized.

This heterogeneity of the elderly with respect to vulnerability to criminal victimization also extends to a variety of other social problem areas that tend to be associated with aging. In general, those who are financially better off and who are relatively healthy have more choices available to them; they are less at the mercy of their social environment.

The term "aging" is used frequently in this book for a specific reason. Although many of the issues with which we deal are primarily applicable to those who are already old, there are other issues which concern people who have started to age, but who are not yet elderly. The discrimination against older workers begins long before they reach retirement age. Similarly, it is not uncommon for people to become quite concerned about the signs of physical aging that appear in their thirties and forties. This concern increases their vulnerability to exploitation by those who offer ways to restore the look of youth.

Finally we address ourselves to the ways in which the aged contribute to the oppression of other age groups. We have tried to do this in such a way as not to blame the aged, but to examine ways in which the social situation of the elderly may contribute to their making victims of other age groups.

A number of our colleagues have read and commented on specific chapters. We are particularly grateful to David Karp and Gretchen Batra in this context, and also to Rosemary Ananis, Barbara Bursk, John Donovan, Linda Evans, Ann Gardner, Barbara George, Lee Mintz, John Mogey, Anne Munley, Joseph Quinn, Henrietta Reynolds, Donald Spence, Elizabeth Tefft, and Michael Useem. We are appreciative of the many hours of stimulating discussions these persons have provided. Others, including Maura Jane Griffin, Louis Lowy, and Steven and Diane Perlmutter, have also helped us. We want to extend special thanks to Elaine Autieri, Alice Close, Shirley Urban, and Colleen Westbrook for typing drafts of each chapter.

We wish to acknowledge the encouragement and advice of Franklin Graham of Holt, Rinehart and Winston. We also appreciate the assistance we received from Yvette M. DeWindt, who managed the book while in production. We found many of the suggestions made by our reviewers of assistance and greatly appreciate their efforts. In this context we would like to thank R. Wayne Kernodle, Michael Creighton, John Henretta, and Ruth Jacobs for their contributions.

We appreciate the interest our families (even Kathryn E. Johnson) have shown in this work.

CONTENTS

CHAPTER 1

Injustices Against The Aging

In recent years television, newspapers, and news magazines have given considerable attention to the plight of the aged. These media often focus on extreme examples of the injustices that some of the elderly are forced to endure. We hear lurid reports of elderly couples found frozen to death in their own apartments, their utilities having been cut off because they were unable to pay the bills. We hear about the elderly who must eat cat food in order to survive on their meager pensions. We are told that even those who were once middle class or even affluent run the risk of poverty in old age. The following is one such report.

Rose Anderson was 90 years old, wispy and frail. She lived in a room filled with yellowed newspapers, magazines and books; it was filthy. There were cockroaches. There was an ugly permeating stench. She was too weary to clean. She gave her energy to caring for her canary.

She had been the wife of a prominent physician but she had the "misfortune" of living to a ripe old age and outliving both the $300,000 her husband had carefully provided for her and her only child, a son, who died at the age of 56 when she was 76. She had given over some of her money to support her daughter-in-law and grandchildren. But most of it went for her own extensive medical expenses. She ended up living on welfare.[1]

Although well-meaning, those who seek to underscore the plight of the aged sometimes contribute to the creation or perpetuation of inaccurate stereotypes. The aged are a heterogeneous group, and for this reason the impact of such problems as poverty, crime, and inadequate health care varies considerably. The injustices that affect one person are often quite different from those that affect another. In the popular press it is common to find problems that affect a small minority of the aged presented as if they affect the majority. For example, overall, the elderly are no more likely to be victims of crime than are younger age groups, despite what many journalists and television commentators would have us believe.[2] This is not to deny that crime is a problem for the elderly; it very definitely is, but to find out why, we have to look to factors other than age differences in victimization rates.

Many of the social problems associated with aging begin long before a person would appropriately be referred to as elderly. For example, discrimination against older persons seeking employment is more the rule than the exception. In some industries there is evidence of discrimination against job applicants who are over age forty-five and many jobs are closed to applicants over fifty-five.[3] Commercial exploitation based on anxieties about changes in physical appearance due to aging often begins before a person is even middle-aged. Media advertising contributes to a heightening of this anxiety and encourages consumers to deal with their anxiety by purchasing products which purport to minimize the physical signs of the aging process. While many people use cosmetics for reasons other than looking youthful, it is clear from the industry's advertising efforts that the desire to appear younger provides one foundation for this multibillion dollar industry. In view of the tendency for many of the problems associated with aging to begin prior to the onset of old age, our concern in this book will be with the social problems and injustices confronting the aging as well as those confronting the aged.

One objective of this book is to describe the various injustices with which the aging and the aged must contend. In this context we give particular attention to four categories of injustice: exploitation, oppression, discrimination, and victimization. To facilitate this objective our discussion focuses on the various social problems associated with aging. Another equally important objective is to deal with the extent of these problems; that is, to make an effort to separate popular myth from the closer approximation to reality which emerges from a balanced analysis of relevant research findings. The myth typically takes the form of a stereotype that is quite valid for some who are aged, but not valid when used to characterize the typical aged person or the aged as a group. Due to the importance of exploitation, oppression, discrimination, and victimization as aspects of the injustices confronting the aged and aging, it is appropriate to begin with a discussion of what we mean by these terms.

EXPLOITATION

As we grow older our vulnerability to certain forms of exploitation increases. We will be using the term "exploitation" in the sense of economic exploitation. Generally the reference will be to the practice of taking economic advantage of those who are particularly vulnerable for reasons of age. On occasion we will also make use of the Marxist definition of the term which refers to the profit the employer (capitalist) makes on the basis of the worker's labor. All the forms of exploitation we consider are perfectly legal; if a practice is illegal, we find it more appropriate to classify it as victimization.

Later in this chapter we will consider the issue of discrimination against older workers in some detail. However, it is worth noting the Marxist analysis that the problem for the older worker is not so much being exploited as it is not being exploited. This somewhat anomalous conclusion follows from the Marxist argument that there can be no exploitation unless the person is actually employed. A capitalist economy is structured in such a way as to put a high premium on efficiency, productivity, and profit maximization. This emphasis, at least in part, accounts for industry's reluctance to hire older workers and the practice of encouraging or even forcing those who are already employed to retire at a certain age. There are, however, reasons other than having fewer productive years left that contribute to the discrimination against older workers; among the most important are salary expectations and pension considerations. While many workers are affected by these discriminatory practices, the injustice involved does not constitute a form of exploitation, at least in the Marxist sense. However, this is not to say that a Marxist perspective is irrelevant to an analysis of the injustices against older workers. Discrimination against older workers puts those who cannot afford to leave the labor force at a disadvantage. Since most jobs are closed to them, they are forced to take what they can get. Typically, those jobs that are open offer poor working conditions and low wages. The effect of discrimination against older workers by one set of employers is to make them highly vulnerable to exploitation by others.

Another type of problem for the older worker can occur when corporations find that costs can be cut and profits increased by moving their operations from one region of the country to another. This has been illustrated by the exodus of the textile industry from the Northeast to the South where labor costs have been lower. Such relocations can deal a major blow to the entire economy of a community; this is particularly so when a substantial proportion of the jobs in the community are either directly or indirectly dependent on the firm that moves.

While such actions affect all age categories, the impact can be particularly severe for older workers. Those who do not wish to relocate can find that their employability is low or even nonexistent. For some it means they will not be eligible for full pension benefits; for others it means there will be no pension benefits. Some face months or even years of unemployment, while for others the result is forced early retirement. On occasion the company offers jobs to those workers who are willing to relocate. However, this involves a major sacrifice for older workers who have a lifelong investment in a family and friendship network in the area as well as a lifestyle built around the peculiarities of the community and region. For those who remain, it is difficult to start over in a new line of work, giving up years of seniority and specialized skills which are not relevant to jobs which are available.

Workers whose jobs are dependent on looking young have good reason to be concerned about age-linked changes in appearance. In our society no one looks upon change in physical appearance due to the process of aging with pleasure. One response to anxiety about these changes is to purchase cosmetics as well as other goods and services designed to minimize the evidence of aging. Since people have the option not to purchase cosmetics, it is reasonable to ask whether those providing these goods are guilty of exploitation. If people choose to spend their money on cosmetics, hair transplants, face lifts, and the like, who are we to say they are being exploited?

We cannot answer these and related questions about commercial exploitation without making some ethical judgments. Is the supplier of these goods and services in some way violating our sense of fairness? Are high profits being made at the expense of providing adequate services to those in a relatively powerless position as in the case of many nursing homes? Are high profits being made by providing services that people must avail themselves of at a time when they are particularly vulnerable as is often the case when dealing with the funeral industry? When our answer to questions such as these is "yes," it is reasonable to conclude that the practice is an instance of exploitation.

The cosmetics industry has taken advantage of anxiety about the physical signs of aging in an effort to increase demand for its products. But isn't this entirely consistent with accepted business practice in a capitalist economy? Are we to hold those who manufacture cosmetics or provide nursing home services to a different set of standards than we apply to those who supply cars? The answer to these questions will depend in large measure upon one's ideology. The conservative would argue that the only social responsibility of business is to do all it can that is within the law to maximize profits.[4] This includes those who sell cosmetics, the services of a funeral home, or used cars.

However, it is consistent with a liberal ideology (which more accurately describes the perspective of the authors) to make distinctions between more and less ethical business dealings. If one party to an economic exchange is particularly vulnerable, the liberal is likely to question the ethicality of extracting unusually high profits. Such transactions are likely to be considered exploitive.

Most liberals would want to hold the cosmetics consumer partly responsible for his or her decision to buy. Even taking into consideration the vast sums cosmetics manufacturers invest in advertising efforts designed to heighten anxiety about one's appearance, the consumer is viewed as having a choice of whether or not to purchase the goods being offered. This situation can be contrasted with that of a recently bereaved widow who must enter into business dealings with a funeral establishment. In this context, the liberal is more likely to classify a high profit transaction as exploitive, particularly if the person is persuaded to spend more than she can afford.

The case concerning exploitation by the pharmaceutical industry is more compelling than the case for the cosmetics industry. Large sums are spent on the development and testing of new drugs, but the discrepancy between what it costs to produce and market these drugs and what the consumer pays is sufficient to keep the industry consistently among the three most profitable in the United States.[5] While all segments of the population are drug consumers, growing older increases the chances of suffering from conditions that require drug therapy. For some of the elderly, the cost of drugs becomes a major economic burden; however, we must still ask whether the elderly are in any sense being exploited by those who produce and sell these drugs. In answering this question, one factor to consider is the practice of selling the same drug under a brand name at a much higher price than under its generic name. Another factor is the nonvoluntary nature of drug consumption for many of the elderly. Some will counter this last argument by pointing out that the elderly consume many drugs that they really do not need. However, such an argument fails to take into consideration the vast sums the industry spends on advertising. This propaganda has undoubtedly contributed to the expectation that there is a drug which can help with just about any physical or psychological problem. In such a cultural milieu it is not surprising that many get "hooked" on over-the-counter or prescription drugs.[6]

The pharmaceutical industry is just one component of what has come to be referred to as the medical-industrial complex, the third largest industry in the United States. Little needs to be said about the profits being made by doctors, insurance companies, medical vendors (for example, the companies that do required laboratory work), and those who produce the sophisticated equipment hospitals use. Since medical problems arise for persons of all ages, we would not want to argue that the exploitation by the medical establishment is explicitly aimed at the aged. This is particularly true in view of the tendency for such services to be covered by third party payments.[7] However, given the correlation between health problems and the process of growing old, it is reasonable to conclude that the medical establishment does find the health consequences of aging a source of considerable profit.

OPPRESSION

Of the injustices associated with growing old, oppression is the most general and comprehensive. A case can be made that the various forms of discrimination, victimization, and exploitation which we consider are all oppressive aspects of growing old. We will often use the term "oppression" to describe the psychological experience associated with these injustices. This psychic oppression is sometimes the result of the actual experience of discrimination, victimization, or exploitation. It can also result from the fear of such experience, as in the case of an elderly woman who lives in terror of being mugged on the way to the grocery store. There are also sources of oppression such as failing health, social isolation, poverty, and the widespread fear of such fates that are not instances of discrimination, victimization, or exploitation. The restrictions of various age roles and age norms are sources of oppression. In addition to considering the subjective experience of oppression, we will consider the objective sources of this oppression. Of particular interest will be institutional sources such as result from living in a nursing home.

Oppressive Age Norms and Roles

In primitive societies age and sex are two of the major determinants of social roles. Typically an elaborate set of normative expectations is associated with the sex roles to be fulfilled at each stage in the life span. In many societies elderly adults have a significant role in child care;[8] this is particularly true of those societies with an extended family structure. In such societies grandparents often take on responsibilities for child care while they in turn are relieved of some of the more strenuous roles of young adulthood. It is common for some of the most important roles—such as those relating to various ceremonial and religious functions—to be reserved for the elders. In a preliterate society, those who have lived the longest are often respected for their wisdom. When an unusual event threatens the community, it may be only the older members who have had experience in dealing with it. They also have significant responsibilities in regard to the transmission of the society's oral tradition.

A contrast is often made between modern societies in which there are few roles for the aged, and preliterate societies in which there were (and in some instances still are) a number of important roles for the aged. However, in many preliterate societies the status of the aged was much less enviable than such a comparison would suggest. Although in some, such as the Aleuts of the Aleutian Islands and the Inland Chukchi of Siberia, the aged were accorded a great deal of respect, more common were societies such as the Yakut of Siberia and the Thonga of South Africa in which the dependent aged were viewed as expendable.[9] This was particularly true of societies living under harsh conditions. If limited food supplies were spread too thinly, all would starve. For this reason, in many primitive societies there were norms supporting ritual murder or abandonment of the aged. Among the Koryak of Northern Siberia, a feast was given in honor of the aged parent who was then killed by a son or other close relative toward the end of the festivities. Among the Siriono in the Bolivian forest, the aged were left behind to starve to death while the rest of the community moved on in search of new food supplies.[10]

In our society there is more flexibility with respect to age and sex roles than in most primitive societies, but even so these roles continue to be major determinants of our behavior. When we encounter a person for the first time, among the first attributes we notice are sex and age. These characteristics tell us a great deal about what we can expect of this person and what they are likely to expect of us. There are shared norms that regulate the kinds of behavior which are considered appropriate in a social encounter as a function of the age and sex of the person involved. In a variety of ways, age roles and the related norms facilitate social interaction and benefit us all. These norms and roles are shaped by, and in turn help maintain the social order, but these same roles and norms can in some contexts become a source of oppression.

The oppressiveness that can be associated with certain age roles and norms is well illustrated by the issue of sexuality in old age. Until quite recently, it was generally assumed by the young that sexual activity was of great interest to themselves, of minor interest to the middle-aged, and of no interest to the aged. An exception was made for a few who were rich or famous, but for most it was assumed that there was little or no sexual activity in old age. Any aged man or woman who was so bold as to boast of an active sex life could expect to meet with disbelief or ridicule. To have even a serious desire for sexual activity was likely to be considered some what improper.

In recent years there has been a dramatic shift in attitudes toward sexuality, including an increase in the acceptance of a variety of forms of sexual behavior which had previously been considered improper, immoral, or perverse. There has been liberalization in attitudes toward premarital sexuality, extramarital sexuality, and homosexuality. As part of a general liberalization in attitudes on such issues, there has been an increase in acceptance of sexuality in old age.[11]

In our society it is considered appropriate for women to select mates who are at least as old as they are and for men to avoid selecting mates who are much older. Minor violations of these norms which do not involve more than a few years generally go without much comment. But any substantial violation becomes an issue worthy of considerable gossip. It would be most interesting to explore why these norms continue with such force today in spite of a marked liberalization in attitudes toward other aspects of sexual behavior. But independent of the reasons why these norms are with us, it is clear that they are no longer functional and that they unnecessarily inhibit the options of both men and women in the selection of mates. The norms result in an unfortunate reduction in the options for persons of both sexes at all ages, but the result is particularly strong for women who outlive their husbands as most women do. For elderly women who wish to find a new mate, men of an "appropriate" age are in very short supply. When this norm is liberalized, a process which may have already begun, there should be an improvement in the options available to elderly women as well as everyone else.

Sexuality is only one sphere of life in which some of the age norms have oppressive consequences. Age norms also regulate and restrict options with respect to friendship formation. We are expected to select our friends from among our associates who are close to us in age. If the age gap between two persons is substantial, in the eyes of many the relationship is suspect. To select as an intimate friend a person of either sex who is either much older or much younger than oneself is not only unusual, it is considered somewhat unnatural. One common interpretation of such relationships is that those involved are acting out certain unresolved early life parent-child fantasies. An even less flattering interpretation is that perverse sexuality is somehow involved.

In addition to the areas of sexuality and friendship formation, labor force participation is also affected by age norms. Some of these norms have been institutionalized as formal regulations, for example, the various mandatory retirement rules. Others operate more informally as subtle or not so subtle pressures on the older worker to retire. The pressure can sometimes result from realistic considerations. For example, in heavy manual work the older worker may no longer carry a full share of the burden; in some situations this increases the burden on the other workers. In bureaucratic organizations there may be younger workers who seek promotions which are not possible until the present division or section heads retire.

Fears: A Source of Oppression

For most crimes the actual victimization rate for the elderly is not greater than for other age groups, but their lifestyles are affected a great deal more than is reflected in crime statistics. [12] Fear of victimization often leads to a radical curtailment of activities. Many who live in cities are afraid to venture out at night, and in some areas the fear extends to going out alone even during the day.

Fear of victimization can lead to social isolation and to a breakdown in informal mechanisms of social control. In some areas the elderly can be counted on to keep track of what is going on in the neighborhood and to report any crime that occurs. This informal mechanism of social control helps keep crime rates down. However, in other areas, particularly the inner cities, many of the younger generation have moved to the suburbs and have been replaced by persons who differ from those who remain in race or ethnicity. This shift in composition has weakened informal mechanisms of social control which then allow crime rates to increase. Among the elderly who have remained in the inner cities, there has been an intensification of the fear of victimization. The response for many of the elderly has been to retreat behind locked doors and drawn curtains. This has further weakened informal mechanisms of social control and contributed to even higher crime rates.

Fear of victimization is only one of a variety of fears that oppress the aging and particularly the aged. There are a number of fears associated with signs of physical aging and the consequences these signs have for one's ability to attract others.[13] These signs also indicate that we are growing older and therefore closer to death. The fear of death and the fear of dying oppress people of all ages; while the evidence suggests that the aged do not fear death and dying more strongly than do other age groups, they think about these issues more frequently and therefore they may be more oppressed by such fear.[14]

Many of the aged and those approaching old age are oppressed by their fear of poverty. With retirement there is typically a sharp drop in income and a corresponding constriction of opportunities to increase that income in the event of economic need. Some widows live long enough to use up what had been a substantial inheritance left to them and end up on welfare. Expenses due to health problems can wipe out a lifetime of savings in a very short time. Many fear that the day will come when they have nothing to live on except social security or welfare.

The aging can be oppressed by the fear that with old age will come social isolation. Some fear that their children will make little or no effort to keep in contact. Many dread the day when they will be left alone due to the death of a spouse. Another common fear is of spending one's last years in a nursing home or other such institutional environment isolated from friends.

Institutional Experience

Between 20 and 25 percent of the elderly are living in nursing homes when they die or enter the hospital to die.[15] For those who do enter a nursing home it is all too often an oppressive experience. Some suffer a reduction in contact with significant others. Their friends and relatives see less of them once they have made the move to a nursing home, finding it inconvenient and unpleasant to visit such a depressing place. This avoidance of those who have moved into a nursing home is an example of what sociologists refer to as "social death," that is, being treated in some way as dead prior to actual death.[16] The resulting social isolation tends to undermine one's morale and identity.

Another reason life in a nursing home is so oppressive is that it involves regimentation of such activities as waking, going to bed, eating, bathing, and toileting.[17] We all develop routines with respect to these activities, but we are free to make changes in them when we see fit. A routine is generally not considered oppressive if one has a sense of control over it, but one has relatively little control over these routines in many nursing homes. They are established by the staff in an effort to maximize organizational efficiency, not patient autonomy. Loss of control over such basic aspects of one's life can deal a blow to one's sense of self-worth; this impersonal treatment represents a dehumanizing denial of one's individual integrity. The more understaffed the institution, the more oppressive the regimentation, but even the best nursing homes severely restrict resident autonomy in comparison to what it had been prior to institutionalization. Even the most deprived of the elderly poor, those living under deplorable conditions in "welfare hotels" located in the worst of inner city slums, live in dread of the day when they will be forced to move into a nursing home.[18] To move to a nursing home is viewed by many as a sign that "normal" life is over; it is seen as a limbo halfway between life and death.

Fortunately most people are able to avoid residency in an institution. But this does not necessarily mean that those who avoid nursing home placement escape the experience of being oppressed by one or another of the other institutions which provide services to the elderly. Many feel stigmatized at having to deal with the welfare bureaucracy to obtain funds to live on or funds to cover health-related expenses. Others must spend extended periods of time in the hospital, an experience that often involves many of the same oppressive characteristics that are associated with nursing homes.

DISCRIMINATION AND VICTIMIZATION

The logic of a competitive market economy calls for employing workers who are as efficient and productive as can be found. This need becomes a rationale for discrimination against older workers. For those who are not protected by seniority rules it becomes a rationale for dismissal; for those who have become unemployed for any reason, it becomes a rationale not to hire. In many instances workers of fifty-five can perform just as productively as workers of twenty-five, but will be passed over because they have fewer years of high productivity left. Older workers are discriminated against to the extent that they are treated differently and less favorably for reasons of age. In actual practice it is often difficult to distinguish between discrimination based on age and discrimination based on other age-linked characteristics. For example, it is not uncommon to find that an older worker is being paid (or expecting to be paid) substantially more than a younger worker of comparable skill. A case can be made that discrimination against such persons is as much due to their being more expensive as due to their being older.

In much the same way, few would deny the desirability of a policy of assuring workers the *option* of retirement at age sixty-five. The debate has been over the policy of *mandatory* retirement at age sixty-five, seventy, or any other specific age independent of a person's ability to do the job competently.

In many instances mandatory retirement policy has been justified on the basis of economic rationality; for many tasks younger workers are as productive and cheaper. In recent years an effort has been made to get mandatory retirement regulations declared discriminatory. Recently, Congress raised the mandatory retirement age from sixty-five to seventy in the private sector and ended the practice altogether for federal employees. This points to a growing awareness of the discriminatory nature of the existing regulations, but does not eliminate the problem in the private sector. It is easy to see why bureaucratic organizations would prefer a simple policy of retiring all workers at a specific age such as sixty-five or seventy to some alternative that calls for an assessment of the competence of each worker on some periodic basis. While the now common policy of using age as the criterion is administratively simple, it does discriminate against older workers, particularly those who are able to continue working and who want or financially need to do so.

Other forms of discrimination against the aging involve the provision of medical care and various other social services. In his study of dying in a large public hospital catering to lower and working class patients, David Sudnow observed that more effort was made to resuscitate (revive) the young than the old. If a young person who had recently stopped breathing and whose heart had stopped beating was brought into the emergency room, typically a great deal of effort was made to resuscitate the patient, but when a very elderly person was brought in with the same symptoms, often no effort at resuscitation was made.[19] It was worth taking "heroic" measures in an effort to save the life of a young patient; however, such measures were deemed less appropriate for the very elderly.

The training of health care specialists often involves inadequate attention to the specific needs of the elderly. Virtually every medical school in the country offers pediatric medicine as a specialty, but very few offer a specialty in geriatric medicine. Discrimination against the elderly in the provision of mental health benefits is illustrated by the preference of psychiatrists for working with younger patients and their hesitancy to suggest long-term psychotherapy for the elderly.[20] Even though the elderly constitute one of the largest population categories for risk of emotional disturbances, they have been in the lowest priority category for need assessment and delivery of community mental health services.

The medical sector is only one of many areas in which the aging are discriminated against in the provision of services. It is often difficult for an older worker to gain admittance to a federally funded job training program, the assumption being that younger workers are in greater need of the limited positions available. The same is true in the provision of educational services. The G.I. Bill, for example, is only available for ten years after a person leaves military service. Children and youth are provided transportation to schools, cultural events, and athletic contests in buses paid for out of public taxes, but most communities have not made a comparable effort to meet the special transportation needs of the elderly.

So far we have considered exploitation, oppression, and discrimination against the aged. We now turn to our fourth and last category of injustice against the elderly, victimization. Included here are those who experience crimes of violence, theft, and various frauds that can in some way be linked to advanced age. Also included are those whose lives are adversely affected by the fear of being so victimized.[21] We will be using the term "victimization" to include criminal victimization and other unethical practices which most would agree should be against the law. For example, consider the legal, but highly disreputable practices used by some land developers in selling "retirement home sites" in swamps and desolate areas without access to roads, to say nothing of public services.

From the attention periodically given to the issue in the mass media, one might be led to conclude that the elderly are more likely to be victimized by crimes of violence than are other age groups; however, this is not the case.[22] Certain subgroups of the elderly, such as those living in the inner city, are disproportionately victimized. In addition, when an elderly person falls victim to a violent crime, the effects of the experience are often more long lasting than in the case of a younger victim. Older people usually take longer to recover and run a greater risk that total recovery will not be possible. The crime statistics also fail to take into consideration the greater precautions, such as not venturing out at night, that the elderly take to protect themselves. The elderly are more likely to be victimized than are equally cautious persons in other age categories.

In addition to violent crime, there are other ways of victimizing the elderly. They are more likely than others to have chronic health problems and for this reason to be highly vulnerable to a variety of health-related frauds. Many entrepreneurs have made fortunes on schemes designed to separate the elderly from their money, some of which are illegal frauds, whereas others are legal but quite disreputable. In some instances a machine or medicine is sold with outlandish promises of effectiveness against everything from arthritis to cancer.[23] Most of these remedies are entirely worthless; some are quite dangerous, as in the case of a quack remedy for cancer which might have been treated successfully with more conventional medical procedures.

Most nursing home residents are not being victimized even though life in such institutions tends to be quite oppressive, but some of those living in very substandard nursing homes are the victims of a wide range of abuses which can be considered criminal. There are a number of laws on the books which were designed to regulate the nursing home industry, but enforcement in many areas has been lax. When nursing home operators have taken advantage of this situation, the outcome has in some cases been appalling living conditions for residents. In such institutions violations of fire and other safety codes are not uncommon.[24] In many of these homes patients are kept highly sedated, not for therapeutic reasons, but rather as a mechanism for social control to make them easier to manage.[25] In her expose of the nursing home industry entitled *Tender Loving Greed*, Mary Adelaide Mendelson documents numerous examples of unsanitary cooking and eating facilities, the use of food that is unfit for human consumption, and a host of flagrant violations of the law, to say nothing of the abuse of personal dignity. In her description of a nursing home in Cleveland she is highly critical of the food the nursing home operator saw fit to feed residents.

> The cook has taken hams, bacon, and wieners and thrown them on Strauss's (the nursing home operator) desk because of their smell, and refused to prepare them. . . . often the cook has thrown away whole baskets of tomatoes Strauss purchased at the market for stewing because they were unfit to eat. And sometimes the cook almost flips a coin to decide whether she should use the contents of a damaged, rusted, and bulging can.[26]

THE ELDERLY AS AGENTS OF OPPRESSION AND EXPLOITATION

To this point our focus has been on the ways in which the elderly are exploited, oppressed, discriminated against, and victimized. We have not considered the possibility that the elderly themselves might in some ways be agents of such injustices. Not only are there ways in which the aged exploit and oppress others, but in addition, there are a number of ways in which they contribute to their own oppression.

The aged are among the staunchest supporters of many norms which specify what behavior is proper for elderly persons. There is a tendency for those who are elderly to give great emphasis to the importance of age as a determinant of what is appropriate behavior.[27] Many if not most of the aged no doubt prefer a social environment in which there is a consensus concerning what is, and what is not, acceptable behavior. However, the security that the elaborate set of norms provides comes at a cost; some of the aged find the limits with respect to what is considered acceptable behavior a source of oppression.

Because many adult children remain involved with their older parents, they are often caught between their own needs, the demands of their own children and spouses, and the demands of their parents. Older parents can make their children's lives more complicated by the guilt they are able to engender either consciously or unconsciously in their children. Children are sometimes expected to be available immediately when needed while at the same time they are expected to remember who is the parent or authority figure. The difficulties that some adult children face as they and their parents grow old together can be stressful for both and can be exacerbated by the history of the relationship. If the parents' personalities have not allowed them to be really supportive of their children over the years, the parents are likely to be similarly unsupportive of their children even when the children are much more responsible for their parents as sometimes occurs in old age. The children may resent the additional burdens, particularly when their parents cannot express their appreciation.

Unlike private health insurance and pension plans, the Social Security system is not set up to assure that on the average people pay in at least as much as they eventually get out in benefits. To the contrary, the Social Security program has been run in such a way that most people get more in benefits than they have paid in during their working years. Given that the aged are getting out more than they paid in and given that the difference is being made up by those who are younger and presently in the labor force, a case could be made that the program allows exploitation of the young and middle-aged by the aged. However, the program is generally not viewed as a mechanism by which the aged exploit those still in the labor force. One reason is that recipients have made substantial contributions to the system; another is that the actual level of benefits provides at best a very modest standard of living. In addition, it is generally accepted that most of the aged do not have other opportunities to support themselves. Some adult children look favorably upon the existence of the program because it provides an alternative to economic responsibility for their aged parents. However, when we look closely there are characteristics of the system that do seem exploitative. For example, there are many poor young families making contributions to the program despite insufficient funds to provide for what most would consider basic necessities of life, and at the same time there are some wealthy elderly persons who receive substantial payments from the system.

CONCLUSION

In this chapter we introduced a number of issues that we will elaborate upon in subsequent chapters. In any analysis of the social problems confronting the aging and the aged, it is important to separate the overgeneralized stereotypes from the very real injustices that certain groups of the aged face. Particular attention will be given to the various forms of exploitation, oppression, discrimination, and victimization with which the aging must contend. For each form of injustice considered we will want to ask such questions as: What are its sources? Who is most adversely affected by it? What can be done to deal with the situation? Answers to questions such as these are often influenced by the theoretical and ideological perspective of the observer. At one time or another most people are agents of oppression just as they are on occasion subjects of oppression. The aged are no exception in this respect and for this reason we will want to consider the evidence concerning the extent to which the elderly are, themselves, agents of oppression and exploitation.

Notes

1. Butler (1975:3).
2. United States Department of Justice (1976).
3. A study by the United States Department of Labor (1965) found that 25 percent of job openings are closed to those above forty-five because of age and that most jobs are closed to those over fifty-five.
4. Friedman (1974).
5. Ehrenreich and Ehrenreich (1970:99).
6. Bernstein and Lennard (1977).
7. One estimate is that in 1970 the elderly paid for an average of 57 percent of their health-care needs out of their own pockets. In 1972 the per capita out-of-pocket expenditure for the elderly was $276 (Butler, 1975:207).
8. Linton (1964:120).
9. For a detailed summary of the ethnographic data describing some seventy-one preliterate societies see Simmons (1945). We use the past tense to describe conditions in these primitive societies because most of the ethnographic studies were conducted fifty to one hundred years ago. While these practices undoubtedly continue in some societies, it is likely that there have been significant changes in others.
10. Material on the Koryak and Siriono is drawn from de Beauvoir (1972:47–50).
11. Burnside (1975).
12. For information on the extent of criminal victimization against different age groups see United States Department of Justice (1976). Also see Gallup Opinion Index (1975). For information on the fear of victimization see Clemente and Kleiman (1976).
13. Bell (1976).
14. For a discussion of age variation in the fear of death see Kalish (1976). For material on age variation in frequency of thoughts about one's own death see Hinton (1972:22–23).
15. At any one time only about 5 percent of the elderly are in institutions, but close to 20 percent spend at least some time in such an institution prior to death. See Kastenbaum and Candy (1973); Ingram and Barry (1977).
16. For a discussion of the concept of social death see Kastenbaum (1977:31–33).
17. For a description of conditions in nursing homes see Gubrium (1975) and Stannard (1973).

18. Stephens (1976:11–12).
19. Sudnow (1967:103–108).
20. Butler (1975:228–29).
21. As will be recalled from our earlier discussion, the fear of being victimized is also a form of oppression.
22. For information on the extent of criminal victimization against different age groups see United States Department of Justice (1976); Gallup Opinion Index (1975); and Goldsmith and Goldsmith (1976).
23. Ducovny (1969:74–89).
24. A 1975 audit by the General Accounting Office found that 72 percent of nursing homes have one or more major violations of fire safety codes. *New York Times,* February 29, 1976.
25. Gubrium (1975:148).
26. Mendelson (1974:90).
27. Neugarten et al. (1965).

References

de Beauvoir, Simone, *The Coming of Age.* Translated by Patrick O'Brian. New York: Putnam, 1972.

Bell, Inge P., "The Double Standard." In Beth B. Hess (ed.), *Growing Old in America,* pp. 150–162. New Brunswick, N.J.: Transaction Books, 1976.

Bernstein, Arnold, and Henry L. Lennard, "Drugs, Doctors, and Junkies." In John B. Williamson, Jerry F. Boren, and Linda Evans (ed.), *Social Problems: The Contemporary Debates,* 2nd ed., pp. 315–324. Boston: Little, Brown, 1977.

Binstock, Robert H., "Aging and the Future of American Politics." *The Annals* 415, 1974: 199–212.

Burnside, Irene M., ed., *Sexuality and Aging.* Los Angeles, Calif.: University of Southern California Press, 1975.

Butler, Robert N., *Why Survive?* New York: Harper & Row, 1975.

Butler, Robert N., and Myrna I. Lewis, *Aging and Mental Health,* 2nd ed. St. Louis: Mosby, 1977.

Clemente, Frank, and Michael B. Kleiman, "Fear of Crime Among the Aged." *Gerontologist* 16, 1976: 207–210.

Ducovny, Amram, *The Billion $ Swindle.* New York: Fleet, 1969.

Ehrenreich, Barbara, and John Ehrenreich, *The American Health Empire.* New York: Random House, 1970.

Friedman, Milton, "The Social Responsibility of Business Is To Increase Its Profits." In John B. Williamson, Jerry F. Boren, and Linda Evans (ed.), *Social Problems: The Contemporary Debates,* pp. 199–205. Boston: Little, Brown, 1974.

Gallup Opinion Index, "Crime." *Gallup Opinion Index,* 1975: 1246–1317.

Goldsmith, Jack, and Sharon Goldsmith (ed.), *Crime and the Elderly.* Lexington, Mass. Heath, 1976.

Gubrium, Jaber F., *Living and Dying at Murray Manor.* New York: St. Martin's, 1975.

Hinton, John M., *Dying,* 2nd ed. Baltimore: Penguin, 1972.

Ingram, Donald K., and John R. Barry, "National Statistics on Deaths in Nursing Homes: Interpretations and Implications." *Gerontologist* 17, 1977: 303–308.

Kalish, Richard A., "Death and Dying in a Social Context." In Robert H. Binstock and Ethel Shanas (ed.), *Handbook of Aging and the Social Sciences,* pp. 483–507. New York: Van Nostrand, 1976.

Kastenbaum, Robert, and Sandra E. Candy, "The 4% Fallacy: A Methodological and Empirical Critique of Extended Care Facility Population Statistics." *International Journal of Aging and Human Development* 4, 1973: 15–22.

Linton, Ralph, *The Study of Man.* New York: Appleton, 1964.

Mendelson, Mary. A., *Tender Loving Greed.* New York: Knopf, 1974.

Neugarten, Bernice L., Joan W. Moore, and John C. Lowe, "Age Norms, Age Constraints, and Adult Socialization." *American Journal of Sociology* 70, 1965: 710–717.

Schulz, James H., *The Economics of Aging.* Belmont, Calif.: Wadsworth, 1976.

Simmons, Leo W., *The Role of the Aged in Primitive Society.* New Haven: Yale University Press, 1945.

Stannard, Charles I., "Old Folks and Dirty Work: The Social Conditions for Patient Abuse in a Nursing Home." *Social Problems* 20, 1973: 329–342.

Stephens, Joyce, *Loners, Losers, and Lovers: Elderly Tenants in a Slum Hotel.* Seattle: University of Washington Press, 1976.

Sudnow, David, *Passing On: The Social Organization of Dying.* Englewood Cliffs, N.J.: Prentice-Hall, 1967.

United States Department of Justice, "Criminal Victimization in the United States: A Comparison of 1973 and 1974 Findings." A National Crime Panel Survey Report, LEAA. Washington, D.C.: United States Government Printing Office, 1976.

United States Department of Labor, *The Older American Worker—Age Discrimination in Employment.* Washington, D.C.: United States Government Printing Office, 1965.

CHAPTER 2

Crime
And
The Fear
Of Victimization

In this chapter we will examine the extent of victimization of older persons and the amount of fear that victimization and its threat generate We will look at whether or not victimization and the fear of it are worse for people as they grow older or if the two are perceived to be worse because of other negative concomitants of the aging process. An attempt will be made to differentiate actual victimization, exposure to victimization, and the perceived threat of victimization, all of which may affect a person's behavior and feelings of life satisfaction.[1]

Criminal victimization is only one of the types of injustice that the aged experience. Other forms including exploitation, discrimination, and prejudice against the aging and the aged are society-wide problems to which many who are not "official" criminals contribute. From this perspective, criminal victimization is just one way in which the aging and the aged are oppressed. It is, however, a visible, frightening, and unfortunate form

VIOLENT CRIMES AGAINST THE ELDERLY

A Law Enforcement Assistance Administration (LEAA) report, based on a representative national sample surveyed in 1973 and in 1974, compared older people with other adult and teen-age groups in terms of victimization rates.[2] In general, the survey results show that there was a decreasing rate of victimization with age; younger groups were more often victimized than older groups in both 1973 and 1974. Eight out of 1000 elderly were victims of violent crimes in 1973 compared with 32 per 1000 people in the general population. The same trend held for theft and household crimes. Furthermore the elderly were not victimized out of proportion to their size in the population. This decreasing rate of victimization with age was also evidenced by a 1975 Gallup Poll in which 20 percent of people age fifty and over, compared with 31 percent of eighteen- to twenty-four-year-olds, reported having been victimized in the prior twelve months.[3] There was not a tendency for the elderly to under-report victimization.

Does this mean that the elderly are less burdened by crime than other age groups? Clearly their overall victimization rates are lower. As clear, however, is the fact that not all of the elderly are homogeneous with respect to a low rate of victimization.

Socioeconomic factors and other personal conditions prevalent among some older people increase the vulnerability of certain groups to victimization. Factors which contribute to the vulnerability of older people are: (1) many older people live in urban areas which are high in crime, (2) the fixed and mostly low income of some older people makes them vulnerable to get-rich-quick schemes, and (3) the loneliness of some older people may predispose them to a stranger's apparent friendliness.[4]

Let's look in closer detail at these factors. For those poor, inner city elderly, both white and black, who live in high crime areas, the risk of being victimized is as high as for other age groups, even though nationwide the crime rate against the elderly is lower than for other age categories. The following information, collected by the Special Committee on Aging in the U.S. Senate vividly illustrates this point: (1) in 1975, 35 percent of New York City's elderly lived in its twenty-six poorest neighborhoods. Of those interviewed in the original survey, which was presented to the Committee, 40 percent reported having been victimized. A member of the Bronx Senior Citizens Robbery Unit, Sgt. James Bolte, remarked that, "The brutality is worse, the beatings are awfully bad." His recent cases have included many so-called "push-in" or "crib job" robberies, where the victims are assaulted as they are entering their homes. In many of those cases the elderly have been locked into closets after being beaten and robbed. Two such victims died of heart attacks, and in one of those instances, a woman remained trapped with the body of her dead husband for three days;[5] (2) in a three-year study of robbery in Oakland, females over sixty-five years of age had a victimization rate of 1 in 24 even though the risk for the general population was only 1 in 146; (3) in Wilmington, Delaware, the victimization rate for street crimes in 1970 of persons sixty years of age or over was about twice the rate for people under sixty; (4) in Detroit, in 1973, persons fifty-five years of age and over represented 22 percent of the population but they experienced 28 percent of the unarmed robberies; (5) in Houston, a three-year study found that the elderly were not overvictimized when all crimes were considered. However, for certain crimes, for example, robbery, swindling, purse snatching, and homicide, those sixty-five and over were more highly victimized than those under sixty-five, and (6) a 1972 study in Boston showed that the elderly experienced 28 percent of all robberies even though they were only 12 percent of the population.[6] An older student in an aging class in Boston reported that an elderly woman whom he knew had seen a television set being loaded on a pickup around noon one day. Since her own television had been operating poorly, she asked the owners of the truck if they would take her set to be repaired. They obligingly agreed. She, of course, never saw her set or the robbers again.

Even more specifically, in high crime urban areas, age-integration in public housing projects results in victimization rates of the elderly that are extremely high. The risk that the immediate environment poses for some people, and particularly for older people, is evident from the following statistics: in 1970, the Bromley-Heath age-integrated housing project in Boston had an assault rate for all ages 783 percent higher than the national average.[7] Elderly people housed in such projects, albeit at a great saving in rent, cannot help but feel like lambs prepared for the slaughter. The following anecdote appeared in a metropolitan newspaper.

> Two kids in sneakers and dungarees, the basic uniform of street crime, came up behind Ethel Lubitz as the old woman made her way along the sloping sidewalk by the projects [in Boston]. One kid grabbed the handbag dangling at her elbow while the other pushed Ethel Lubitz's back as if it were a revolving door.
>   The woman hit the pavement thinking only that she had been run over by a truck. A bag of groceries spilled out on the street, the bag splitting. Cans rattled along the gutter.[8]

The high risk that their living environment poses for elderly persons is further supported by the fact that half of the violent victimizations occurred in or near their homes, whereas younger adults were more often victimized in locations away from their homes.[9] The implication is that the elderly limit their community involvement, but when they do leave their dwellings for necessary errands, they are likely to be victimized. Younger people may more often take part in activities away from their homes causing them to be in more dangerous public places more frequently. In contrast, the urban elderly cannot feel secure even in their own homes and neighborhoods.

The offenders in these street and household crimes against the elderly are usually male, under thirty years of age, most often teen-agers, and black.[10] Their elderly victims are also, slightly more often, black.[11] The offenders are sometimes members of families who live in the same public housing projects as their elderly victims. The younger families may live under such stressful conditions that their children project their frustration and anger at objects weaker than themselves; those objects are often their elderly neighbors. Unemployment and its correlate, boredom, may contribute to the high amount of crime committed by the young. From one perspective, it appears that the young are victimizing the old. However, the economic system which allows unemployment to be so high, especially among minority groups, may indirectly contribute to the victimization of the elderly population by the young. As long as there are great inequalities in the distribution of wealth in society, those groups that are perceived as weakest will be victimized by those equally oppressed but physically stronger. The victimization that is part of the lives of many inner city elderly will not change as long as other inner city residents perceive that they have nothing to lose, that in fact, the 99 chances in 100 of not being jailed for having committed a crime are far better odds than any others for getting ahead.[12]

Further disaggregation of the data on victimization from the LEAA surveys shows that elderly men are victimized more than elderly women except for purse snatching. While arrest and conviction procedures against criminals are not good, they are particularly bad against purse snatchers. The fact that the victims are older women and the snatchers are often juvenile males may combine to facilitate limited enforcement procedures in our youth- and male-oriented society. Elderly women may also fear retribution and avoid informing authorities of purse snatchers, as the following newspaper excerpt suggests.

After what must have been only a minute or two but what seemed like an hour, a telephone repair truck pulled over to the curb where the old woman was now sitting, surrounded by the small statistics of life in the city, 1978: a missing handbag, an increased pulse rate and a growing distaste for the young.

"You OK, lady?" the telephone man asked.

"I think so," Ethel Lubitz said.

"Stay here and I'll get the cops," the man said.

"No. No, that's all right," she said. "I want to go home, that's all. I just want to go home ... "

"Lady, you should really come with me and we'll get the cops."

"No. No. I don't want any more trouble," she said ... [Later at home, a friend said]

"They would find out that she went to the police and they would do it again ... "

"They knocking us down and robbing us. All the time it happens. What can the police do? They can never catch them and when they do they get right out again. They never go to jail or nothing."[13]

Elderly women are also more likely to be residents of nursing homes where they may sometimes be physically abused and/or be victims of theft. Although it is unclear whether the pilfering that occurs is the result of the actions of staff or other confused residents, the result can be very demoralizing for the victims. The complaints of the residents about abuse or stealing may too often be dismissed as paranoia.

The other two conditions which cause the elderly to be more vulnerable to victimization are their desire for greater financial security and their loneliness. The contributions of each of these conditions to the victimization of the elderly will be examined in greater detail in the following section.

FRAUDS AGAINST THE ELDERLY

In addition to victimization which includes physical danger, the elderly are good targets for con "artists" because of their fixed incomes. The lower education level of many of the present generation of elderly increases their susceptibility to fast-talking swindlers. The offenders in confidence games are usually younger adults, male or female, and white.[14] One of the more often discussed and practiced cons is the "bank-examiner swindle." In this "game," a person, often an older woman living alone, is telephoned and told that there is someone embezzling money at her bank and she can help the authorities catch the thief. All she has to do is withdraw her money from her account. After she does this, she is told that the thief has been caught and in consideration the bank will send a messenger to pick up her money. A messenger is sent, but not from the bank. By the time the woman realizes what has happened, the thieves are far away. To compound the problem, some victims are reluctant to report that they have been defrauded because they feel they would look foolish.

In the "pigeon-drop swindle," also perpetrated largely against older people, a young woman goes up to an older person on the street. She tells the older person that she has just found a suitcase (or wallet) with a huge amount of money in it. She then says that she has to go out of town for a few days and she has nowhere to leave the money, but if the older person will take care of it for her, she will split it when she returns. However, in order to insure the good faith of the older person, she requests that he or she give her a deposit of $1000 or so. Once the older person provides the deposit, the wallet is given over for safekeeping and the young woman leaves, promising to return in a few days. She never does and the wallet is found to contain real dollars on either end of a wad of phony money.

A less grandiose but equally distressing con is played by crooks who read obituary notices and attempt to collect from the widow or widower on a "debt" owed by the deceased. A modified version of this game is to inform the surviving spouse that the deceased had ordered a Bible or some other sentimental item, to deliver it, and request payment. In still another situation, thieves masquerading as door-to-door salespeople select a person who is visually handicapped. Then when they make change, they cheat the person.

While many of us might discount the prevalence of the bank examiner and other cons as fictions in the mind of a television scriptwriter, the seriousness of the crimes is illustrated by the following statistics.[15] Within the Los Angeles Police Department's jurisdiction, in one six-month period almost twice as much money was lost by older people through the bank-examiner and pigeon-drop con games as was lost by the banks in L.A. through robberies in that same period. More concretely, in the last four months of 1965, thirty-eight older women in L.A. were swindled out of $200,000 through the "bank-examiner" fraud alone.[16]

Other victimizing schemes which also are not fictitious, are those in which Social Security agents are impersonated. They promise to obtain higher payments for the older person if they are paid a fee. The fee is taken and the "agent" is never seen again.

Another version of swindlers posing as Social Security agents is provided by the following case study.

Two young men identifying themselves as Social Security agents approached two elderly citizens, aged eighty-six and eighty-four, and told them there had been an overpayment and the government demanded the excess amount immediately. The eighty-six-year-old beneficiary turned over $750 to the impersonators. The eighty-four-year-old told them he didn't have the $1,628 demanded but he could have it for them the next day. He then called the Social Security office. The matter was reported to the FBI[17]

Another type of fraud to which middle-aged and older people are vulnerable involves land. In one type of con, the person is told that he or she has won a plot of land somewhere in the sunbelt. However, it then turns out that the plot of land is very narrow and in order to build on the site another adjoining lot must be purchased. In another situation, land which is virtually uninhabitable is sold as a retirement homesite. One investigator's report of such land misrepresentation which was reported to a Senate Committee graphically depicts the difference between the customer's perspective and that of the sales agent.

I spent almost two days, using a slow plane and a four-wheel-drive radio-equipped jeep, to try to locate a certain parcel in a development called University Highlands, being sold by a corporation named First America Corp., located approximately ten miles west of Daytona Beach in a dismal swamp.

After some of the roughest riding, we had to give up, as it was impossible to penetrate deep enough into the swamp to a point which we had spotted from the air. The land had been sold to a woman from Syracuse, New York, who had intended to use it as a homesite for a trailer house.

All of these frauds can be perpetrated on people of any age. However, when the knowledge that the future includes a fixed income combines with the hope of a good deal for retirement, the result is that older groups are more vulnerable to economic exploitation by smooth-talking, hope-engendering swindlers.

Although these get-rich-quick or get-something-for-nothing schemes are not literally forced on anyone, the internal pressure that results from the uncertainty of one's ability to make ends meet when income is reduced, coupled with the fantasy of spending one's retirement in a desirable climate, may figuratively force peole to do things that they otherwise would approach more cautiously, if at all.

The ultimate answer to many of these misrepresentations and frauds is increased opportunity for older people to earn money in the later years, as well as more consumer education and a lower tolerance for those who use deceitful sales methods. Laissez-faire attitudes which caution the "buyer to beware" are not sufficient. Unfortunately, the public's right to know how to evaluate these marginal activities may make even legitimate businesses nervous, since most sales are not strictly based on people's needs, but on needs which have been facilitated by advertising. Even legitimate businesses may feel that once the issue of consumer education has been raised, the body of regulatory mechanisms for all businesses cannot be far behind.

ANOTHER WAY TO LOOK AT VIOLENT CRIME: FEAR OF VICTIMIZATION

Is the lower rate of violent victimizations of the elderly a result of the greater esteem in which the elderly are held by offenders? Much more likely, it is partially a result of the greater precautions to avoid victimization that the elderly take. It is clear that older people alter their lives to a greater extent than other age groups in order to protect themselves against crime. The elderly may go out only during the daylight hours and even stay inside more during the day.

A Gallup Poll in 1975 found that nonwhites and women residents of large cities were the most afraid of walking alone at night.[18] These same groups felt the least safe in their homes at night. The following example illustrates the fear that some women feel.

An older woman leaving a temple in Los Angeles was robbed at knife point and also had her finger broken. She says, "It was frightening, of course. It is not only the fear, it is the insult. I was insulted, hurt that this should happen in our country, a free country. We walk to church . . . I live here . . . I am not a person to be afraid . . . I go wherever I have to go on the bus, in the streets. But in the evening, after 7 o'clock, I am afraid to go out . . . "[19]

In the Gallup survey, fear for personal safety appeared to be related more to factors such as race, sex, education level, and city size, than to age *per se*. However, there are many elderly who fit the characteristics of those who are especially fearful. The fact that black, urban elderly live in the highest crime areas may in fact be responsible for their high levels of fear. However, their high fear may indicate, at the same time, a breakdown in traditional black patterns of respect for the aged, since the victimizers in the inner cities also are more often black.[20] The situation is exacerbated by the fact that at least within age-integrated public housing projects, there is a high turnover of younger families. The result is a nonexistent sense of extended family or even community, a sense which many younger and older blacks used to share. This lessened community spirit can have wide implications, as the following suggests.

> Each time that a handbag is grabbed or someone is mugged and decides to give up, to move to a rest home in [a suburb], the city dies a little bit more. Every time a 74-year-old woman hits the pavement during an assault, a little more life oozes through the cracks.
>
> Another room becomes vacant. Another human being gets closer to giving up. And fear moves in as the next-door neighbor.[21]

Those female, black, and urban elderly who have the highest fear rates, are the elderly who are likely to be living alone in age-integrated public housing projects or in deteriorating age-integrated urban neighborhoods.[22] The results of a survey in Albany-Troy, New York, showed that 42 percent of the residents of age-segregated or age-mixed housing (age-mixed housing is age-homogeneous housing surrounded by housing for younger families) wanted to move.[23] The case against age-integrated housing projects may seem less than newsworthy; however, there have been many discussions in the gerontological literature regarding the desirability of age-heterogeneous versus age-homogeneous housing. Those who have favored age-heterogeneous housing have often argued that it is desirable for the elderly to live with other age groups, that all groups are better for the experience. Some of the elderly voice the same opinion. Advocates of age-homogeneous housing have noted that elderly in such communities develop more friendships than those elderly in age-heterogeneous housing. It is important, however, to note that when public housing is involved, high actual and feared victimization rates of the elderly in age-integrated projects may be more basic to life quality than some of the other factors which are often mentioned.

In addition to violent victimization, elderly residents in age-integrated housing projects can also be targets of malicious mischief. For example, in one age-integrated housing project, women participants in an elderly day-care program asked the van driver to drop them off at the rear entrance to their building because they did not wish to face the taunts of the teen-agers who hung out in front of the building. In this case, no "crime" was feared; however, psychic abuse was feared. Consequently, while intervention strategies such as escort patrols and self-help techniques can make it easier for the elderly to go out and to maintain the quality of their lives, they cannot totally alleviate the mental anguish that many elderly experience because of the lack of respect shown by society for the old, as evidenced by the malicious mischief perpetrated by the young on the old.

On the other hand, age-segregated housing offers a social environment that is considered defensible space.[24] While the elderly living in age-segregated housing (in high crime areas) may possibly interact less with other age groups than the elderly living in age-integrated housing, at least their imagined or real interaction will less often be as victims of muggings. Additional support for the perceived security of age-segregated housing comes from another study which found that older residents of a retirement community had the lowest fear of victimization while inner city residents had the highest. A third group who lived in suburbia fell in between on the fear dimension. Fear of victimization was not directly related to having been a victim, but to the perceived safety of the neighborhood which is known from the experiences of others as well as self.[25]

While the elderly seek to move to safe neighborhoods, the financial cost as well as the necessity of giving up life-long associations are usually balanced against the fear of victimization. In any case, to freely come and go in the old neighborhood often is not possible.

The fear of victimization can be related to a realistic belief that injury, whether as a victim of crime or in some other way, for example, slipping in the bathtub, has great potential for decreasing independence and even for hastening death. The need to remain independent is strongly ingrained in our culture and goes back to Colonial America. It is expressed in *Poor Richard's Almanack* as, "God helps them that help themselves."[26] This ethic of the need to be independent can be particularly oppressive when one's vulnerability is exaggerated as one grows physically and economically weaker in old age.

The ethic of independence is a factor in the desire of many older people to live independently of their families. For many women, this means living alone once their husbands die. Unfortunately, because they live alone, the effects of victimization can be particularly stressful. A survey of elderly victims of residential burglary in Los Angeles almost always showed a long-lasting residual fear that the researchers felt was related to the anonymity of the invasion as well as the latent threat it created.[27]

As a result, fear of victimization is not only related to what might be stolen, but also with the indirect consequences that a purse snatching or mugging can have. When an older person is knocked off balance and falls down, the health-related consequences, which usually involve decreased independence, can be much more serious than for a younger person. Sometimes a broken hip is the precipitating factor to nursing home placement; nursing home placement can lead to the funeral parlor earlier than otherwise might have been expected.[28]

Although the indirect effects of victimization can be life threatening, the direct consequences can also have significant impact on the quality of life of the older person. Little is lost in an absolute monetary sense by the elderly who are robbed—an average of $39 is stolen—however, the fact that many elderly women are living on less than $3000 per year makes the loss more pronounced.[29] For example, a television set is a very important article to many elderly who live alone. If that television is stolen, paying for a replacement may be difficult if not impossible. A relatively small theft may mean very extensive changes in the lives of some of the elderly.

Older people are fearful of victimization because of their vulnerability due to reduced income, limited or nonexistent opportunities for increasing income, and lesser physical strength. Compounding this diminished strength is the lack of confidence in their physical selves that many older women have because of societal notions regarding strength and femininity. For both men and women, retirement encourages passivity; passivity may result in less ability to respond to a potential attack.[30]

Even if older people are not victimized in greater proportion to their numbers than other age groups, and even if they do not under-report victimization, the constraining effect of the threat of victimization on their freedom to come and go as they please appears to be considerable. This constant stress may lead to physical illness and to a general fear even when there is no discernible cause. Among people who have some sensory deficiencies, as many of the elderly do, such paranoid types of reactions are reasonable responses to make to a feared environment. The quality of the lives of older people is also affected by the fact that others are less interested in coming to them because of the threatening neighborhood in which they live. Doctors are more reluctant than usual to make house calls in high crime areas where many older people live. In fact in a study of a home medical service, healthy, young, male medical students expressed resentment at having to make house calls in neighborhoods that they felt were dangerous.[31] In addition to the doctors' reluctance to visit, stores often will not deliver goods, taxis do not want to pick up, sometimes even the ambulance refuses to come.[32] The police may attribute the complaints of some of the elderly to senility and fail to appreciate their concerns.

What all of this means is that the life styles of older people who live in some urban communities may be only marginally better than the lives of those who live officially segregated from the community in nursing homes. While the lack of integration of nursing home residents within the greater community is beginning to be realized, the lack of integration of community-housed elderly within the community remains hidden.

Would greater police protection provide the kind of environment in which older people would be able to leave their apartments and not fear victimization? To some extent it would help. However, an important point to keep in mind is that technological innovations and increased police protection are only one aspect of reducing the crime rate. People who are fearful and retreat behind closed blinds and locked doors may marginally reduce their own potential for victimization, but they increase the chances that a neighbor will have her purse snatched right in front of her apartment building because the attacker realizes that all the neighbors are sequestered behind their drawn blinds and locked doors. The enforced seclusion of urban elderly persons within their apartment walls not only contributes to their own isolation, but also to the breakdown of social controls over the potential victimizer. While technological advances may hamper the criminal and slightly reduce crime, criminals are freer to act when communities are not organized and residents exert little vigilance control over their neighbors' lives. This supports the notion that a vicious circle exists, where the elderly are afraid to be victimized and therefore stay behind their locked apartment doors, with the result that they are less aware of others being victimized in their vicinity.

The extent of the fear of victimization and the oppression that it creates in the lives of the elderly, more than for other age groups, is illustrated by the following testimony taken by the Select Committee on Aging of the U.S. Congress.[33]

> I am coming before you to say my little bit in behalf of the senior citizens . . . The problems we are having . . . are vandalism [and] nonsecurity . . . when I say vandalism, you name it, that is what we have . . . The old, the new, it is demolished . . . I have not been attacked myself . . . but my wife has been attacked. And speaking about going to church or anywhere at any time—that is a problem . . . you can't hardly live for being afraid that you will be ill-treated by the same kind of animal you are, a human being. I just can't see why the senior citizens of America . . . who have worked hard for this country . . . can't be respected . . . wherever you go you will find the same thing . . . people will be looking for security.

The effect of fear of victimization on the life styles of the elderly results in a social problem *in addition* to that created by actual victimization. As previously noted, studies have shown that for most criminal categories, the elderly are victimized less than other age groups. However the elderly, being fearful of victimization, alter their life styles more than other age groups do and resent their ill-treatment. If all thirty-year-old women stayed behind locked doors as often as seventy-year-old women do, society would long ago have recognized the magnitude of the social problem that fear of victimization creates for the elderly and for all of society. Because they do not "have" to be out at jobs, PTA, or cub scout meetings, it is not regarded as peculiar or unfortunate that they are not out more. In other words, society is able to overlook a social problem of great magnitude because there are so few important or necessary roles that the elderly play. In effect, as society is currently structured, it really does not matter if the elderly exist at all.

FEAR OF CRIME VERSUS FEAR OF VICTIMIZATION

In a national survey, 47 percent of the respondents who were age sixty-five or over reported that fear of crime was either a somewhat or a very serious problem for them personally.[34] The issue of fear may not be related simply to a concrete fear of personal victimization but may, like free-floating anxiety, be a more general, diffuse issue. Some provocative ideas about the fear of crime have been suggested by Frank Furstenberg.[35] He makes an interesting distinction between the fear of crime and the fear of victimization. On the basis of a reanalysis of Louis Harris survey data regarding crime and victimization in Baltimore, he concluded that the ranking of crime as a major problem in the United States by the elderly was related more to changing social conditions, while fear of victimization was related more to feelings of personal security. In other words, when older people were asked to rank crime as a serious problem and when they were asked how fearful they were of being victimized, the responses were not highly correlated for all subgroups. Those most concerned about the problem of crime were no more or less afraid of being personally victimized than anyone else. The 40 percent of those most threatened by change, compared with only 19 percent of those most committed to change, ranked crime as the number 1 problem. Very few people who lived in high crime areas were unafraid of victimization, while those who lived in low crime areas were mostly unafraid. Furstenberg notes that few political leaders have undertaken the task of educating the public to the idea that crime is not a necessary by-product of social change. This education might be particularly relevant for an older population whose values and beliefs may be entrenched though not unchangeable. The need for educational efforts is supported by data from a survey carried out with elderly residents of the model cities area of Rochester, New York.[36] Older whites were disturbed about the influx of older blacks into their neighborhood. Older blacks, on the other hand, were bothered by crime and other neighborhood conditions, but not about the racial composition of the neighborhood.

Downwardly mobile people of all ages have been found to be more prejudiced against people who are different than the valued group.[37] For the elderly, the valued-group may be those who are affluent, healthy, and middle-aged. To the extent that many of the elderly, particularly older women, are forced into downward mobility, they may be fearful of changing social conditions, as expressed in their fear of crime. The task of society therefore is two-fold: safer living environments for urban elderly and better educational efforts aimed at reducing anxiety about changing social conditions.

CONCLUSION

Criminal victimization of the elderly is a visible and frightening form of injustice. Although the rate of victimization against the elderly is lower than for most other age groups, the problem is not adequately expressed in statistics which treat the elderly as a homogeneous group, or which ignore the effects the fear of victimization has on their life styles.

Inner city elderly, often those who are members of minority groups, have victimization rates as high as those for other age groups. Those elderly who live in age-integrated public housing projects are particularly vulnerable to victimization. The offenders are often young residents of the same projects. Social conditions, including inadequate living environments and lack of employment opportunities, contribute to the preying of the young on the old.

In addition to violent crimes, the elderly are also victims of swindlers. Although there are many varieties of confidence games and frauds, they generally offer the apparent opportunity for greater financial security in old age. Because retirement includes a fixed income, older people and the middle-aged are particularly vulnerable to con artists.

The fear that victimization plays in the lives of the elderly is evident from the alteration in their life styles. Many elderly, particularly those in urban areas, go out only for necessary errands and only during the day. The fear of those inside their locked and shuttered dwellings facilitates the victimization of neighbors who are out on errands. The lack of community control increases the opportunity for criminals to escape notice. The social problem that is created when a large segment of the population remains cloistered within their dwellings goes largely unnoticed because of the lack of important and necessary roles for the elderly in society.

The constant stress which fear creates can lead to paranoia and even to physical illness, especially among people who already have some sensory deficiencies, as many of the elderly do. The quality of their lives is not only affected by the restriction on their own life styles, but also by the reluctance of the community to come to them.

There has been some evidence that the fear expressed by the elderly is related to changing social conditions. To the extent that perception of crime as a major problem is not concretely related to fear of personal

TABLE 2-1a Personal Crimes: Change in Victimization Rates for Persons Age 12 and Over, by Sex, Age, and Type of Crime, 1973 and 1974—Females (Rate per 1000 persons in each age group)

Sex and age	Number of persons in the group	Crimes of violence	Rape	Robbery			Assault			Crimes of theft	Personal larceny	
				Total	With injury	Without injury	Total	Aggravated	Simple		With contact	Without contact
1973 rate	85,056,000	21.6	1.8	3.8	1.5	2.3	16.1	5.2	10.9	80.3	3.4	76.8
1974 rate	86,368,000	21.7	1.8	4.3	1.4	2.8	15.6	5.2	10.4	82.3	3.2	79.1
Percent change		+0.2	+4.0	+13.3	-0.7	+22.4	-3.4	-1.5	-4.2	+2.6	-5.8	+2.9
12–15												
1973 rate	8,151,000	35.8	1.3	3.3	0.6	2.6	31.3	9.3	22.0	158.3	2.1	156.2
1974 rate	8,143,000	35.6	2.7	5.2	1.5	3.7	27.7	6.4	21.3	155.8	2.2	153.6
Percent change		-0.8	+102.2	+58.8	+132.8	+41.2	-11.4	** -31.0	-3.1	-1.6	+3.3	-1.7
16–19												
1973 rate	7,860,000	39.2	4.6	4.5	2.1	2.5	30.1	9.2	20.9	139.1	3.6	135.5
1974 rate	8,015,000	43.0	4.9	5.5	1.4	4.0	32.7	10.7	21.9	136.7	3.1	133.6
Percent change		+9.9	+5.9	+20.6	-31.4	+63.4	+8.7	+16.7	+5.1	-1.7	-15.0	-1.4
20–24												
1973 rate	9,011,000	45.6	6.2	5.9	2.9	3.0	33.5	12.0	21.6	113.6	4.6	109.1
1974 rate	9,157,000	37.0	4.0	6.4	2.6	3.8	26.6	8.6	18.0	121.5	4.0	117.5
Percent change		* -18.8	** -35.2	+9.6	-9.1	+27.3	* -20.8	* -28.3	-16.5	+7.0	-11.9	+7.8

25-34												
1973 rate	14,429,000	23.4	2.4	4.0	1.7	2.3	17.1	5.8	11.3	86.6	3.4	83.2
1974 rate	14,998,000	27.9	2.5	5.2	1.8	3.5	20.4	7.1	13.0	90.1	1.9	88.2
Percent change		**+19.1	+5.8	+31.2	+3.5	+52.0	+18.1	+23.6	+15.2	+4.0	*-43.6	+6.0
35-49												
1973 rate	17,554,000	16.1	10.4	3.2	1.0	2.3	12.5	4.4	8.0	69.4	2.7	66.7
1974 rate	17,526,000	14.9	10.4	3.5	1.2	2.3	11.0	4.6	6.4	74.6	2.5	72.1
Percent change		-7.3	+10.8	+8.4	+22.7	+2.7	-11.8	+3.4	-20.2	+7.5	-9.1	+8.1
50-64												
1973 rate	16,158,000	7.8	10.1	2.6	0.8	1.7	5.2	1.1	4.0	45.5	4.0	41.5
1974 rate	16,301,000	3.2	10.6	3.0	0.6	2.4	4.5	1.7	2.8	44.6	4.8	39.8
Percent change		+4.1	+342.9	+18.0	-28.4	+39.1	-12.0	+50.9	**-29.4	-2.1	+18.1	-4.1
65 and over												
1973 rate	11,893,000	6.9	10.2	4.3	1.8	2.5	2.4	0.9	1.5	18.1	3.6	14.5
1974 rate	12,228,000	7.0	10.3	3.0	1.7	1.3	3.7	1.2	2.5	20.2	4.1	16.1
Percent change		+1.8	+65.0	-30.8	-9.8	*-46.3	+55.3	+29.2	+71.0	+11.7	+14.4	+11.2

* Percent change is significant at the 2 standard error or 95 percent confidence level.
** Percent change is significant at the 1.6 standard error or 90 percent confidence level.
Z Less than .05.
1 Rate, based on about 10 or fewer sample cases, is statistically unreliable.

a Copied from United States Department of Justice, Table 4 (1976).

TABLE 2–2a Personal Crimes: Change in Victimization Rates for Persons Age 12 and Over, by Sex, Age, and Type of Crime, 1973 and 1974—Males (Rate per 1000 persons in each age group)

Sex and age	Number of persons in the group	Crimes of violence	Rape	Robbery			Assault			Crimes of theft	Personal larceny	
				Total	With injury	Without injury	Total	Aggravated	Simple		With contact	Without contact
1973 rate	77,128,000	44.1	¹0.1	9.9	3.3	6.7	34.1	15.2	19.0	102.9	2.6	100.2
1974 rate	78,194,000	45.1	¹Z	10.3	3.3	7.0	34.8	16.0	18.8	108.7	3.0	105.7
Percent change		+2.3	−20.0	+3.6	+1.5	+4.8	+1.9	+5.3	−0.8	*+5.7	+12.1	*+5.5
12–15												
1973 rate	8,425,000	74.2	¹0.2	19.1	5.1	14.0	54.9	20.7	34.1	185.2	2.2	183.0
1974 rate	8,384,000	69.2	¹0.3	20.0	5.1	14.9	49.0	19.1	29.9	177.2	4.0	173.2
Percent change		−6.7	+17.4	+4.7	Z	+6.4	−10.8	−7.9	−12.5	−4.3	+81.0	−5.3
16–19												
1973 rate	7,717,000	84.1	0.0	14.2	4.2	10.0	70.0	37.6	32.4	184.1	5.0	179.0
1974 rate	7,777,000	93.5	0.0	17.3	5.6	11.7	76.2	37.1	39.1	183.6	4.4	179.2
Percent change		+11.1	0.0	+21.9	+34.5	+16.7	+8.9	−1.2	+20.6	−0.3	−13.5	+0.1
20–24												
1973 rate	8,305,000	84.1	¹0.1	17.2	5.5	11.7	66.8	30.6	36.1	154.9	4.6	150.3
1974 rate	8,452,000	87.2	0.0	15.4	4.1	11.3	71.8	36.6	35.2	173.2	2.7	170.5
Percent change		+3.8	−100.0	−10.3	−25.1	−3.5	+7.6	+19.6	−2.6	*+11.8	*−41.7	*+13.5

25-34												
1973 rate	13,699,000	45.9	10.1	7.0	2.0	5.1	38.8	16.9	21.9	112.1	2.0	110.2
1974 rate	14,213,000	49.9	10.1	9.0	2.4	6.5	40.9	18.3	22.5	123.1	3.4	119.7
Percent change		+8.9	+28.6	+27.3	+22.3	+29.0	+5.5	+8.5	+3.1	*+9.8	+71.4	**+8.7
35-49												
1973 rate	16,279,000	27.2	0.0	7.0	3.1	3.9	20.2	9.0	11.2	74.1	1.1	73.0
1974 rate	16,257,000	27.3	0.0	7.6	3.0	4.6	19.6	9.6	10.1	84.2	2.6	81.6
Percent change		+0.2	0.0	+8.3	-3.8	+18.0	-2.6	+6.6	-10.0	*+13.7	*+140.0	*+11.8
50-64												
1973 rate	14,329,000	18.8	0.0	6.5	2.7	3.8	12.3	4.4	7.9	48.0	2.8	45.3
1974 rate	14,546,000	15.8	0.0	5.4	2.5	2.9	10.4	3.9	6.5	54.7	2.0	52.7
Percent change		**-16.1	0.0	-17.5	-8.8	-23.8	-15.3	-11.1	-17.6	**+13.9	-26.1	*+16.3
65 and over												
1973 rate	8,374,000	10.7	0.0	5.9	1.8	4.1	4.8	1.3	3.5	28.4	2.8	25.6
1974 rate	8,565,000	11.9	0.0	5.2	2.3	2.9	6.7	2.1	4.6	24.3	2.5	21.8
Percent change		+10.9	0.0	-12.2	+25.4	-28.4	+39.2	+59.9	+31.3	-14.3	-11.2	-14.7

* Percent change is significant at the 2 standard error or 95 percent confidence level.
** Percent change is significant at the 1.6 standard error or 90 percent confidence level.
Z Less than .05.
1 Rate, based on about 10 or fewer sample cases, is statistically unreliable.

a Copied from United States Department of Justice, Table 4 (1976).

TABLE 2-3. Household Crimes: Change in Victimization Rates, by Age of Head of Household and Type of Crime, 1973 and 1974 (Rate per 1000 households)

Age of household head	Number of households in the group	Burglary				Household larceny			Motor vehicle theft		
		Total	Forcible entry	Unlawful entry	Attempted forcible entry	Total	Completed	Attempted	Total	Completed	Attempted
12–19											
1973 rate	1,079,000	218.2	62.0	129.6	26.6	195.1	176.9	18.1	37.9	26.8	11.1
1974 rate	1,080,000	217.3	59.2	115.9	42.2	204.8	186.9	17.9	54.0	33.5	20.5
Percent change		–0.4	–4.5	–10.6	+58.7	+5.0	+5.7	–1.2	+42.5	+25.2	+84.3
20–34											
1973 rate	19,707,000	122.4	41.5	51.2	29.7	145.6	134.4	11.2	28.3	18.4	9.9
1974 rate	20,459,000	127.3	44.4	54.2	28.7	174.2	162.5	11.7	27.8	17.2	10.5
Percent change		+4.0	+7.0	+5.8	–3.3	*+19.6	*+20.9	+4.3	–1.9	–6.3	+6.4
35–49											
1973 rate	18,264,000	98.6	29.4	50.0	19.1	126.2	119.3	6.9	21.1	14.3	6.8
1974 rate	18,322,000	99.0	30.6	49.8	18.7	145.9	137.9	8.1	20.8	14.2	6.6
Percent change		+0.5	+3.8	–0.5	–2.1	*+15.6	*+15.6	+17.0	–1.5	–0.4	–4.0
50–64											
1973 rate	17,663,000	70.0	22.1	32.5	15.4	83.7	77.0	6.7	15.8	10.5	5.3
1974 rate	17,938,000	69.0	23.7	30.3	15.1	88.9	82.2	6.7	14.2	8.7	5.6
Percent change		–1.4	+7.4	–6.8	–2.5	+6.2	**+6.7	–0.3	–9.8	**–17.5	+5.7
65 and over											
1973 rate	13,591,000	55.0	19.0	23.5	12.5	47.3	43.7	3.6	5.4	3.5	1.9
1974 rate	14,036,000	54.4	16.6	24.4	13.4	57.9	54.3	3.6	5.7	3.7	2.0
Percent change		–1.2	–12.8	+3.5	+7.7	*+22.5	*+24.2	+1.7	+5.6	+4.9	+7.0

* Percent change is significant at the 2 standard error or 95 percent confidence level.
** Percent change is significant at the 1.6 standard error or 90 percent confidence level.

victimization, outside efforts might help change the situation and reduce the oppression of the elderly from this source.

In the long run, the problems of crime, victimization, and fear of victimization among the elderly require more education for the oppressed, better opportunities than are available through crime for the victimizers, as well as more immediate apprehension and prosecution strategies. Many of the elderly are victims of crime because they are too financially limited to live in better neighborhoods. Their decline in physical strength and their fear of personal injury make them particularly vulnerable targets. Lower educational levels and insecurity about the future combine to make many of the elderly susceptible to fast-talking con artists.

Because the elderly have fewer necessary roles to play in society, their isolation is easily overlooked. Victimization and the fear that it generates are highly visible aspects of a network of unfortunate social conditions which the aging and the aged experience.

Notes

1. See Lawton et al. (1976).
2. See the United States Department of Justice survey which will be referred to in future footnotes as the LEAA (1976) survey. Tables 2-1, 2-2, and 2-3 are reproduced from that survey.
3. See the Gallup Opinion Index (1975).
4. See Loether (1975). The Harris - NCOA (1975) survey found that approximately 29 percent of a national sample of adults age sixty-five and over felt that they personally had a very serious or somewhat serious problem with loneliness.
5. See United States Senate Special Committee on Aging (1977:126).
6. See United States Subcommittee on Housing and Consumer Interests of the Select Committee on Aging (1977:12-16).
7. See Loether (1975).
8. See Mike Barnicle's column, "The Elderly, Easy Targets for Teenagers", published in *The Boston Evening Globe*, Friday, June 16, 1978, p. 2.
9. See Antunes et al. (1977).
10. See United States Subcommittee on Housing and Consumer Interests of the Select Committee on Aging (1977:21-37).
11. See Gubrium (1974).
12. See Butler (1975).
13. See Mike Barnicle's column cited in footnote 8.
14. See United States Subcommittee on Housing and Consumer Interests of the Select Committee on Aging (1977:35).
15. See Younger (1976).
16. See Loether (1975:116).
17. See Ducovny (1969:182). The example of land fraud which follows is from page 174.
18. See Gallup Opinion Index (1975).
19. See United States Subcommittee on Housing and Consumer Interest of the Select Committee on Aging (1977:40).
20. See Sussman (1976).
21. See Mike Barnicle's column cited in footnote 8.

22. See Clemente and Kleiman (1976).
23. See Sherman et al. (1976); Rosow (1967) found that older people within age-homogeneous housing had more friends.
24. See Van Buren (1976).
25. See Sundeen and Mathieu (1976).
26. See Benjamin Franklin's *Poor Richard's Almanack,* written in 1733, reprinted in Bradley, Beatty, and Long (1962:127).
27. See Cunningham (1976).
28. See Blenkner, Bloom, and Nielson (1971).
29. See Cunningham (1976).
30. See Lawton, Nahemow, Yaffe, and Feldman (1976).
31. See Johnson (1976).
32. See Conklin (1976).
33. See United States Subcommittee on Housing and Consumer Interests of the Select Committee on Aging (1977:39).
34. See the Harris-NCOA survey of the myths and realities of aging (1975).
35. See Furstenberg (1971).
36. See Sterne, Phillips, and Rabushka (1974).
37. See Rokeach (1960).

References

Antunes, George E., Fay Lomax Cook, Thomas D. Cook, and Wesley Skogan, "Patterns of Personal Crime against the Elderly: Findings from a National Survey." *Gerontologist* 17, 1977: 312–327.

Blenkner, Margaret, Martin Bloom, and Margaret Nielson. "A Research and Demonstration Project." *Social Casework* 52, 1971: 483–499.

Butler, Robert N., *Why Survive?* New York: Harper & Row, 1975.

Clemente, Frank, and Michael B. Kleiman, "Fear of Crime Among the Aged." *Gerontologist* 16, 1976: 207–10

Conklin, John E., "Robbery, the Elderly, and Fear: An Urban Problem in Search of Solution." In Jack Goldsmith and Sharon Goldsmith (ed.), *Crime and the Elderly,* pp. 99–110 Lexington, Mass.: Heath, 1976.

Cunningham, Carl L., "Pattern and Effect of Crime against the Aging: The Kansas City Study." In Jack Goldsmith and Sharon Goldsmith (ed.), *Crime and the Elderly,* pp. 31–50. Lexington, Mass.: Heath, 1976.

Ducovny, Amram, *The Billion $ Swindle.* New York: Fleet, 1969.

Franklin, Benjamin, "Poor Richards Almanack." In S. Bradley, R. C. Beatty, and E. H. Long (ed.), *The American Tradition in Literature (revised),* p. 127. New York: Norton, 1962.

Furstenberg, Frank J., "Public Reaction to Crime in the Streets." *American Scholar* 51, 1971: 601–610.

Gallup Opinion Index, "Crime." 124, 1975: 6–17.

Gubrium, Jaber, F., "Victimization in Old Age: Available Evidence and Three Hypotheses." *Crime and Delinquency* 20, 1974: 245–50.

Harris, Louis, and Associates, *The Myth and Reality of Aging in America.* Washington, D.C.: NCOA, 1975.

Johnson, Elizabeth S., "Home Medical Service: The Program of the Boston University Medical Center." Prepared for the Edna McConnell Clark Foundation. Boston: Boston University Gerontology Center, 1976.

Lawton, M. Powell, Lucille Nahemow, Silvia Yaffe, and Steven Feldman, "Psychological Aspects of Crime and Fear of Crime." In Jack Goldsmith and Sharon Goldsmith (ed.), *Crime and the Elderly*, pp. 21–30. Lexington, Mass.: Heath, 1976.

Loether, Herman J., *Problems of Aging* (2nd ed.). Encino, Calif.: Dickenson, 1975.

Rokeach, Milton, *The Open and Closed Mind.* New York: Basic Books, 1960.

Rosow, Irving, *Social Integration of the Aged.* New York: Free Press, 1976.

Sherman, Edmund A., Evelyn S. Newman, and Anne D. Nelson, "Patterns of Age Integration in Public Housing and the Incidence and Fears of Crime among Elderly Tenants." In Jack Goldsmith and Sharon Goldsmith (ed.), *Crime and the Elderly,* pp. 67–76. Lexington, Mass.: Heath, 1976.

Sterne, Richard S., James E. Phillips, and Alvin Rabushka, *The Urban Elderly Poor.* Lexington, Mass.: Heath, 1974.

Sundeen, Richard A., and James T. Mathieu, "The Fear of Crime and its Consequences among Elderly in their Urban Communities." *Gerontologist* 16 (3), 1976: 210–211.

Sussman, Marvin B., "The Family Life of Old People." In Robert H. Binstock and Ethel Shanas (ed.), *Handbook of Aging and the Social Sciences.,* pp. 218–243. New York: Van Nostrand, 1976.

United States Department of Justice, "Criminal Victimization in the United States: A Comparison of 1973 and 1974 Findings." *A National Crime Panel Survey Report, LEAA.* Washington, D.C.: National Criminal Justice Information and Statistical Service, 1976.

United States Senate Special Committee on Aging, " A Call for Action on Crime." In *Developments in Aging Part I:* 1976, pp. 124–131. Washington, D.C.: United States Government Printing Office, 1977.

United States Subcommittee on Housing and Consumer Interests of the Select Committee on Aging, "Profile of the Victim and the Offender." *In Search of Security: A National Perspective on Elderly Crime Victimization.* Washington, D.C.: United States Government Printing Office, 1977.

Van Buren, David P., "Public Housing Security and the Elderly: Practice Versus Theory." In Jack Goldsmith and Sharon Goldsmith (ed.), *Crime and the Elderly,* pp. 153–157. Lexington, Mass.: Heath, 1976.

Younger, Evelle J., "The California Experience in Crime Prevention Programs with Senior Citizens." In Jack Goldsmith and Sharon Goldsmith (ed.), *Crime and the Elderly,* pp. 159–168. Lexington, Mass.: Heath, 1976.

CHAPTER **3**

Economic Status: Poverty Or Relative Deprivation

For many, one of the costs of living to a ripe old age is the humiliation of falling into poverty. The experience is not uncommon among those who have been solid members of the working class throughout their early and middle years. However, even those from a middle-class background sometimes suffer the same fate. Rose Anderson, the ninety-year-old woman mentioned in Chapter 1 who ended up living on welfare despite having been left $300,000 by her physician husband, is one example. While cases as dramatic as that of Rose Anderson are rare, even those who have managed to acquire substantial assets are not entirely protected against the possibility of a marked reduction in living standard if they live long enough.

There are many ways to describe the economic status of the elderly. Some indicate that the aged are economically disadvantaged; others suggest that as a group the aged are not disadvantaged. We will first propose a resolution of these apparent inconsistencies and then go on to argue that despite recent advances the aged continue to face a great risk of poverty. As we shall see, it can be misleading to consider statistics describing poverty rates for the aged as a whole, as the rates vary considerably from one category of the aged to another. The poverty which many of the elderly experience is in itself a major source of oppression, but equal, if not more important, is the evidence that poverty contributes to the victimization and exploitation of the aged in a variety of other spheres.

In Colonial America there were very strong norms concerning the filial responsibility of children to their parents and the veneration of age. At the end of the eighteenth century most Americans lived on farms, and the less than 2 percent of the population who were age sixty-five or older usually lived with one or more of their as yet unmarried children. Very few lived alone or in extended three-generation households. Those who had a farm and a family typically could expect to be adequately cared for in their old age. However, the same was not true of the elderly poor who did not have children who could provide care for them in their old age. By modern standards the treatment of such persons often reflected callous indifference.

Between the middle of the nineteenth century and the middle of the twentieth century the nation was transformed from a predominantly rural agricultural society to a predominantly urban industrial society. This transformation was associated with very substantial economic growth and increases in the standard of living, but these increases were not shared equally by all segments of the population. During much of this period the economic status of the elderly relative to others was declining.[1]

There were a number of social developments that contributed to this decline. One was the sharp increase in life expectancy. Another was the decline in family size. As a result, a higher proportion of parents became economically dependent on a smaller number of children for a longer period of time. Given the general weakening of family ties with the move from the farm to the city, this meant that a higher proportion of the elderly could not count on adequate support from their children in their old age.

Further complicating the plight of the elderly was the transformation in the nature of work. On the farm it was possible to reduce one's work effort gradually over a period of years. This made it possible for many to continue working until a ripe old age. But the aged factory worker was in a very different situation. Many were forced to quit work because of health problems and few were eligible for pensions of any kind. For those who had been forced to retire, there were few alternative employment opportunities available.

By the early 1900s the issue of old age poverty had become a major social concern. The first effort to study the economic status of the elderly was carried out in Massachusetts in 1910. The investigators found that nearly one quarter of the aged were public paupers, inmates of almshouses, or dependent on some other form of institutional support.[2] In the years that followed conditions got worse, not better.

By roughly comparable measures, dependency of elderly Americans was 23 percent in 1910, 33 percent in 1922, and 40 percent in 1930—before the Great Depression began to take effect. When the Depression struck, the situation grew even worse. Old age dependence rose nearly to 50 percent in 1935, and to two-thirds in 1940.[3]

With the Great Depression of the 1930s poverty among the elderly reached crisis proportions. This was a major factor contributing to passage of the Social Security Act in 1935. The Social Security program has come to have a far greater impact on the economic status of the elderly than had originally been anticipated. When it was introduced only a small minority were eligible; today almost everyone is.

THE ECONOMIC STATUS OF THE ELDERLY

Are the elderly (persons age sixty-five and over) getting less than a fair share of the nation's economic resources. Some argue that they are already getting more than their due. Others feel that the aged are being unfairly denied an adequate share. As a group, the aged receive a proportion of the nation's aggregate personal income (the sum total for all persons combined) about equal to their proportion of the population. In 1973 approximately 11 percent of the nation's $849 billion in personal income went to the elderly.[4] In the same year they constituted approximately 10 percent of the total population. Between 1969 and 1979 the fraction of the federal budget spent on programs for the elderly increased from 22 to 31 percent.[5] Evidence such as this has been used by some to argue that economic deprivation is not a serious problem among the elderly.

As is indicated in Table 3–1, one of the largest sources of the aggregate personal income received by the elderly is retirement benefits (37 percent). Of this, the largest portion comes from Social Security benefits (31 percent). These statistics do not surprise us. They fit right in with the common conception of the elderly as being retired and living on Social Security, with their income being supplemented by private pensions, if

TABLE 3–1. Sources of Aggregate Personal Income of the Aged, 1972[a]

Source	Percent
Retirement Benefits	37
Social Security (31 percent)	
Other[b] (6 percent)	
Earnings	39
Income from Assets	16
Welfare	2
Other Income	7
Total	101

[a] Head or spouse age 65 or over.
[b] This includes government and veterans' pensions.
Source: Moon (1977:8).

they are lucky. Of greater interest is the evidence that there may be some serious flaws in this stereotype. In reality, we find that 39 percent of the aggregate income of the elderly is derived from earnings. Clearly, earnings are a significant source of income for a substantial minority of the elderly. We also find that another 16 percent of the elderly's aggregate income is derived from assets. By "assets" we mean property and other economic resources. Asset income includes dividends paid on shares of common stock, bonds, and mutual funds; interest on savings; and rent on property.

One limitation of statistics that describe the economic status of the elderly in the aggregate is that the picture produced may be distorted by the impact of a small number of people. In the case of Social Security income, the problem is not too serious because most of the elderly do derive substantial income from this source. However, when interpreting the 39 percent of the aggregate income derived from earnings, it is important to keep in mind that it is all going to the minority, 20 percent of men and 8 percent of women, who continue in the labor force. In the case of asset income the problem is even more serious. Most of this income goes to a very small proportion of the elderly. Very few of the elderly derive anywhere near 16 percent of their income from assets.[6]

Median income statistics can be used to obtain a more representative description of the economic status of the elderly. The "median" (family) income is the income of those families that have 50 percent of all families above them in income and 50 percent below them. Median income is a more representative statistic because it is not influenced by the very high incomes of a small number of families. In 1976 the median income for elderly families was $8,000. As is indicated in Table 3–2, this was far below the median for all families ($15,000). As we can see, the description we get on the basis of these median income statistics is very different than that obtained on the basis of the elderly's aggregate share of the nation's personal income. The discrepancy is due to the tendency for a small number of very prosperous elderly to contribute disproportionately to the aggregate income that goes to the elderly as a group.

However, even median income statistics can be misleading if we do not

TABLE 3–2.   Median Family Income by Race, Age of Head, and Size, 1976

	All Races	Whites	Blacks
Aged Families[a]	$ 8,000	$ 8,300	$5,000
All Families	$15,000	$15,500	$9,200
Two-person Families with Head under Age 65	$14,200	$14,800	$8,100

[a] Head age 65 or older.
Source: Based on Table 22, Bureau of the Census (1978a).

take into consideration the reality that the elderly population is made up of a variety of subgroups in very different economic situations. Three of the most important factors specifying such subgroups are race, sex, and employment status. As indicated in Table 3–2, the $5,000 median income for elderly black families is considerably below the $8,000 median for elderly white families.

Based on what we know about relative incomes in the general population, we would expect to find lower incomes for elderly females than for elderly males. The relevant statistics confirming this expectation are presented in Table 3–3. We find that the $3,100 median income for elderly females is much below the $5,500 median for elderly males. We have found, as might have been expected, that the income effects of past discrimination based on race and sex follow one into old age.

When considering the economic status of the elderly, it is essential to take into consideration the extent of the person's participation in the labor force. Most persons over age sixty-five have retired, but a substantial minority are still at work and, in some instances, earning more than at any prior time in their lives. The $13,800 median income for elderly men who work fulltime all year round is far greater than the $5,500 median for all elderly men. Similarly, for elderly women the $7,800 median income for those who are fully employed is far greater than the $3,100 median for all elderly women.

It is often difficult to determine whether an older person is retired. This is particularly true of those who are presently out of work, but who would return to work were they able to find a suitable position. It is also difficult to decide what to do with those who have been able to find a job for a few hours a week, but would prefer to be working full-time. This is one of the reasons why it is difficult to offer a precise estimate of the decrease in income that occurs with retirement. A reasonable estimate is that incomes typically drop by 40 to 50 percent at retirement.[7] This decline continues

TABLE 3–3. Median Income of Persons[a] by Sex, Work Status, and Age, 1977

	All Persons	Fully Employed Workers[b]
Males		
Age 65 and over	$ 5,500	$13,800
Age 14 and over	$10,100	$15,100
Females		
Age 65 and over	$ 3,100	$ 7,800
Age 14 and over	$ 3,900	$ 8,800

[a] Excludes persons without any income.
[b] Persons employed full time all year.
Source: Table 7, U.S. Bureau of the Census (1978b).

throughout the retirement years, being further exacerbated by increases in income levels for those still in the labor force.[8]

Most people do not require as much income after retirement as they required prior to retirement in order to maintain their accustomed standard of living. There tend to be reductions in certain costs associated with employment such as clothing and transportation. According to one estimate, the typical retired couple can maintain their previous standard of living on approximately 75 percent of their preretirement income.[9] However, less than 10 percent of male workers retire with Social Security and other pension benefits that equal as much as 70 percent of their preretirement income.[10]

In recent years, has the economic status of the elderly been getting better, getting worse, or has it remained virtually unchanged? The way in which we answer this question depends to a large extent on how we measure change in economic status. If we look at trends over time in the median income for the elderly, we find evidence of considerable improvement. In 1947 the median income for elderly families was $4,900 (measured in 1977 dollars); by 1977 it had increased to $9,100. This represents an increase of 86 percent in purchasing power. However, if we focus on the incomes of the elderly relative to other age groups, we get a different picture. In 1947 the median income for elderly families was 60 percent of the median for all families; in 1977 it was 57 percent of the median for all families. Over this period of thirty years there has been no net improvement in the economic status of the elderly relative to other age groups; in this sense, they remain as disadvantaged today as they were in 1947.[11]

The elderly have a higher poverty rate than does any other adult age group. In 1977, of the 22 million persons age sixty-five and over, 3.2 million or 14 percent were classified as poor by the federal government.[12] This is significantly above the 12 percent poverty rate for all age categories and it is more than double the 7 percent poverty rate for those forty-five to fifty-four, the age group with the lowest risk of poverty. In 1977 the federal poverty line for a non-farm family of four was $6,200. For an elderly couple it was $3,700 and for an elderly person living alone it was $2,900. Some critics point out that the government's poverty measure fails to take into account many of the "hidden poor," that is, elderly persons who would be classified as poor on the basis of their own income, but who have been taken in by relatives who are not poor. One estimate is that if the hidden poor were counted, as many as 5 million or nearly one-quarter of the elderly would be classified as poor.[13]

As we argued earlier, the elderly population is made up of a variety of subgroups in very different economic circumstances. On the basis of our previous analysis of median income statistics, it would be reasonable to expect a higher poverty rate among elderly women than among elderly men and a higher rate among elderly blacks than among elderly whites.

TABLE 3–4. Poverty Rates[a] among Aged Persons[b] by Race and Sex of Head, 1959 and 1977

	1977 (Percent)	1959 (Percent)
Male Head		
Whites	7	28
Blacks	28	59
Female Head		
Whites	21	47
Blacks	48	70

[a]Percent poor.
[b]Head age 65 or older.
Source: Table 16, U.S. Bureau of the Census (1978b).

In 1976 some 18 percent of elderly females in contrast to 11 percent of elderly males were poor. In the same year 35 percent of elderly blacks in contrast to 13 percent of elderly whites were poor. When we consider these characteristics simultaneously as we have done in Table 3–4, we find even greater discrepancies. Only 7 percent of families headed by elderly white males are poor in contrast to 48 percent of those headed by black females.

There are a number of other observations that can be made on the basis of the information presented in Table 3–4. Probably the most important of these is the evidence of a sharp reduction in the prevalence of poverty since the late 1950s. In 1959 some seven out of ten families headed by black women were poor; by 1977 less than five out of 10 were poor. In 1959 almost half of families headed by white women were poor, but today less than a quarter are poor. There are also corresponding decreases for families headed by elderly males of both races. These statistics point to the marked improvement in the economic status of the elderly that has taken place in recent decades. However, these same statistics also point out that poverty continues to be a very common fate to many of the elderly, particularly white women and blacks of either sex.

To the extent that we are interested in economic well-being as opposed to income status alone, it is necessary to take into consideration the various nonmoney government transfers to the elderly. Of relevance here are health insurance benefits, food stamps, public housing subsidies, and a wide variety of social services. Similarly, we would want to consider the value of food, personal services, transportation, and lodging provided by relatives. Needless to say, it is all but impossible to make reliable estimates of the economic value of all these benefits.[14] While we cannot expect to make actual adjustments for more than a few of these benefits, it is important to keep in mind that they are not taken into consideration in the income statistics generally used when describing the economic status of the elderly.

SOCIAL SECURITY

The Social Security program contributes more to the economic well-being of the elderly than do all other federal, state, and local income programs (such as Supplemental Security Income) and in-kind programs (such as public housing) combined. Today most of the elderly are eligible for at least minimal Social Security pension benefits. Many of those who are not, such as people who have not contributed to the program for the required minimum of ten years, are eligible for pension or welfare benefits from other sources. For example, federal government workers and railroad workers have their own independent pension programs; they do not participate in the Social Security program. Of those who are not eligible for either Social Security or one of these alternative pensions, many are eligible for benefits from Supplemental Security Income (SSI), a program administered by the Social Security Administration. It was introduced as a replacement for several earlier public assistance programs.

The Social Security Act was passed in the midst of the Great Depression of the 1930s. A major objective of the old-age pension program created by the act was to reduce the extent of economic destitution among the elderly.[15] However, another important objective was job creation. Old-age pensions were seen as a mechanism to encourage older workers to leave and remain out of the work force.[16] The goal was to open up new positions for younger workers, positions that were at a premium when one quarter of the labor force was out of work.

The first Social Security old-age pensions were paid in 1940. At that time only a small fraction of the elderly were eligible for benefits, but many of those who were got a very good return on their "investment."[17] This was particularly true for Ida Fuller, a legal secretary who became the first person to receive a Social Security pension check. She became eligible for pension benefits after having contributed less than $100 in Social Security taxes. Her pension was $22 per month in 1940, but it increased over the years. By the time she died in 1975, after living to be one hundred years old, she had been paid more than $20,000 in Social Security benefits.[18]

Over the years there has been a marked increase in the proportion of the working population covered by the Social Security program. In 1940 it was restricted to approximately 60 percent of the labor force, those in industry and commerce. During the 1950s and 1960s coverage was steadily expanded to other categories of workers. Among those added were regularly employed domestic and agricultural workers as well as most of the self-employed. Today more than 90 percent of workers are in "covered" employment. Those still not covered include agricultural and domestic workers who do not hold regular jobs, as well as housewives and self-employed persons with very low incomes. Also excluded are the railroad workers and civilian government employees mentioned earlier who have their own pension programs.

There has also been expansion with respect to categories of persons eligible for Social Security benefits. When first enacted in 1935 the program, Old Age Insurance (OAI), was to provide benefits only to retired workers. However, before any pension benefits were actually paid, it was modified in 1939 to extend benefits to a covered worker's dependents and surviving spouse. To reflect this change the program was renamed Old Age and Survivors Insurance (OASI). In 1956 benefits were extended to disabled workers and their dependents (OASDI). In 1965 health insurance (Medicare) was added (OASDHI), and in 1974 the Supplemental Security Income (SSI) program went into effect. Although the program is administered by the Social Security Administration, it is kept as a separate program. The name Social Security has not been modified to include this component. The conscious effort to keep SSI as a distinct program is due to its being so explicitly a welfare program.

As a consequence of this expansion of the Social Security program there has been a steady increase in the proportion of the elderly who are eligible for Social Security pension benefits. In 1948 only one out of eight of the elderly were eligible; today nine out of ten are eligible.

In 1940, the average Social Security pension to a retired worker was $271 ($1,172 in 1977 dollars) per year; by 1977 it had increased to $2,916. There has been a marked increase in both Social Security pension benefits and in average (median) family incomes since 1940. The ratio of the Social Security pension benefits to the average family income can be interpreted as a measure of the relative purchasing power this pension provides. This ratio was relatively constant between 1950 and 1970, but it has increased substantially during the early 1970s, suggesting an improvement in the relative purchasing power of Social Security pensions. That is, in 1970 the average Social Security benefit to a retired worker was $1,417, which would buy 14 percent as much as would the average family income of $9,867. By 1977 the Social Security benefit had increased to $2,916, which would buy 18 percent as much as the $16,009 average family income at that time.

When we consider the period from 1940 to 1977 we find that Social Security benefits increased at a rate greater than the cost of living (inflation) during each decade (Table 3–5).[19] However, these increases in pension benefits did not always keep pace with increases in the overall standard of living as much as average family income. During the 1940s and 1960s, the overall standard of living (as reflected in median family income) increased more rapidly than did Social Security pension benefits, but dur-

TABLE 3–5.   Percentage Increases in Social Security Pension Benefits, the Cost of Living, and Median Family Income, by Decade 1940–1977

	Percent Increase in Social Security Retired Worker Pension Benefit[a]	Percent Increase in Cost of Living[b]	Percent Increase in Median Family Income[c]
Decade			
1940–49	94	72	170
1950–59	69	23	69
1960–69	60	31	76
1970–77	106	56	62
1940–77	976	332	1200

[a]Source: Table M–13, U.S. Dept. of Health, Education and Welfare (1978:43). These figures are based on estimates of the average benefit to retired workers. They do not include spouse benefits.
[b]As measured by increases in the Consumer Price Index.
[c]Source: Table 2, U.S. Bureau of the Census (1978b), for 1950 through 1977. The statistics for 1940–49 were estimated on the basis of data from U.S. Bureau of the Census (1975:303). The 1940 estimate is based on wage income only: this would tend to give an upward bias to out estimate of the percent increase for the decade.

ing the early 1970s Social Security pensions increased more rapidly than did the overall standard of living. During each decade since 1940 there has been an increase in the absolute purchasing power of the Social Security pension, but it was not until the 1970s that there was an increase in the relative purchasing power of this pension, that is, an increase relative to the purchasing power of the average family.[20]

As the number of Social Security recipients and the level of pension benefits have increased, so has the cost of the program. In 1950, less than 1 percent of the nation's GNP was spent on the Social Security program. Today, if we include the health insurance component, more than 5 percent of GNP is spent on the program. In 1940, it was paid for by a payroll tax of 1 percent on the first $3,000 of the employee's income and by a corresponding contribution by the employer. By 1978, the tax on both the employer and employee had increased to 6 percent of the first $17,700 of the employee's income. Present legislation calls for continued increases in the Social Security tax through the 1980s. By 1987 the tax is scheduled to be 7.1 percent of the first $42,600.

For many years Social Security was one of the least controversial federal programs, but in recent years this has changed. The sharp increase in cost is one reason. The combined impact of the trend toward earlier retirement, increased life expectancy, and smaller families is creating a situation in which the number of those who are retired and drawing pension benefits relative to those who are in the labor force and paying for these benefits is increasing. The resulting increase in the tax burden on those in the labor force could become a very explosive issue in the not too distant future. Another reason that the Social Security program has become controversial is the increase in awareness that it is being financed by a regressive payroll tax. A regressive tax is one in which those with low income are taxed more than those with high incomes. In 1978 those who earned $10,000 paid just over 6 percent of their income as a Social Security payroll tax, but those who earned $100,000 paid just over 1 percent of their income.[21]

Social Security has some of the characteristics of private insurance programs and some of the characteristics of public welfare programs.[22] The conflict between these two aspects of the program has become increasingly evident in recent years. When first enacted, the insurance objectives were predominant, but over the years Social Security has been modified to accommodate an increasing number of welfare objectives.

A major source of Social Security's popularity has been in its image as an insurance program. Covered employees are required to make "contributions" to this "social insurance" program which are paid into a "trust fund" during their working years. Upon reaching retirement age, they in turn can expect to be paid a pension out of this trust fund. In general those who have higher preretirement incomes and who have made larger contributions to the program over the years can anticipate a larger pension upon retirement. Being a Social Security recipient has none of the stigma associated with being a welfare recipient. One reason is that these pension benefits are viewed by all as having been earned. Another reason is that the benefits are not restricted to those with low incomes. In fact, there are some very wealthy people who collect Social Security pension benefits.

However, this is only part of the picture. The program has a number of characteristics that are not at all consistent with principles of private insurance.[23] In private insurance programs there is a clear actuarial correspondence between the amount people pay in premiums and the size of the pension they are eligible for upon reaching retirement age. While some will live longer than others and end up collecting more in pension benefits, on the average the expected pension benefit corresponds to the premium one has paid. However, with the Social Security program, the relationship between prior contribution and the size of the pension benefit is more tenuous. One example of this is the spouse benefit which increases the effective pension income for recipients who are married. Another example is the provision for replacing a larger share of preretirement income for those with low incomes. This results in a better return on "contributions" for those who have paid in less. The tenuousness of the link is most clearly illustrated by the provision that calls for at least minimal pension benefits to all persons over age seventy-two independent of whether they have ever paid Social Security payroll taxes.

Social Security pension levels are set by Congress and can be modified at any time. The extent to which these benefits reflect prior contributions is entirely up to Congress, and is influenced as much by political as by actuarial considerations. Benefits are automatically adjusted each year to correct for increases in the cost of living (inflation), but adjustments for increases in the overall standard of living (median income) are still at the discretion of Congress.

In a private insurance program money paid in by policyholders is set aside in some form of trust fund that will eventually be used to pay benefits to them. If for some reason the insurance company were to stop taking in new policyholders, this would not adversely affect those who had retired and were already drawing pensions. There would be no problem because such pensions are financed by money already paid into the trust fund, not out of funds obtained from those currently making payments.

However, with Social Security the "contributions" made by workers today are paid right out in the form of benefits to those currently retired. While the Social Security trust fund is worth billions of dollars, it would only provide benefits to today's recipients for a little over a year were those presently in the labor force to cease making their contributions through payroll taxes. Where did the money go? It was paid out over the years to those who were retired at the time the contributions were made. This pay-as-you-go financing system is quite inconsistent with the principles of private insurance. Today's workers are being taxed to pay the pensions of today's recipients. They are not contributing to a trust fund from which they will one day draw benefits that correspond in any direct actuarial sense to the contributions made over the years.

Some people pay Social Security taxes for thirty years or more and end up with the same pension benefit for which they would have been eligible had they not contributed any Social Security taxes at all. This is often the case with widows. A woman often finds that she is eligible for a larger pension based on her deceased husband's work history than based on her own work history. In such a situation she has a choice. She can select whichever pension is larger, but she is not eligible for both.

The Social Security program includes a retirement test. In 1978 persons under age seventy-two who were eligible for Social Security pension benefits could not earn more than $4,000 per year without having benefits reduced $1 for every $2 earned above this amount.[24] This provision helps cut Social Security pension costs, but it does so by discriminating against lower income recipients. People who have had low incomes over the years are likely to have little in the way of outside unearned income, such as interest on savings or stock dividends, to supplement their generally lower Social Security pension benefits. Many of these people are forced by economic necessity to remain in the labor force despite the penalty associated with the retirement test. This provision is entirely inconsistent with private insurance which would pay the pension regardless of any other sources of income the policyholder might have.

By now it should be evident that the Social Security program is based on a somewhat contradictory mixture of welfare and insurance objectives. However, it is unlikely that any major effort will be made to resolve these contradictions in the foreseeable future. There is little interest in either turning Social Security into an outright welfare program consistently structured around welfare objectives, or in eliminating the welfare provisions that contradict the basic principles on which private insurance programs are based.

If the program were to be restructured more in accordance with social welfare objectives, one of the first changes would be in the mechanism used to finance it. A shift would be made away from the payroll tax which tends to have a regressive impact (taxing those with the lowest incomes the most) to financing it out of general federal revenues.[25]

However, some fear that if this change were made Social Security would take on some of the stigma presently associated with welfare programs. It is generally argued that the clear link between the payroll tax and the pension benefit is necessary to avoid the stigma of a welfare program.[26] If changes were made in the structure of Social Security programs that did increase the stigma associated with being a recipient, it is possible that many of the elderly would do without rather than apply for benefits they clearly needed. Today many more older persons are eligible for Supplemental Security Income benefits than the 14 percent currently on the rolls. Some argue that one reason for this under-enrollment is that SSI carries the stigma of welfare despite its being administered by the Social Security Administration.

Suppose on the other hand that the Social Security program were restructured in accordance with the principles of private insurance. Pension benefits would then be actuarially based on prior contribution. One consequence would be that those with poor work histories, who tend to have the lowest Social Security pensions, would end up with even less adequate Social Security pensions than they get today. It would be necessary to substantially expand the Supplemental Security Income program to compensate for this drop in Social Security pension benefits. Many who today can make ends meet on their modest Social Security pension would have to apply for SSI benefits. Some fear that the elderly poor would in the long run be worse off because there would be less support in Congress for incrementing SSI benefit levels than there is for incrementing Social Security benefits. The poor tend to do better when included as recipients of more universalistic (applying to everyone or everyone who is aged) programs such as Social Security and Medicare than they do when special programs such SSI are created to provide income or in-kind benefits just for the poor.

Because of the tenuous link between contributions in the form of Social Security tax contributions and the pensions retired workers are eventually paid, the selection of Social Security benefit levels is very much a political matter. In arriving at a decision, it is necessary to strike a balance between the interests of the retired elderly and the interests of persons presently in the labor force. Many of the elderly find themselves with few if any options for supplementing this pension income should it prove inadequate to meet their needs. On the other hand, many of those who are being asked to pay for these benefits have their own legitimate economic needs. Under the present system some workers who are attempting to provide for a growing family on a near poverty income are paying Social Security taxes that get distributed, at least in part, to elderly persons who are financially much better off then they will ever be.

How do we decide on the minimum standard of living that it is reasonable to ask the elderly to accept in this society? How in turn do we decide what it is fair to tax those in the labor force in an effort to assure the elderly this standard of living? Important as these questions are, there are no simple answers. They call for ethical and political judgments that are unavoidably colored by one's age, social class, and ideology.

The Social Security program has been a major social change agent in recent decades. One of the most significant effects has been on labor force participation among aged males. In 1940 some 42 percent of elderly males were still in the labor force, but there had been a decline to 20 percent by 1976.[27] While Social Security is not the only factor which has contributed to this decline, it is certainly an important one. Some view this decline with favor, others with disfavor. The liberal is likely to point out that many of those who in the past would have continued to work would have done so at a high personal price. Many have health problems that make continued employment an oppressive experience; in some instances continued employment is a serious health hazard. By contrast the conservative would be likely to point to those who are retired, but still in good health. The argument from this perspective is that those who are physically fit should be in the labor force carrying their own weight, not sitting idly at home increasing the already heavy tax burden on others.

Another major consequence of the Social Security program has been the impetus it has provided for the introduction of mandatory retirement regulations. Prior to enactment of the Social Security program it was rare to require that employees retire at any specified age. Most worked until they could no longer function effectively on the job. But when the Social Security program set the age of sixty-five for pension eligibility, this age was soon adopted by many corporations for mandatory retirement. Instead of being the age at which a worker would have the option of retiring, it became the age at which the worker had to retire. The availability of this pension eased the conscience of the employer and undercut organized resistance from workers. Recently these mandatory retirement regulations have been called into question. Mandatory retirement has been eliminated for federal civilian employees and the minimum age in private industry has been raised from sixty-five to seventy. However, it is reasonable to assume that the principle of mandatory retirement will remain with us for some years to come in the private sector.

Although we have considered only a few of the social consequences of the Social Security program, it should be clear that this change in economic status for so many of the elderly has had a variety of social ramifications. Since Social Security is only one factor among many that have contributed to these changes, it is difficult to estimate with any precision just how much of the observed change can be attributed to Social Security alone. For example, since the enactment of Social Security in 1935 there has been a great deal of economic growth in the country. This growth has increased personal incomes and the funds available for various social programs. Thus we might ask how much of the improved economic status of the elderly is due to the Social Security program and how much is due to this economic growth? As it turns out these two alternatives are not entirely independent. The substantial increases in Social Security benefits have been made possible, at least in part, by economic growth. This is just one illustration of the way in which macroeconomic phenomena such as inflation, unemployment rates, and economic growth have an impact on the elderly's standard of living.

THE IMPACT OF THE ECONOMY ON THE ELDERLY

Inflation, unemployment levels, and rates of economic growth are all aspects of the economy which affect the lives of the elderly.[28] It is common knowledge that inflation is a threat to the elderly's standard of living, but as we shall see, the degree of vulnerability varies considerably across different income groups. A substantial minority of the elderly are still in the labor force and for this reason are vulnerable to fluctuations in unemployment rates. Economic growth turns out to have both positive and negative consequences for the standard of living available to the elderly.

Many older persons find themselves living entirely or in part on fixed incomes, such as pensions, that are not periodically adjusted for inflation. Many private pensions specify that the recipient is entitled to a fixed monthly benefit for life without any provision for the reduction in purchasing power that will occur over the years. Even a pension which provided an adequate income at the time of retirement may fall far short of adequacy some fifteen or twenty years later. As an increasing proportion of workers are retiring earlier and living longer, the erosion of purchasing power due to inflation becomes an increasingly serious problem.

In discussions of categories of persons living on fixed incomes, it is common to mention those who depend primarily on their Social Security pension, but this example is not entirely accurate. As noted earlier in the chapter, Social Security pension benefits have more than kept pace with inflation over the years. For the past several years, legislation has been in effect which calls for automatic increments in benefit levels each year to compensate for reductions in purchasing power due to inflation. Similar escalator clauses are being written into an increasing proportion of private pension plans, but today many of the elderly are still dependent on pensions which have no such provision.

Those who are in the middle income category just prior to retirement are likely to be more adversely affected by inflation than are those with relatively high incomes. This middle income category includes many who have little in the way of asset income from savings and stocks, but who do have a private pension to supplement Social Security benefits. While their Social Security income is protected against inflation, their private pension income often is not. As a result they are likely to experience a reduction in purchasing power over the years.

Those with low preretirement incomes are likely to have little more than their Social Security pension to live on. While their purchasing power at the time of retirement will be lower than that of the middle income retiree, it is well protected against inflation. Such persons are not as likely to suffer an erosion in their purchasing power over the retirement years. Similarly, those with high preretirement incomes are likely to have acquired substantial income-producing assets. These assets tend to increase in value at a rate that at least keeps pace with inflation. For this reason retirees with either low or high preretirement incomes are likely to be more protected against the effects of inflation than are those in the middle income category.

Since many of the elderly are no longer in the labor force, the elderly as a group tend to be less vulnerable than other age groups to shifts in unemployment rates. However, to the 20 percent of elderly males and the 8 percent of elderly females who are in the labor force, high unemployment rates are as much a threat as they are to other age groups. Many elderly workers are forced to look for new jobs because of mandatory retirement regulations. Due to discrimination against older workers in the hiring process, they typically find that most jobs are closed to them. The employment opportunities available to the elderly are likely to be particularly limited during periods of high unemployment. By contrast, during periods of unusually low unemployment, the elderly find their services very much in demand; this was the case during World War II.

While automatic cost-of-living increments protect Social Security pensions against any erosion in absolute purchasing power due to inflation, this increment does not deal with any erosion in relative purchasing power due to economic growth and the tendency for incomes to increase with growth. During periods of economic recession there is no growth in the economy; that is, there is no increase in "real" GNP.[29] However, over the long run our economy continues to grow. This growth is reflected in the increase in real GNP, the Gross National Product after adjusting for inflation. This real increase in GNP contributes to an increase in personal income over and above the increase due to inflation. Not only do people have higher incomes, but they can also buy more with these incomes; their purchasing power has increased. Economic growth is generally looked upon favorably as it increases the purchasing power of workers and provides the funds necessary for expanding government benefits to the elderly and other economically deprived segments of the population.

Ironically, economic growth, which is so important as a factor contributing to the increasing standard of living available to the elderly, does have some adverse consequences for those who are retired. The increase in incomes due to economic growth tends to go disproportionately to those who are in the labor force.[30] Economic growth contributes to increases in the absolute standard of living available to the elderly, but the increase is generally not as great as that to persons still in the labor force. Thus, the income gap between the retired and those still at work tends to increase during periods of economic expansion. This would not be a serious problem if the elderly could avoid making comparisons between their own purchasing power and that of the typical American family. Many cannot avoid making such comparisons, and as a result they are vulnerable to feelings of "relative deprivation." For those who have been retired twenty years or more the reduction in relative purchasing power can be quite substantial.

CONCLUSION

Today the aged receive at least their proportionate share of the nation's aggregate personal income. However, the favorable aggregate income picture for the elderly is due in part to the high incomes of a small proportion. For this reason, average (median) income statistics present quite a different picture. The average income for the aged is between 50 and 60 percent of that for the general population. However, even median income statistics can be misleading when the aged are treated as one homogeneous group. When we compare the incomes for various race, sex, and employment status subgroups, we find substantial differences.

Not all of the aged are victims of economic deprivation, but 14 percent of the elderly have incomes that fall below the federal poverty line, more than double the poverty rate for the forty-five to fifty-four age category. Poverty rates are higher for families headed by women and blacks; almost

50 percent of families headed by black elderly females fall below the poverty line.

The economic deprivation that many of the aged experience is itself a source of oppression, but more importantly, it is at the root of a variety of other injustices they face. In a society which places a high premium on economic self-sufficiency and in which income is a major determinant of social status, the economic deprivation in old age can have devastating consequences for one's self-esteem. Those who have lost many of their former sources of self-esteem are particularly vulnerable to the added burden of poverty. Even those who do not find themselves below the poverty line may experience a severe sense of relative deprivation due to a very real reduction in living standard.

For most of the elderly poor much more than their self-esteem is at stake. Economic deprivation has profound implications for the quality of their lives in many other spheres. Consider, for example, the issue of crime and fear of crime discussed in the last chapter. Victimization rates for the inner city elderly, particularly those living in public housing, are substantially higher than the rates for the elderly living in the suburbs. Many of the elderly remain in inner city slums of economic necessity, not by choice. Here the link between poverty and exposure to criminal victimization is all too evident.

Similarly, we find that those who are most likely to end up in the most oppressive nursing homes are the aged poor. Those who can be expected at least to pay their way for the first few years are often able to get into a better quality home. Poor nutrition is found among all subgroups of the elderly, but it is particularly problematic among those who are most economically deprived. Today the elderly poor are eligible for Medicare and Medicaid, which have substantially improved the quality of the medical care available. However, these programs do not cover all medical costs and they do not assure the elderly poor the same quality of medical care that is available to those who can afford to pay more than these programs provide. Some physicians refuse to treat patients who cannot supplement Medicare payments. Others provide medical care, but with less attentiveness and consideration than given to those who are in a position to pay the higher fees the physician considers appropriate.

The standard of living available to the employed aged tends to be substantially higher than that available to those who are no longer in the labor force. Recent legislation may lead to some reduction in the extent of discrimination against older workers, particularly those protected by seniority rules, but it would be naive to assume that the problem is going to disappear in the case of those who for one reason or another become unemployed. Employers can easily find ways to discriminate against older workers regardless of legislation which prohibits such practices. It is all too easy to attribute discriminatory treatment to some factor other than age.

Ours is a society based in large measure on one's ability to pay. While our welfare state does provide a variety of services to those who are poor, these services generally are not of the same quality and not provided with the same sense as dignity as those provided to those who are in a position to pay for these services themselves. A case can be made that it is no accident that a welfare state has evolved over the years to provide at least a minimally adequate standard of living to the elderly poor. If workers believe that in old age their basic needs will be taken care of by the state, they will probably not push as hard as they otherwise would for wage increases and income redistribution programs.

Notes

1. See Pechman et al. (1968:29).
2. Fischer (1977:157).
3. Fischer (1977:174).
4. See U.S. Bureau of the Census (1974:2). Also see Fried et al. (1973) for a somewhat higher estimate of 14 percent for 1972.
5. It is important to keep in mind that much of the money referred to here goes to nursing home operators, hospitals, physicians, and others who provide services for the elderly, rather than going directly to the elderly themselves. Also, some of the recipients for such programs as Social Security are dependents under age sixty-five and in some cases under age eighteen.
6. In 1967 some 26 percent of couples and 42 percent of unrelated individuals had no financial assets. Another 17 percent of couples and 19 percent of unrelated individuals had less than $1,000 in assets. In 1967 two thirds of elderly couples had less than $5,000 in income-earning assets. Assets of $5,000 would bring in an income of $250 a year if earning 5 percent interest in a savings account. Those with $20,000 or more in income-producing assets begin to have substantial asset income, but this included only 13 percent of couples and 5 percent of unrelated individuals. If we take into consideration equity in a home, the asset position of the elderly is somewhat better, but this has little to do with the issue of asset income (Murray, 1972).
7. See Schulz (1976a:569).
8. In 1967 some 50 percent of nonmarried persons aged sixty-five to sixty-nine had incomes of less than $2,500. In the same year, 61 percent of those aged seventy to seventy-four, 71 percent of those aged seventy-five to seventy-nine, and 84 percent of those aged eighty and over had incomes of less than $2,500 (Schulz, 1976a:17).
9. Henle (1972).
10. The study referred to was conducted in 1970. Only about one half of the workers were eligible for pension benefits other than Social Security. Of this group, 47 percent had pension incomes equal to at least one half their preretirement earnings. Of those eligible for Social Security only, 19 percent had pension incomes equal to at least one half of their preretirement earnings and 60 percent had pension incomes equal to between 31 and 50 percent of preretirement earnings (Schulz, 1976a:569–570).
11. However, if we were to take into consideration the money value of Medicare and other such service programs for the elderly, we would have to conclude that the elderly's relative standard of living has also improved over the thirty year period referred to.
12. For a discussion of the way in which the government measures poverty, a critique of this measure, and some of the alternatives that have been suggested, see Williamson et al. (1975:13–18) as well as Williamson and Hyer (1975).

13. U.S. Senate (1977).
14. However, this does not stop son   ̃m trying. One study attempts to come up with a more accurate estimate of the prevalence of poverty among the elderly (U.S. Senate, 1977:6). To this end the income estimates are adjusted for the value of various in-kind and third party payments such as food stamps, Medicare, and rent supplements. The study also adjusted the income estimates to take into account the net effect of taxes.
15. The goal was to provide an income floor for the elderly. It was assumed that people would need income from other sources if they were to maintain their preretirement standard of living. Today the Social Security pension for the average recipient replaces approximately 40 percent of earnings just prior to retirement.
16. Schulz (1976b:89).
17. One estimate is that persons who retired in 1974 could expect a return on their contribution to Social Security equivalent to interest at a rate of between 6 and 17 percent, depending on such factors as marital status, preretirement earnings, and years of covered employment. By contrast, those entering the labor force in 1974 could expect a return on their contributions of between 1 and 8 percent, depending on various assumptions (see Chen and Chu, 1974).
18. Schulz (1976b:88).
19. Because the median income statistics for the years prior to 1950 are not entirely comparable to those for 1950 and after, it makes the most sense to base our comparison of the long-term trends for the three components on the data for the period from 1950 to 1977. During this period Social Security pension benefits increased by 454 percent, the cost of living increased by 152 percent, and the median family income increased by 382 percent.
20. To calculate the increase in "absolute" purchasing power, subtract the increase in the cost of living from the increase in Social Security benefits.
21. The employee who earned $10,000 was taxed at a rate of 6.05 percent on all of this income. The employee who earned $100,000 was taxed at the same rate, but only on the first $17,700; this comes to $1,070, approximately 1.1 percent of $100,000.
22. Many life insurance companies provide policies for those who want to be assured an annuity income when they reach retirement age. The annuity is a pension usually paid for life. The size of the pension is based on the amount of income paid into the program as premiums over the years and on the policyholder's life expectancy at the time when payments started.
23. The reference here is to such principles as: (1) benefits actuarially linked to the amount one has contributed and (2) benefits paid independent of the amount of income one has from other sources.
24. The amount is scheduled to increase gradually to $6,000 by 1982. There is no retirement test for persons age seventy-two and over.
25. General federal revenues includes the federal personal income tax, federal corporate taxes, and federal excise taxes. The net effect of general federal revenues is progressive, that is, taxing those with more income at higher rates.
26. Some have proposed that the pensions for retired workers continue to be funded on the basis of the Social Security payroll tax, but that the expenses related to health insurance and disability be shifted to general federal revenues. The goal is to reduce the burden on the payroll tax while at the same time avoiding any stigma that might result were the link between the payroll tax and benefits entirely eliminated.
27. Two qualifications are in order when interpreting this trend data. The labor force participation for women has been relatively stable (around 10 percent) with no such long-term decline. It is also of note that labor force participation for males had been on the decline for many years prior to the introduction of Social Security pensions. Between 1890 and 1940 labor force participation among elderly males declined from 68 to 42 percent (Atchley, 1976:17).

28. In this section we draw extensively on the work of Juanita Kreps (1976).
29. GNP may show an increase, but the increase is due to inflation rather than increased output (real growth).
30. Kreps (1976).

References

Atchley, Robert C., *The Sociology of Retirement.* New York: Wiley, 1976.

Chen, Yung-Ping, and Kwang-Wen Chu, "Tax Benefit Ratios and Rates of Return under OASI: 1974 Retirees and Entrants." *Journal of Risk and Insurance,* 41, 1974:189–206.

Fischer, David H., *Growing Old in America.* New York: Oxford, 1977.

Fried, Edward R., Alice Rivlin, Charles L. Schultz, and Nancy H. Teeters, *Setting National Priorities—The 1974 Budget.* Washington, D.C.: U.S. Government Printing Office, 1973.

Henle, Peter, "Recent Trends in Retirement Benefits Related to Earnings." *Monthly Labor Review* 95, 1972: 12–20.

Kreps, Juanita M., "The Economy and the Aged." In Robert H. Binstock and Ethel Shanas (ed.), *Handbook of Aging and the Social Sciences,* pp. 272–285. New York: Van Nostrand, 1976.

Moon, Marilyn, *The Measurement of Economic Welfare.* New York: Academic Press, 1977.

Murray, Janet, "Homeownership and Financial Assets: Findings from the 1968 Survey of the Aged." *Social Security Bulletin* 35 (August 1972): 3–23.

Schulz, James H., "Income Distribution and the Aging." In Robert H. Binstock and Ethel Shanas (ed.), *Handbook of Aging and the Social Sciences,* pp. 561–591. New York: Van Nostrand, 1976[a].

———*The Economics of Aging.* Belmont, Calif.: Wadsworth, 1976[b].

U.S. Bureau of Census, "Household Money Income in 1973 and Selected Social and Economic Characteristics of Households." *Current Population Reports,* Series P-60, No. 96. Washington, D.C.: U.S. Government Printing Office, 1974.

———., *Historical Statistics of the United States, Colonial Times to 1970.* Washington, D.C.: U.S. Government Printing Office, 1975.

———., "Money Income in 1976 of Families and Persons in the United States." *Current Population Reports,* Series P-60, No. 114. Washington, D.C.: U.S. Government Printing Office, 1978a.

———., "Money Income and Poverty Status of Families and Persons in the United States. 1977 (Advanced Report)." *Current Population Reports,* Series P-60, No. 116, Washington, D.C.: U.S. Government Printing Office, 1978b.

———., "Characteristics of the Population Below the Poverty Level: 1976." *Current Population Reports,* Series P-60, No. 115. Washington, D.C.: U.S. Government Printing Office, 1978c.

U.S. Department of Health, Education and Welfare, "Current Operating Statistics." *Social Security Bulletin* 41 (October 1978):31–71.

U.S. Senate Special Committee on Aging, *Developments in Aging: 1976.* Washington, D.C.: U.S. Government Printing Office, 1977.

Williamson, John B. et al., *Strategies Against Poverty in America.* New York: Wiley, 1975.

Williamson, John B., and Kathryn M. Hyer, "The Measurement and Meaning of Poverty." *Social Problems* 22, 1975: 652–663.

CHAPTER 4

Work
And Retirement:
Preference
Or Accommodation

The idea of working is oppressive to some people; the idea of retiring is oppressive to others. If you are young, you probably wish that someone would pay you to retire so that you could do what you prefer. If you are older, you may wish that the time you had left to do paid work was longer. In recent years, the topic of retirement has attracted substantial public and academic attention. The transition to and adjustment within retired status have been the primary interests of many social scientists. Their research areas have included the desirability of preretirement programs, the influence of retirement on male identity, the economics of retirement, and more recently, the effects of retirement on women.

Until 1978, mandatory retirement regulations legalized discrimination against some workers who reached their sixty-fifth birthday.[1] In addition, society viewed age sixty-five as the appropriate age for retirement even when mandatory regulations did not apply. As a result, older workers had a difficult time locating new employment or holding onto old jobs. Such workers were (and still are) often exploited—they were (are) paid lower wages and offered jobs which younger workers did not want. The psychological oppression that results when people realize they have virtually no way to augment a small income from Social Security or savings can contribute to a less than satisfactory retirement. On the other hand, a financially adequate retirement can provide an opportunity to enjoy life in a way that was not possible when the drudgery of the "job" was ever present. These topics and others will be discussed in more detail in succeeding sections of this chapter.

A BRIEF HISTORY OF RETIREMENT

Prior to the implementation of retirement programs, people worked until they were no longer physically able. The absence of formal retirement as a concept was not necessarily due to the greater enjoyment that people took in their work—although for some that was the reason for continuing to work—but to the lack of an alternative means for obtaining life's necessities. The coming together of several societal conditions within the industrialized world resulted in the phenomenon of retirement. Increasing numbers of people lived to old age as science developed means to conquer early deaths from infectious diseases. Older workers in physically demanding industrial jobs were perceived to be less capable than those who were younger and stronger. Finally, the world-wide depression of the 1930s produced too many people competing for too few jobs. These conditions existed within the framework of a standard of production sufficiently high to allow a portion of the population to be financially supported even though they were not directly contributing work to society. What emerged was the phenomenon of retirement, a mechanism which, in addition to opening up jobs for younger workers, providing older people with a guaranteed income, and controlling the total number of workers, diminished the impact of the death of the older individual on society's total productivity and functioning.[2,3]

Let us examine these retirement facilitating factors more closely. As a larger proportion of the population lived to more advanced ages through progress in medical technology, greater numbers were then vulnerable to debilitating or chronic health conditions. This produced a growing mass of older people who needed some form of support beyond that which they could generate themselves through employment. This was a new problem. Previously, the survival of the fittest assured a relatively healthy, though small, population of elderly. However, the new and growing ranks of the aged may not have been as physically fit. The perception of the older worker as incapable of completing jobs which required the expenditure of physical energy under difficult working conditions was sometimes appropriate.

The Great Depression of the 1930s, with its profound unemployment problems, served to crystallize the need for some sort of societal planning to avoid repetition of this large-scale economic disaster. The Social Security Act was conceived as a means to provide income to supplement savings for individuals during their old age. However as economist, James Schulz argues, "... the major motivating force behind the passage of the Social Security Act in 1935 was not the provision of adequate income in retirement but the creation of jobs" by removing people from the labor market when they reached age sixty-five.[4] Having accepted the need to retire older individuals from those jobs which were physically demanding,

Social Security now allowed society to view the removal of all older workers from their jobs as a sign of progress.

At the present time, most people including retirees agree that a government sponsored plan such as Social Security or some other suitable alternative should provide income for older people who are no longer employed.[5] However, the adequacy of Social Security benefits as a financial base in retirement has been a source of recurrent controversy. More people have come to realize that Social Security is not an insurance plan but a pay-as-you-go system in which those presently employed "pay" those who are currently retired. This knowledge may elicit anxiety based on an awareness of the statistical threat to future Social Security benefits which is posed by the declining birth rate. Under the present system, future Social Security taxes will have to be much higher to perpetuate the scheme. Will workers be willing and/or able to pay the costs? Due to the declining birth rate, the age structure of society is also changing to produce an increasing proportion of older people. Historically, industry has felt it advantageous to remove older people from the labor force. Even though mandatory retirement policies have not affected the majority of workers, the projected lower numbers of available youthful workers has generated some long-range rethinking. Is it purely coincidental that the reconsideration of mandatory retirement policies occurred at a time when projected numbers of future employees were showing decreases and Social Security expenditures were reaching dangerously high levels?

Even without mandatory retirement, social pressure toward retirement can be almost as effective as official policy. A vocational rehabilitation worker recently told one of the authors about the difficulty she was having in keeping a seventy-two-year-old retarded man on the job in a sheltered workshop. Although he was healthy and the work he did was virtually his only means of maintaining ongoing contact with other people, he announced one day that he wished to terminate his employment because everyone his age was retired. He felt stigmatized by having a job.

The push to entirely eliminate mandatory retirement policies coexists with the trend toward increasing use of early retirement options. Differing interpretations of retirement, based on the meaning of work to the individual as well as the changing importance of the work ethic, influence the view of retirement as positive or negative. Underlying the disagreement in attitudes toward retirement is the fact that for many people work is still the best way to obtain money and a role.[6]

SOME CHARACTERISTICS OF WORK

Currently we are told that the days of hard physical labor are gone, that the postindustrial age of work is upon us. However, the integration of work and leisure which is the ideal of the postindustrial age is not yet available to most people.[7] Many adults continue to be employed in the types of jobs that developed during industrialization, jobs which have not changed significantly in their characteristic repetitiveness and lack of worker autonomy.[8] However, in spite of some undesirable job characteristics, survey research has found morale to be generally unconnected to work or retirement, but to be more influenced by health, family situation, and other personal conditions.[9]

The underlying factor that emerges from surveys of different types of workers and their wishes regarding working conditions is the need for a variety of rewards or incentives in addition to adequate wages. One issue that has been considered to be important is meaningful involvement. For many people this is best obtained on the job. For others, who are wealthy or who have roles outside of paid employment which are meaningful to them, nonemployment situations can be rewarding. Data from the New Jersey negative income tax experiment show that married, white women took the option of not working to a greater extent than other groups when they were guaranteed a certain income. With an average of four children, these women presumably had sufficient work to do at home, a role which was meaningful to them, and the guaranteed income afforded reasonable compensation.[10]

The quality of working life and specifically of job satisfaction has usually been considered within the framework of a system which encourages economic competition, growth, and utilitarianism. Given these parameters, recent research evidence tends to discount the fact that employees want more involvement on the job. Workers do say that they want more autonomy, which is difficult in many cases to increase because there is an "assumption that ownership of capital conveys the right to control significant aspects of the lives of employees."[11]

One of Studs Terkel's interviewees, a "felter" in a luggage factory, in describing her job, provides a vivid illustration of this power imbalance between owner and worker.[12] The characteristics of her job may also offer a clue as to the growing popularity of early retirement when income is adequate.

> The tank I work at is six-foot deep, eight-foot square. In it is pulp, made of ground wood, ground glass, fiberglass, a mixture of chemicals and water. It comes up through a copper screen felter as a form, shaped like the luggage you buy in the store.
> In forty seconds you have to take the wet felt out of the felter, put the blanket on—a rubber sheeting—to draw out the excess moisture, wait two, three seconds, take the blanket off, pick the wet felt up, balance it on your shoulder. . . . get the hose, spray the inside of this copper screen to keep it from plugging, turn around, walk to the hot dry die behind you, take the hot

piece off with your opposite hand, set it on the floor—this wet thing is still balanced on my shoulder—put the wet piece on the dry die, push this button that lets the dry press down, inspect the piece we just took off, the hot piece, stack it, and count it—when you get a stack of ten, you push it over and start another stack of ten—then go back and put our blanket on the wet piece coming up from the tank . . . and start over. Forty seconds. We also have to weigh every third piece in that time. In the summertime, the temperature ranges anywhere from 100 to 150 degrees . . .

For many people, especially those men who have traditionally been expected to work outside of the home, work and the conditions of work can be oppressive. For some others, work is enjoyable and/or gives meaning to life. This spectrum of variations in the experience of work makes it less surprising that retirement from work is perceived differently by different people.

THE MEANING OF WORK

Individual perspectives on retirement are influenced by the different meanings that work holds for people. Interpretations of the meaning of work have been influenced by a traditional view of sex roles. Men have primarily been engaged in being breadwinners for their families. Their primary role has been seen as the work role. The sociological position of the 1950s and early 1960s is reflected in the following statement.

The contemporary American worker has been socialized in a milieu which has defined work as a central life task and interest for the male. In addition to his source of income, a man's job means a point of personal and social anchorage with considerable significance, both for the emergence and maintenance of a satisfactory self-identity, and for the experience of adequate social intercourse with his family and peers.[13]

Women, on the other hand, have been primarily identified with the family. Even if they worked outside the home, women were seen only as returning to their primary role once they left work or retired, hence no psychological difficulties at retirement were assumed or even looked for among women. They were often excluded from studies of the impact of retirement and the meaning of work.[14] More recent research on women and retirement will be discussed in a later section of this chapter.

Consistent with the identification of men with work, retirement for them has been viewed as the loss of their primary role. As a result, men have been assumed to experience difficulties in retirement. One approach to getting at the potential problem that retirement presents is to understand the meaning of paid work to the individual. In one study, which became a landmark in spite of the fact that women were not included, Friedmann and Havighurst concluded that work had meaning in addition to that dictated by the necessity of earning a living.[15] They reported that work provided an opportunity to be useful, to associate with others, to fill time, to gain respect, and to find intrinsic enjoyment. The meaning of work seemed to vary for the different occupational types which were included in the study: for steel workers, it was money; for crafts and sales people, it was activity; for coal miners, work meant routine and association with fellows; and for physicians, it was the service aspect that was important. Given these characteristics of the meaning of work, it is not surprising that retirement or its contemplation can be oppressive to some people.

A later study, which corrected for Friedmann and Havighurst's lack of identical questions for the various occupational subgroups and which used a larger national probability sample, found not surprisingly that all employed men said that the most important thing about their work was money.[16] However, when asked about the noneconomic meaning of work, white-collar workers were more likely to say that the people at work were important; agricultural workers said the work itself was important; and blue-collar workers felt that both the people at work and the work itself were important. When these blue-collar workers retired, they often said that money was what they missed most about their jobs. When retirement income was adequate, a significant proportion of retirees, including those who had been white-collar and professional, said that they missed nothing about their work.

More recent evidence for the overriding importance of work as a source of income is available from data on respondents in a national panel survey of Social Security recipients. About one half of the retirees aged sixty-two to sixty-seven who are participants have reported that they have health limitations which would preclude their return to work whether or not they would so desire.[17] Ten percent of the respondents who had no work limitations said that they would like to return to work, an additional 23 percent were ambivalent, and the remaining 67 percent did not want to return to work. Low retirement income seemed to be the single strongest motivating factor for desire to return to work for workers with no physical limitations. Happiness in retirement also appeared to be most strongly correlated with size of income.[18] It is apparent that economic security overrides the importance of the loss of the work role for many people.

Robert Atchley, a sociologist, reports that slightly less than a third of retirees have difficulty adjusting to retirement and that only about 7 percent of these have problems because they miss their jobs. The rest are affected by difficulties due to financial limitations, health problems, and death of a spouse.[19] The traditional belief, true for some but certainly not for all, that retirement has negative effects beyond the loss of income has facilitated the view that retirement negatively affects health. In an attempt to analyze the relationship between retirement and health, sociologists Streib and Schneider compared retirees with individuals who continued to work but who were the same age as the retirees.[20] They concluded that advancing age, rather than retirement *per se,* was responsible for reported health declines. Health status appeared to influence the decision to retire rather than vice versa.

Attitudes toward work have been changing in recent years so that the importance of work as a primary source of meaning and satisfaction in life has come to be questioned by some people. Social scientists who place emphasis on the loss of self-identity in retirement because of the loss of the work role may possibly be reflecting, at least in part, their own more advantaged employment positions.[21] Once economic security is possible, the importance of the work role seems to be lessened for some.

Supportive evidence for this belief is provided by the growing popularity of early retirement, particularly among industrial workers; although it is important to note that at least some early retirees involuntarily leave their jobs because of health declines or the inability to find a job.[22,23] One estimate places the proportion of involuntary early retirees at around 11 percent, although others would undoubtedly place it much higher, particularly for minority group members.[24] The following quotation, from a fifty-one-year-old automobile worker who voluntarily retired early, is typical of at least some of that group: "I was working since I was ten years old. I thought of all the years I've been working, and I want a rest."[25] Although it is not difficult to imagine that people in physically demanding, dangerous, or dirty jobs might want to retire early, statistics collected by General Motors indicate that salaried office employees who work in more pleasant surroundings are also opting for the "thirty and out" option.[26] These early retirees are often able to take their modest to comfortable pensions and engage in the kind of work or leisure activities that are meaningful to them.

While ability to structure retirement is likely to reflect coping behavior at earlier life stages, it is important to stress that even if coping styles were adequate at earlier life stages, certain extreme changes in health, finances, or other environmental situations may result in an inability to adjust successfully.[27] For those people who are in relatively good health with adequate retirement incomes and who have others with whom to interact, retirement from punching a clock can be entirely positive. Problems in retirement for many people appear to stem from a lack of adequate income, health problems and, to a lesser extent, to the lack of good friends or family with whom to "do things."

There also appear to be different styles of retirement, as Robert Havighurst and his colleagues report. In their study of teachers and steelworkers in six countries, the particular culture interacted with occupation to produce a specific retirement pattern. Furthermore, Chicago interviewees appeared to spend their retirement in ways that were related to the expectations that had been held for them in their jobs. For example, retired teachers were involved in activities that required more initiative and autonomy than were the retired steelworkers.[28]

VOLUNTARY WORK

The idea that people want meaningful activity has not really changed; however, the situations in which older people can find meaning may have broadened to include alternatives which do not involve pay or the notion of a "career," provided that an adequate income is available from some other source. Ralph Helstein, president emeritus of the United Packing-house Workers of America said to Studs Terkel:

Learning is work. Caring for children is work. Community action is work. Once we accept the concept of work as something meaningful—not just as the source of a buck—you don't have to worry about finding enough jobs. There's no excuse for mules any more. Society does not need them. There's no question about our ability to feed and clothe and house everybody. The problem is going to come in finding enough ways for man to keep occupied, so he's in touch with reality.[29]

As increasing numbers of middle-class women return to the labor force, a potential source of meaningful involvement for older people is beginning to emerge. Organizations, which in the past have relied heavily on volunteers drawn largely from the ranks of middle-class women, have had to reappraise their situations. Some of these organizations have reached a "new" conclusion: to recruit from groups not traditionally encouraged as volunteers, namely retired people.[30] If basic expenses of transportation and meals eaten away from home were to be reimbursed, it is possible that those retirees who do not need or want paid work would find new meaning in life through volunteering. Voluntary organizations would be able to continue their programs with a minimal readjustment.

On the other hand, there are those who regard voluntary work as exploitive. Just as some middle-class women have come to feel that they should be compensated for their activities, some older people may feel that if organizations value their volunteer efforts, those efforts should be acknowledged with a monetary reward. An older woman in an aging class expressed that view. She had been forced to retire from a job with the state's welfare department and although she could do volunteer work, she would have felt exploited. In our income-conscious society it may be difficult to take unpaid work seriously for either the volunteer or the "employer."

In spite of possible exploitive elements inherent in volunteering, a national survey found that 22 percent of people sixty-five and over regularly volunteer. An additional 10 percent said they would like to volunteer.[31] If voluntary organizations could reimburse the expenses of their older volunteers, the option of voluntary work might become attractive to more older people who have chosen to retire from their regular jobs.

WOMEN, WORK, AND RETIREMENT

Women's traditional role has been that of caretaker of family and home, a role which was economically functional to the family unit. After industrialization, the participation of women in the labor force continued to be viewed as a supplementary role, secondary to their primary familial role.[32] Married women were viewed as working just to get extra money, unlike men who were presumed to work for more profound reasons. Consequently, the belief that paid work has little intrinsic meaning to women has been prevalent, in marked contrast to the belief that for men the work role is central to identity.

For many women, this view has resulted in a general education aimed at developing good wives and mothers. Available employment has often been restricted to those jobs which allow women to move in and out of the labor market with as little disruption as possible to the employer. While this perceived need for employment flexibility for some women and their employers may have been and may still be accurate, less desirable effects prevail, such as lower wages, limited benefits, and fewer job opportunities for all women. The needs of those women who want paid work on a long-term basis have not been considered separately; opportunities and rewards for all women have been similar.

Traditionally, women have been excluded from studies on retirement, again partly due to the view that their labor force participation was secondary to their roles as wives and/or mothers. The self-identification of women as workers was questioned. Women who left work, including those who retired, were seen as returning to their primary role and no difficulties with the transition were assumed. However, because of the lesser importance attached by society to the work role for women, women who retire may experience confusion over who they are or were. While a man in retirement may continue to identify with the work he did, a woman may have a more difficult identification: is she a retired secretary or a mother/wife/widow who also happened to work as a secretary?[33]

Survey data have begun to appear which further question the assumption that women retirees do not experience difficulty at retirement. New studies have found that women who have had careers, in the sense that their work life has been relatively long term, show lower morale in retire-

ment than men, at least initially. In Atchley's study of telephone workers
and teachers, women reported feeling lonely more often than the men,
even after marital status, education, age, and income adequacy were controlled.[34] They were more sensitive to criticism and more likely to be
depressed. They also more often reported their incomes as inadequate.
Even after financial status was controlled, the longer time to adjust to
retirement held.

If present trends continue, retirement will increasingly affect more
women. Greater numbers of women are in the paid labor force than ever
before. Women are returning to employment in greater numbers after
their youngest child enters school and even earlier, yet they continue to
be employed in a narrower range of jobs than men, to receive lower
average wages than men, to be eligible less often for pensions than men,
and to remain in lower level positions regardless of their individual
capabilities. At least some of these women persevere in the nonsupportive
environment of the labor force because they need the money and/or
enjoy working outside the home for pay—however inadequate—more
than they enjoy working inside the home and not receiving any direct
remuneration. For women who do not enjoy household activities on a
full-time basis, employment outside of the home is preferable. For many
other women, working outside of the home is not a choice but a necessity.

When women reach retirement age, it is assumed they will be able once
again to enjoy, full-time, their primary role as homemakers even though
many are by then widowed. When their employment ends, they are denied the socially acceptable excuse "that they work" to avoid baking for
the food sale or entertaining at home. When women are reconfronted
with the primariness of a role that they had long ago relegated to a
secondary position either by choice or by necessity, they may experience
depression. Streib and Schneider report that more women than men say
they feel useless in retirement.[35] Housekeeping, which was a taken-for-
granted, lesser role when they were employed, becomes their major contribution.[36] The feeling of uselessness was expressed to one of the authors
by a woman retiree who said, "If you were in a job in which you served
others, when you retire, at first, you feel bad that you are not doing that
anymore even if you enjoy housekeeping."

The traditional pattern of women and employment has had significant
consequences for women's lives at all ages, but especially as they approach
old age. One result of our cultural tradition is that women receive lower
average retirement benefits, including Social Security, than do men.[37]
Those women who were employed generally earned less than men, consequently, they retire with lower benefits. Although recent changes in Social
Security legislation enable a widowed spouse to receive 100 percent of the
benefits of the deceased partner, provided that benefits were not begun
for the surviving spouse before age sixty-five, many women claim early

benefits because they are usually younger than their husbands who take their benefits at or before age sixty-five. Private pension programs are usually not as generous as Social Security to the widowed spouse.

The aged widow's average monthly Social Security benefit in 1976 was $208.[38] For those women who reach retirement age and have a spouse still living, the financial situation is somewhat better. In 1976, married couples received an average monthly Social Security benefit of $371. However, the percentage of women who face retirement widowed is four times higher than for men.[39] The financially precarious situation of many older women is evident from the fact that, of those retirees who receive the minimum Social Security benefit, half are single women, another one fourth are widows or single men, and one fourth are married couples.[40] It is clear that retired women, and older women more generally, are often involved in life situations which include very limited incomes.

The importance of income adequacy *per se* for women in retirement, exclusive of any meaningful involvement through employment, is illustrated by the fact that in 1976 women sixty-five and over who were still employed had higher morale than retirees when income in retirement was less than $5,000. However, when retirement income was $5,000 or more, retired women had higher morale than women sixty-five and over who were still employed. In fact when the combined effects of age, income, general health, and physical incapacity were controlled in a national sample of older women, continued employment accounted for less than 1 percent of the variance in morale.[41]

The difficulties that inadequate finances present for older women can be even more painful if there is a realization that cultural norms regarding women and work have unjust and negative consequences in terms of life experiences many years later. Because benefits to employees are based on the male model of labor force participation, that is education oriented toward work, continuous work history, and progressive job responsibility, retirement benefits including those provided through Social Security penalize women. Women's earnings have often been lower than those of men because of sex discrimination in job opportunities and pay differentials on the job. Retirement benefits for women based on those earnings continue to exploit older women. In summary, older women often live out their lives in financially precarious situations because of their work histories and inadequate pension coverage from their own employment or from that of their deceased spouse. Any unexpected expense can cause anxiety.

However, the picture is not completely bleak for the older woman retiree. Women who retire after having been employed much of their lives report having more social outlets than long-term housewives.[42] Data on women over sixty-five who have retired or who have never worked also show that those who have never worked outside of the home tend to have lower morale.[43] It is clear that employment decisions made at earlier ages can have ramifications on many areas of the older woman's life. With changing norms for women and employment, one might expect more women in the future to have been employed and to have better financial situations in their old age. However, as long as earnings continue to be lower for women, retirement incomes will also continue to be lower.

The removal of the mandatory retirement age or the raising of that age can also have a positive effect for women by extending the work life of those women who drop out of the labor force while their children are young and who return to work when the children are older. Some of the difficulties that these women have in meeting their own career goals could be alleviated by the increased time available within which to fulfill their objectives.[44] A longer possible work life may also enable these women to put in the necessary time on the job to receive an adequate retirement income. Extending pension coverage to part-time workers and increasing the transferability of pensions from one job to another would also benefit many women (and men).

AGE DISCRIMINATION

The "prime age labor force" is a term used to refer to those people twenty-five to fifty-four years old, the age category having the greatest concentration of workers. Unemployment rates for men tend to be lowest in the thirty-five to forty-four year age range and to rise with increasing age.[45] As a side effect of the increased sensitivity to racial discrimination, age discrimination, as a factor in the increasing unemployment rates with age, was formally recognized in 1967 when Congress passed the Age Discrimination Employment Act (ADEA). The law protects workers forty to sixty-five years old. With the passage of other laws removing mandatory retirement at age sixty-five, it protects workers up to the raised retirement age. Although there has been increasing enforcement of the law, age discriminatory practices are thought to be so widespread in business that enforcement is difficult although not impossible.[46] The trend in industry toward making work physically easier not only results in fewer unskilled workers needed, but also contributes to the use of selection criteria which are unrelated to the ability to perform the job. Older workers who are displaced by modern technology, by industries relocating to states with lower taxes, by their own limited schooling, which in a high labor supply situation excludes them from jobs which require a high school diploma, may find it difficult or impossible to find a new job in the community where they have spent much of their lives.

Evidence of the discrimination against older workers is provided by the following statistics: in 1969, one tenth of the participants in Manpower

Development and Training Act programs were forty-five years of age or older, while one third of the long-term unemployed were in that age category. Some underrepresentation may occur because older workers are seen as possessing adequate job skills, that is, they are not perceived to need retraining. Other underutilization of older workers for training programs results from the employment counselor's reluctance to place older workers in such programs. Some may feel that if older workers are retrained and then are still unable to find employment, they will be even more disheartened than by the lack of employment before training.[47]

A survey of aerospace employees provides another concrete example of discrimination against older workers.[48] Respondents fifty-five years of age and over were much more likely to report that they had experienced age discrimination in employment. Because the aerospace industry is one where full employment in any particular company is likely to fluctuate according to the availability of government contracts, there are fairly frequent large-scale layoffs. Consequently, older workers have significant potential to experience discrimination because of their age alone.

Another situation, known personally to one of the authors, involved discrimination against older workers, specifically older women textile workers. They had been allowed, even encouraged, to continue working past age sixty-five in part because the nonunion mill paid nonunion lower wages and because the women were hard workers. However, when the company decided to replace its traditional looms with new equipment from Japan, a decision was made to let the old women go because they were felt to be unretrainable. In this situation, the company was not dissatisfied with the older women's performance as long as the company's profit was perceived to be maximized. When the issue of retraining developed and the potential profit margin of employing the women was lower, stereotypes regarding older workers, involving factors which can never be guaranteed even with younger workers, entered the picture and the older women were laid off.

There is evidence that discrimination in employment against older workers exists. It is also clear that growing numbers of workers are choosing to remove themselves from the labor market provided they are guaranteed a retirement income that they feel will adequately meet their present and future needs. The existence of the early retirement trend does not negate the fact that age discrimination exists. The real issue is that workers should have choices regarding continued employment: if older people want to continue to work and if they are physically and mentally able to, they should not experience discrimination in employment.

However, statistics show that older male workers tend to be overrepresented as an age category among the long-duration jobless.[49] There is speculation regarding the fact that the growing popularity of early retirement may be, at least for some of these individuals, a response to the inability to find a decent job at an older age once a previous job has terminated. Having depleted their employment compensation benefits, older males may find it easier to wait a few months and apply for reduced Social Security benefits at age sixty-two than to continue to face the humiliation caused by the fact that no one wants to hire them. This discrimination against older workers has been intensified by a more positive social trend: the growth of private pension plans. Because their time on the job will be relatively short term and because the company will have to contribute proportionately more to their retirement pensions, newly hired "older" workers are less desirable to employers from a pragmatic economic standpoint.

On an individual basis, some older people continue to find jobs while others cannot. While age discrimination is a reality, there is evidence in the literature that there may be other factors operating in the inability of older workers to find new jobs. After working at jobs that are physically hard and/or mentally unengaging, some older workers may lose their interest in finding other work. Their low motivation may be at least partly responsible for their inability to find work.[50] On the whole, individual characteristics do not change the fact that systematic biases operate to exclude the older worker from finding new employment.

Older workers often have fewer resources to exchange for a job. In general, their education levels are lower; they have fewer years to work for a new company; their physical attractiveness has lessened, particularly devastating for women because they no longer approach the youthful ideal. The fact that they often have strong, positive work habits, high dependability, and loyalty is not regarded with as much value as more immediate economic factors.

PENSIONS

Government policy has usually assumed that workers are saving enough during their employment years so that, with the addition of Social Security and other pension benefits, a reasonable standard of living can be maintained in old age. One study of the reasonableness of such an assumption about the saving ability of many people found that a majority of the respondents anticipated financial problems in retirement with 85 percent planning to use savings and 70 percent planning to work at a supplementary job. However, in order to have the amount saved that they expect to need in retirement, they would have to save much more than they currently do.[51]

Alice Washington, an order filler in a shoe factory, told Studs Terkel,

... I'm able to save very little, and I do mean very little. You have to pay rent, lights, and telephone bills. You have to clothe your children, you have to feed them. It's very hard. If you get a nickel or two, something comes up and you have to spend it. My son just got off to college. Every time he picks up the telephone, this has to be done, that has to be done ... it's rough ...

How long will I be able to hold up at this? That is my main worry....[52]

The traditional view that Social Security supplements savings seems to be unrealistic for many people, who find it difficult to save enough or to make their savings in retirement go as far as they had planned in less inflated times. Private pension funds are a positive additional source of retirement income, and yet as recently as 1971, it was estimated that only 1 in 20 pension-fund holders who had left their employment due to plant shutdowns, transfers, store closings, and fund termination in the preceding twenty years would actually receive a pension upon retirement.[53] According to James Schulz, passage of the Employee Retirement Income Security Act (ERISA) in 1974 resulted in "standards for participation, vesting and funding, plan-termination insurance, and extensive reporting and disclosure information" which previously had been largely unavailable.[54] However, there has been criticism that even two years after its passage, established enforcement procedures still were lacking.[55] ERISA, even when enforcement is provided, does not deal with the major problem in private pension programs: a majority of the work force is not covered by such plans.

In order to deal with the lack of universal pension-plan coverage in a way that would also encourage the traditional American ethic of self-reliance, a tax-incentive system was legislated in 1974. This system allows individuals not covered by private pension plans to set up their own individual retirement accounts. In 1977, the amount an individual could save tax-free until disbursal in retirement was 15 percent of earned income up to a maximum of $1,500. The same legislation increased the amount that self-employed individuals, those generally not covered by Social Security, can save tax-free until retirement.

Unfortunately, given the evidence for the inability of many people to save in inflationary times, it is not clear how many people who really need such a private plan will be able to take advantage of a program which encourages "choices" between saving and spending. For many people, particularly for some single women and minority members, those whose incomes are well below the national median, there can be little choice but to spend the money for necessary living expenses at the time. If pension plans become more prevalent in the future and do not require continuous employment on the same job, but are transferable to new jobs and available even for part-time workers, then more people might enjoy an income level in retirement that produces less anxiety.

CONCLUSION

There are at least two ways to view retirement. On the one hand, retirement moves older workers out of the labor force and makes room for younger workers. On the other hand, once workers reach a certain age, they are no longer required to work outside of the home in order to receive an income.[56] It is apparent that forcing people from their jobs because they have reached a certain age is discriminatory, particularly since the guaranteed income which is available to people after they reach a certain age is often inadequate. To compound the problem, retirement age has come to be viewed as the point when people are less capable of working. Individual differences in ability and preference are disregarded. The arbitrariness of the age for retirement is forgotten when older workers are stereotyped as less able with or without mandatory retirement regulations. As a result, those individuals who find their retirement income inadequate find themselves victims of age discrimination, either formal or informal, and are unable to augment their incomes through employment. Sometimes when they do locate employment, they are exploited.

On the more positive side, retirement with a guaranteed income and medical coverage is an improvement over the situation which existed not too long ago. Historically, older people were forced to work, even in declining health, because there were no alternatives to the poorhouse. Only affluent societies have been able to provide support for their members who no longer work.[57] The more positive aspects of retirement have sometimes been left out by social scientists. The availability of unstructured leisure in retirement has been viewed as a problem, particularly by sociologists who have emphasized the importance of the work role.[58] Adequate finances and good health may, in fact, be the key elements which allow the individual to maintain the identity that Atchley maintains does not dissipate with retirement.[59]

While women's culturally influenced work patterns and job opportunities have caused them to enter retirement with inadequate incomes, the presence of sufficient financial resources also appears to be the single most important factor in the satisfaction of men with retirement. Although much attention has been paid by social scientists to the other-than-money meaning of work, the ability of healthy retirees to enjoy the leisure of retirement appears to have been increasing in recent times. The growing number of voluntary early retirees from industries which provide adequate pensions offers some evidence that the structure of work is sometimes oppressive rather than meaningful to workers.

Unfortunately, early retirement is not always a positive event. Some workers choose to retire early because their health has declined or because they have been unable to locate employment due to age discrimination. Rather than continue to face the humiliation of being turned down, some people may choose to take reduced retirement benefits at an age earlier than they would have desired.

Notes

1. See Harris (1975:211–226) for responses of older persons and those of other ages regarding retirement. The Harris Survey reports that of all companies without pension plans, 95 percent have had flexible retirement policies. Of those with pension plans (less than half of all employers), a little over one third have mandated a fixed retirement age. These data are based on the responses of individuals regarding their employers. Schulz (1976) notes that estimates of the proportion of workers covered by private pension plans may vary between 35 and 50 percent. If one third of the highest estimate of 50 percent have been affected by mandatory retirement, that is about 17 percent. If only 5 percent of the other half of all workers, those uncovered by private pension plans, were subject to mandatory retirement, approximately 22 percent of all workers may have been affected by such regulations, In 1973, legislation was passed which raised to seventy the age at which mandatory regulations could take effect. Such regulations were disallowed altogether for federal employees.
2. Juanita Kreps provides a discussion of the background of retirement in the United States (1972).
3. Blauner presents an interesting discussion of the way that various societies contain the impact of death (1966).
4. See Schulz (1976) for an elaboration of this argument. The quote is from page 89.
5. The Harris Poll (1975) included several questions regarding retirement. All questions were asked of individuals younger than sixty-five and those sixty-five and over. The response cited is from p. 222.
6. Harold Sheppard discusses work and retirement in his chapter in *The Handbook on Aging and the Social Sciences* (1976).
7. Miller notes the postindustrial integration of work and leisure (1965).
8. See *Work in America* (1973). Albert Camus is quoted: "Without work all life goes rotten. But when work is soulless, life stifles and dies."
9. See Simpson, Back, and McKinney (1966). Except for a slight tendency for those in highly automated, monotonous jobs to dislike their work, Terkel's (1975) interviewees were also similar. George and Maddox (1977) found that the loss of the work role did not lead to lower morale in their longitudinal analysis of fifty-eight people.
10. See Watts and Rees (1977).
11. See Nord (1977); the quote is from page 1027.
12. Grace Clements, one of Studs Terkel's interviewees (1975:384–389), probably has one of the least attractive jobs described in the book. However, the characteristics of Clement's job are found in other assembly-type work. The quotation is from pages 384–386.
13. See George Maddox (1966). The quote is from page 123.
14. For some early work on retirement, see Donohue, Orback, and Pollack (1960).
15. Friedmann and Havighurst's (1954) study is regarded as a classic.
16. Ethel Shanas (1972) presents an enlightening discussion of her own and other earlier research on work and retirement.
17. See Motley (1977). Her data are part of the Social Security Administration's Retirement History Study. Interviews are being held every two years for a period of ten years. The data used in the reported analysis are from interviews completed in 1973 with unemployed men who had been employed at the time of the initial interviews in 1969.

18. Gayle Thompson (1977) bases her conclusions on data from the same Social Security Administration Retirement History study on which Motley's report is formulated.
19. See Robert Atchley (1976b) for an interesting and comprehensive treatment of the subject of retirement.
20. Gordon Streib and Clement Schneider (1971) present a detailed analysis of their data on retirement.
21. Glamser takes the academics to task (1976).
22. See Jerry Flint's article, "Early Retirement is Growing in U.S.," which appeared in *The New York Times* on Sunday, July 10, 1977: 1,22. Schulz notes that since provisions for early retirement were introduced, more than half of men and women who receive Social Security benefits have begun to receive them before age sixty-five (1976); see also Barfield and Morgan (1969) and Barfield (1970).
23. Sheppard (1976) reports that the Social Security Administration's Retirement History Study found that 60 percent of early retirees said their health was poorer than that of others their age. This is in contrast to the same response being given by only 12 percent of workers still on the job. It is not clear, however, whether or not people said their health was poorer because of a need to find a socially acceptable reason for not working.
24. See Fields (1970); also Sheppard (1976).
25. See Flint referenced in footnote 22. The quotation is from page 1.
26. See Flint referenced in footnote 22. The statistics reported by General Motors appear to differ from those provided in earlier years by Ford Motors to Sheppard (1976). The Ford data suggest that workers in more physically demanding jobs were the early retirees. Barfield (1970), and earlier Barfield and Morgan (1969), studied decision making in early retirement among automobile workers. In both studies adequate financial prospects were the single strongest factor in the decision to retire early. Retired automobile workers appeared to be overwhelmingly pleased with their situations.
27. Powell Lawton (1974) cautions against the environmental docility hypothesis which minimizes the effect that changes in the environment can have on an individual's coping style.
28. See Havighurst et al. (1970).
29. Ralph Helstein speaks to Studs Terkel (1975). The quotation is from page xxviii.
30. The changing picture regarding volunteers appeared in *The Boston Evening Globe* in an article "Age-Old Volunteer Image Falls" written by Tony Chamberlain (Jan. 9, 1978:3).
31. See Harris (1975).
32. See Lopata and Steinhart (1971).
33. For a discussion of the identity-continuity theory see Robert Atchley (1971).
34. See Atchley (1976a) and Streib and Schneider (1971): it is possible that both men and women suffer equally from retirement but that women are more expressive of their discontent.
35. See Streib and Schneider (1971).
36. Judith Huff Fox presents interesting data on women and work (1977).
37. See Schulz (1976).
38. The benefit levels were published by the United States Senate Special Committee on Aging (1977: 2).
39. See Atchley (1976b).
40. Atchley (1976b).
41. See Jaslow (1976).
42. See Fox (1977).
43. See Atchley (1976a); Jaslow (1976); Streib and Schneider (1971).
44. This possibility was suggested by Don Spence, a colleague at the University of Rhode Island.

45. Rashelle Axelbank looks at the position of the older worker in the labor force (1972).
46. See Patricia Kasschau for a discussion of age discrimination among aerospace employees (1976).
47. See Sheppard (1972).
48. See Kasschau (1976).
49. See Axelbank (1972).
50. See Sheppard (1972).
51. For a provocative article on saving for retirement see Morrison (1976).
52. Alice Washington was interviewed by Studs Terkel (1975:357–361). She seems to be typical of many people who work hard for low pay, people who have little left over to save once they have paid their expenses. The quote is from page 360.
53. See United States Senate Special Committee on Aging for an update of ERISA (1977:171–174).
54. See Schulz (1976).
55. See United States Senate Special Committee on Aging (1977:171–174).
56. Although some housewives do not work outside of the home in order to obtain money with which to obtain life's necessities, their support depends on a relationship and is not an entitlement in its own right.
57. See Kreps (1972).
58. See Shanas (1972).
59. Atchley (1971).

References

Atchley, Robert C., "Retirement and Leisure Participation: Continuity or Crisis." *Gerontologist* 11, 1(I), 1971: 13–17.
———"Selected Social and Psychological Differences between Men and Women in Later Life." *Journal of Gerontology* 31(2), 1976a: 204–211.
———*The Sociology of Retirement.* New York: Halsted Press, 1976b.
Axelbank, Rashelle G., "The Position of the Older Worker in the American Labor Force." In Gloria M. Shatto (ed.), *Employment of the Middle-Aged,* pp. 17–27. Springfield, Ill.: Charles C Thomas, 1972.
Barfield, Richard E., *The Automobile Worker and Retirement: A Second Look.* Ann Arbor, Mich.: Institute for Social Research, 1970.
Barfield, Richard E., and James Morgan, *Early Retirement: The Decision and the Experience.* Ann Arbor, Mich.: Institute for Social Research, 1969.
Blauner, Robert, "Death and Social Structure." *Psychiatry* 29, 1966: 378–394.
Donohue, Wilma T., Harold Orbach, and Otto Pollack, "Retirement: The Emerging Social Pattern." In Clark Tibbits (ed.), *Handbook of Social Gerontology,* pp. 330–406. Chicago: University Press, 1960.
Fields, Theron J., "Company-Initiated Early Retirement as a Means of Work-Force Control." *Industrial Gerontology* 1970: 36–38.
Fox, Judith Huff, "Effects of Retirement and Former Work Life on Women's Adaptation in Old Age." *Journal of Gerontology* 32(2), 1977: 196–202.
Friedmann, Eugene A., and Robert J. Havighurst, *The Meaning of Work and Retirement.* Chicago: University of Chicago Press, 1954.
George, Linda K., and George L. Maddox, "Subjective Adaptation to Loss of the Work Role: A Longitudinal Study." *Journal of Gerontology* 32(4), 1977: 456–462.

Glamser, Frances D., "Determinants of a Positive Attitude Toward Retirement." *Journal of Gerontology* 3(1), 1976: 104–107.

Harris, Louis and Associates, *The Myth and Reality of Aging in America.* Washington, D.C.: National Council on the Aging, 1975.

Havighurst, Robert J., Joep. M. A. Munnichs, Bernice L. Neugarten, and Hans Thomae, *Adjustment to Retirement.* Assen, The Netherlands: Van Gorcum and Company N.V., 1970.

Jaslow, Philip, "Employment, Retirement, and Morale among Older Women." *Journal of Gerontology* 31(2), 1976: 212–218.

Kasschau, Patricia Lee, "Perceived Age Discrimination in a Sample of Aerospace Employees." *Gerontologist* 16(2), 1976: 166–173.

Kreps, Juanita M., "Lifetime Tragedies between Work and Play." In Gloria M. Shatto (ed.), *Employment of the Middle-Aged,* pp. 31–41. Springfield, Ill.: Charles C Thomas, 1972.

Lawton, M. Powell, "Social Ecology and the Health of Older People." *American Journal of Public Health* 64, 1974: 257–260.

Lopata, Helen Z., and Frank Steinhart, "Work Histories of American Urban Women." *Gerontologist* 11(II), 1971: 27–36.

Maddox, George, "Retirement as a Social Event in the United States." John C. McKinney and Frank T. DeVyver (ed.), *Aging and Social Policy,* pp. 117–135. New York: Meredith, 1966.

Miller, Stephen J., "The Social Dilemma of the Aging Leisure Participant." In Arnold M. Rose and Warren A. Peterson (ed.), *Older People and Their Social Worlds,* pp. 77–92. Philadelphia, Pa.: Davis, 1965.

Morrison, Malcolm H., "Planning for Income Adequacy in Retirement." *Gerontologist* 16(6), 1976: 538–543.

Motley, Dena K., "The Availability of Retirees for Return to Work." Paper presented at the 30th Annual Meeting of the Gerontological Society, San Francisco, November 18–22, 1977.

Nord, Walter H., "Job Satisfaction Reconsidered." *American Psychologist* 32(12), 1977: 1026–1035.

Schulz, James H., *The Economics of Aging.* Belmont, Calif.: Wadsworth, 1976.

Shanas, Ethel, "Adjustment to Retirement: Substitution or Accommodation." In Frances Carp (ed.), *Retirement,* pp. 219–243. New York: Behavioral Publications, 1972.

Sheppard, Harold L, "Some Contributions of the Social Sciences to Industrial Gerontology." In Gloria M. Shatto (ed.), *Employment of the Middle-Aged,* pp. 5–12. Springfield, Ill.: Charles C Thomas, 1972.

Sheppard, Harold L., "Work and Retirement." In Robert H. Binstock and Ethel Shanas (ed.), *Handbook of Aging and the Social Sciences,* pp. 286–309. New York: Van Nostrand, 1976.

Simpson, Ida H., Kurt W. Back, and John C. McKinney, "Work and Retirement." In Ida H. Simpson and John C. McKinney (ed.), *Social Aspects of Aging,* pp. 45–54. Durham, N.C.: Duke University Press, 1966.

Streib, Gordon F., and Clement J. Schneider, *Retirement in American Society: Impact and Process.* Ithaca, N.Y.: Cornell University Press, 1971.

Terkel, Studs, *Working.* New York: Avon, 1975.

Thompson, Gayle B., "The Impact of Receipt of an Employee Pension on the Psychological Well-Being of Retired Persons." Paper presented at the 30th Annual Meeting of the Gerontological Society, San Francisco, November 18–22, 1977.

United States Senate Special Committee on Aging, "ERISA: Progress on Pensions." In *Developments in Aging Part I: 1976,* pp. 171–175. Washington, D.C.: United States Government Printing Office, 1977.

———"How Far Short of Adequacy Is Social Security Now?" In *Developments in Aging Part I: 1976,* pp. 2–3. Washington, D.C.: United States Government Printing Office, 1977.

Watts, Harold K., and Albert Rees (ed.), *The New Jersey Income-Maintenance Experiment Volume 2.* New York: Academic Press, Institute for Research on Poverty Monograph Series, 1977.

Work in America: Report of a Special Task Force to the Secretary of Health, Education, and Welfare. Cambridge, Mass.: MIT Press, 1973.

CHAPTER **5**

Attractiveness,
Aging,
And
Sexuality

In this chapter, we will explore some of the ways that attractiveness, sexuality, and aging are intertwined throughout the adult life span, particularly the way that certain cultural norms about physical appearance and the appropriateness of sexuality at older ages oppress some people.[1] The idea of economic exploitation presents itself in the marketing of goods and services purported to diminish the signs of aging. Discrimination is evident when employers exclude job applicants because of their older appearance. Psychological oppression accompanies the signs of physical aging for both men and women, but women express more anxiety.

The experience of a sexual identity, of being male or female, is one that is biologically begun at conception and culturally reinforced throughout life. As a result, sexuality is a very complex phenomenon. To discuss sexuality and aging and focus primarily on the physiological processes involved would be to vastly oversimplify the issue; the result would be more appropriately considered sex and aging. In order to avoid this narrow perspective, we have chosen to examine also the changes in physical appearance that occur with the aging process, the subjective perception of those changes which can be different for men and women, and the way that the sexual identity of the person can be affected by this very individual though societally orchestrated experience. We have not explicitly considered the issues of homosexuality, lesbianism, or transsexualism. In passing we note that there is some evidence that aging gay men experience problems similar to those of aging people generally.[2] Specifically, older gay men lose people close to them, are stigmatized by age, and fear institutionalization. They also face additional discrimination problems because of their sexual identities.

ATTRACTIVENESS AND SEXUAL IDENTITY

Feelings about attractiveness and appearance, particularly as they influence our sexual identities, can contribute to positive experiences as well as to difficulties and instabilities in relationships that extend over the entire life span, not just to those that occur during adolescence and young adulthood. Appearance itself, or the "power" it suggests, is important as a foundation for interactions that take place between individuals.[3] As they approach middle age, some people may begin to experience anxiety stemming from their "aging" appearance as a result of the cues they receive from others; in turn, their anxiety may further increase the negative responses of others.[4]

Aging-related changes in physical appearance, such as wrinkles, gray hair, flabby skin, and increased weight, occur in varying degrees and are changes that some people find difficult to accept as part of a "natural" process. "Most people want to look younger—and why not? Youth is a time of freshness, energy, endless possibilities. As the years close in, we long to recapture the sense of promise that youth gave us," says a makeup artist.[5]

With regard to aging, particularly for women, our culture perceives natural as young or youthful; that is, smooth-skinned, not gray-haired, and slender. There are strong attempts, and often stronger desires, to "fix" appearance earlier in time, much as we might fix a biology specimen in a zoology laboratory. Some individuals try to preserve their youthful appearance with cosmetics, face lifts, diets, exercise, vitamins, hair products, clothing, and almost anything that they think will help. One of Sharon Curtin's interviewees in *Nobody Ever Died of Old Age* offers a pertinent observation.[6]

Now I live in an affluent section of the city. And the women around here— women my age—do these amazing things to themselves. Their hair is tinted some pastel color, some color no one was ever born with, and is worn in some style about ten years behind the times. Or maybe they just all wear ten- year-old wigs. And they lift and paint their faces just so, until they peer at the world through a mask. They dare not laugh or cry; all the junk would run off into their collars. I think a woman has a duty to try and be attractive, but a seventy-year-old woman makes a fairly ridiculous imitation of Marilyn Monroe. And the bodies below are clothed in garments far too youthful for most of us. Why do old women feel so pressed, so forced to look young?

Many of the points that Susan Sontag made in her classic article, "The Double Standard of Aging," are relevant as responses to Curtin's interviewee.[7] Sontag notes that women identify with their faces: after adolescence they have to launch a holding operation against the natural changes in appearance that come with age. At the same time, the standards for male attractiveness conform to what is possible or natural with age. Men have a wider range of both acceptable facial characteristics and opportunities for gaining status supplements from sources other than their appearance as they grow older. The anxiety that some men feel about aging appears to be primarily associated with the need to be successful in their careers. For women, aging is not only destiny, as it is for men, it is also vulnerability to failure.

Sontag notes that with the increase in average life expectancy, the vulnerability extends over much more of a women's lifetime. Women try to maintain their attractiveness not simply for intrinsic reasons, but also to keep avoidance by others at a minimum. The double standard of aging establishes women as property whose value declines with age. Sontag feels that when women lie about or mask their aging appearance they are participating in their own underdevelopment as human beings and proposes that women refuse to participate in this process, eventually freeing themselves from the humiliation of the aging experience. Proponents of the Women's Movement have in fact advocated other bases than physical attractiveness for the development and maintenance of women's self-esteem. One outcome of their advocacy may be that women of all ages will be able to age more gracefully.

THE DEVELOPMENT AND MAINTENANCE OF A DOUBLE STANDARD OF AGING

A norm in our own and in many other cultures which has recently started to change is for most married women to derive their positions from their husbands.[8] Beginning at least as far back as the Greek and Roman Empires, women have been granted more status when they possessed a husband and were able to bear children, perhaps because they were then less of a threat to the social order.[9] Although 50 percent of American women are now employed, and career opportunities are expanding for women, the trend has been for women to continue to depend on men for much of their social position.

Initial pairings between men and women have generally been made between individuals of similar attractiveness levels.[10] Since aging men have traditionally had greater opportunities for enhancing their attractiveness through employment, wages, and other sources, their female partners have needed to maintain some parity by preserving their physical appearance. If the relationship became too asymmetrical, the risk of insensitivity, oppression, or abandonment increased.[11]

Glen Elder, a sociologist, addressed this exchange value of women's attractiveness.[12] He said,

Depending on the society, the status determining qualities of women include shade of skin color, facial and morphological features, and relative age. We don't yet know the preferential value (or utility) of these qualities within differing cultures, when compared to each other or the weight attributed to other commodities of exchange, such as termperament, interests, values, wealth, and social origin. Nevertheless, throughout human history some women have been able to exchange their physical beauty for a young man's family lineage, accomplishments, or mobility potential.... There is substantial research evidence that American men rank physical attractiveness at or near the top among qualities they desire in women, and this seems to be especially true of upwardly mobile or strongly ambitious men.

Elder noted that a woman's beauty, however culturally defined, has been an avenue for upward mobility in Eastern Indian and Negro cultures in addition to white cultures.

The period of maximum physical beauty in Western and non-Western cultures for both sexes has been youth. Simone de Beauvoir notes in *The Coming of Age* that the Manbikwara Indians have a single word that means "young and beautiful" and another that means "old and ugly."[13] In virtually all societies younger females have been preferred to older ones. In earlier times, this preference was undoubtedly tied into the fact that then as now only younger women could bear children. However, even today when reproduction by every couple is not crucial to the survival of the species, we continue to take the youthful beauty standard so much for granted that we sometimes fail to recognize it as a criterion by which all women are frequently judged.[14]

Within our own culture, when we hear someone say, "She certainly looks her age," we know that the speaker is expressing pity for, or criticism of, some woman who has not been successful in maintaining a youthful, or at least a younger than her age, appearance. Since knowledge of physical attractiveness is at least partly a result of the cues that are received from other people, like Snow White's wicked stepmother, few people want to be told by their mirrors, or by the mirrored responses of others, that they are no longer as attractive as they once were.[15] Women have been and still are taught from the earliest ages that it is important to be pretty; men also learn that it is important for women to be pretty. As women grow older they are beset by aging processes that have effects which are frequently not considered attractive. Simone de Beauvoir writes that she was not able to find literary references from any culture which alluded to beautiful old women except to refer to women who once were beautiful.[16]

When women realize through their interactions with others that they are no longer considered pretty, anxiety may begin to intrude into their aging process. One result of this anxiety can be a desire to change the body to a more idealized form. This urge appears to be strongest when bodily features are the least ideal and the individual is still strongly concerned with what others think.[17] Research data suggest that for many women this time occurs in the period shortly before age 60. However, the desire for bodily change, the beginning of being bothered by the discrepancy between the actual and the ideal body, begins much earlier. "Somewhere in the later twenties, probably at around 27, you'll look in the mirror and realize with a start that changes are taking place and you're not going to stay a young girl forever," warned one popular women's magazine as recently as "liberated" 1978.[18]

A parallel for men of the identification many women have with their physical and particularly with their facial attractiveness, may be the need that they have been socialized to feel for an attractiveness based on power: sexual, economic, intellectual, muscular, interpersonal, and/or organizational.[19] Power has been described as the "capacity to participate effectively in the decision-making process."[20] In some cases, increases in economic, intellectual, interpersonal, or organizational power can offset declines in power that some men experience from aging changes in their sexual and muscular strength. In addition, some men who might not have been particularly attractive to women at an earlier age find themselves, by virtue of their powerful positions, sought out by desirable women. Henry Kissinger while he was Secretary of State was one such example.

Although power in any form may begin to have meaning in itself, most people need to feel that their power is known to others. One of the surest ways for men to let women and other men know that they are powerful is to acquire certain symbols of power such as fancy cars, expensive ski or other sports equipment, "good" clothing, or whatever else assures being treated as a special person. The implication is that having the item, whether it is a "regal" brand of Scotch, an "executive" watch, or an "imperial" car, means having prestige, or power.

Similarly youth is symbolic of both sexual and muscular energy and vigor. One of the developmental tasks of that youthful period is mating. In somewhat circular fashion, men who feel their aging weighing heavily on them may find that they feel more attractive, more energetic, more powerful, at least temporarily, when they have a new and younger mate.

In fact, second marriages are often carried out between substantially older men and younger women, just as most marriages at younger ages are carried out between women and same aged or slightly older men. Twenty percent of grooms sixty-five and over marry women under the age of fifty-five; only 3 percent of older brides marry spouses that young.[21] Older man-younger woman marriages, whether in old or middle age, represent one way in which the crisis of aging can be resolved or at least postponed: a man who changes careers or who takes a new spouse can experience a surge in power.[22]

In other words, it may be a reaffirmation of youthful forms of power to the older man to have a younger mate. The myths suggest that if the older man can still satisfy a younger woman, then he must not be all that old. Choosing a younger woman companion is often a denial of the reality of aging. As anthropologist Leo Simmons reports, "to forestall or at least to delay old age, the Xosa [a South African tribe] recommended the removal of all gray hairs and frequent marriage with fresh young wives. A Xosa patriarch with the advance of age takes another wife or concubine and then another to keep up eternal youth, for he is never supposed to grow old so long as he can obtain a youthful bride."[23]

In addition to these benefits which some men have received from the exaggerated but traditional age pattern for mate selection, it is not surprising that, from the female perspective, older men who have substituted economic or intellectual power for more youthful forms are attractive to younger women. There are some notable exceptions to this rule, such as that provided by Jennie Churchill, Winston's mother, whose second and third husbands were much younger than she was.[24] Women such as movie or television personalities, those who have inherited a lot of money, or more recently those who have important careers, that is, women whose economic and social positions give them independent sources of power, may be able to have relationships with much younger men. However, when women confer status on men through their interpersonal relationships, the men may be devalued and considered gigolos.

In addition to career or spouse changes, less drastic methods of power enhancement for men can include a preoccupation for some with physical fitness or with more specific athletic abilities. Some men who have few or no opportunities to gain power from their employment may bolster their masculine identities as they lose their youthful energy through traditional male hobbies, including spectator sports. Through their identification with certain sports figures or teams, they may experience a vicarious enhancement of their power.[25]

These as well as other opportunities to develop and display power may allow some men to postpone or deny the reality of aging changes; however, women face not only changes in physical appearance which may be cosmetically or surgically treated or sometimes disregarded, but also undeniable changes in the reproductive system which make it virtually impossible to deny that youth has ended and the possibility of maintaining youthful attractiveness has diminished. Once the external signs of aging have begun to appear, every woman must also confront the impending loss of her ability to bear children. Some women who have not had children may begin to think seriously and sometimes even feel panic about whether they should; those who already have children may think about having more.

In the past, female mental disorder rates including depressions were reported to rise at age thirty-five.[26] More recently, an analysis of depressed and nondepressed institutionalized women age forty to fifty-nine found that the depressed middle-aged women were more likely to have suffered maternal role loss.[27] In other cultures, research has suggested that problems were also apt to occur at menopause when there were no equally sanctioned female roles subsequent to maternal function. The increasing trend for women to re-enter the labor force after their youngest child enters school may begin to offset, at least to some extent, the negative consequences of physical aging and maternal role loss.

While expanding employment opportunities for women may allow them to exert more control over their economic and social situations and to develop sources of status other than youthful attractiveness as they grow older, the culture, until recently, has held the notion that women must be careful not to become too successful in their careers or they would jeopardize their femininity.[28] While these attitudes may be changing, some men still cannot relate to women who have more status than they do. This difficulty men have had in relating to higher status women has in part been due to a tendency for some women, even successful ones, to respect the traditional standard of male superiority: they have had a hard time respecting men who were not successful in their careers, and men knew it. Status and power often seem to act as aphrodisiacs for men. Consequently, until women can accept men who have less status than they do as companions and friends, and until men can accept women who have more status than they do, the movement toward sexual equality and status achievement through employment for women has a long way to go. In addition, the willingness of those men who have status and power to share them with women is unknown; some think such sharing unlikely. Furthermore, if men are able to receive support for their power needs through their sexual relationships with women, then women who participate in those relationships are reinforcing their own inferior status and are likely to continue to do so.

A pragmatic obstacle to women achieving status from their employment in the immediate future is economic. Census data show that in 1974 the median income for female-family heads was $6,400, while the median family income for husband-headed families where the wife was not in the paid labor force was $12,000.[29] And rather than an improvement with time, the trend is for the economic disparity between men and women to be increasing slightly, as shown by census data for 1963 and 1973.[30] Thus, the need that married or single women have had to maintain their physical appearance at a peak has continued to exist because avenues for achieving significant power and status independent of relationships with men have just begun to seem possible. The system is such that physical appearance has been a central resource for women. But, as Sontag notes, the full realization of women's potential may require them to acknowledge the double standard and then to reject it.

PHYSICAL APPEARANCE AND ECONOMIC EXPLOITATION

Some women try to preserve their youthful appearance as do some men; other men try to match their appearance to the increased power and status that are expected with age for a man. Those who stand to profit from the anxieties of the aging public and the promotion of the youthful beauty standard or a power image include many businesses such as the cosmetics and toiletries industry.

Statistics show that the cosmetics and toiletries industry is at least a $5 billion business, of which approximately $6 million is spent on men's items.[31] The difference is not totally allocated to women's products, but includes shampoo, toothpaste, and other unisex items. Regardless of the size of the expenditure, is the anxiety of individuals, particularly women, about aging being exploited by the cosmetics industry? The question is difficult to answer because women buy cosmetics at all ages, with adolescent girls and young adult women being big consumers.[32] These younger women may actually be trying to look older with cosmetics. If there is nothing good about looking older for women, why do young women try to look older? In many cases, they are trying to communicate a certain worldly wiseness which only a slightly older woman would have; Miss Jean Brodie was not supposed to be "in her prime" until her early forties.[33] In addition, is it fair to talk about exploitation when the choice to buy the product is voluntary? To the extent that individuals have been conditioned by advertising to believe that they need the product when they do not, certain consumers are being exploited. Women who hear over and over that "today, a younger looking face is within reach of all of us . . . No, you will never look sixteen again, but to drop a decade from your face is not difficult at all," certainly are being urged to pursue the makeup and clothing fashions that are presented as a way to look younger.[34]

A cosmetics saleswoman interviewed by Studs Terkel offered a pertinent comment.[35] She said,

> I sell cosmetics to women who are trying to look young. They are spending more on treatment creams than they did years ago . . . Appearance. Many times I think, thirty dollars for this little jar of cream. I know it doesn't have that value . . . A cosmetic came out that was supposed to smooth out the wrinkles, for five or six hours. It puffs out the skin. The wrinkles would return . . . a woman came in one morning, she said, "I'm going for a job interview and I'm past forty. I want to look nicer." . . . It might bring her a job . . .

There is always the competition of keeping their husbands interested. You see the fear in their faces—becoming lined. They all discuss this: "Look at me. I look terrible." They will talk about seeing it on television—the cream that erases lines. Television is the thing that has brought all this. More anxiety.

Although men and women buy cosmetics and toiletries to try to look what they think is their best at all ages, there is no doubt that advertising strategies are aimed at exploiting insecurities. Many of these attempts exploit anxiety about sexuality and more generally the signs of aging. Even young women are affected by such advertising when they believe that if they "moisturize" their skin each day they will not get wrinkles, even though the largest basis for the onset of wrinkles is heredity.

In addition to moisturizing, other strategies are promoted in the wrinkle and aging war. Mike Royko, a Chicago newspaper columnist wrote: "A physician has published a highly publicized book saying that if you regularly eat lots of sardines, your wrinkles will disappear, you will get bounce in your step and you will almost explode with youthful energy. That, plus a $250 hairpiece, and you can go to a disco and pinch all the nice young things."[36] The diet referred to has created a great deal of interest both among the aging public and among nutritionists who claim that it is pure quackery, although they do admit that eating quantities of sardines might make your skin look smoother. Because sardines are high in salt content, eating them causes the body to retain water and results in a slightly bloated puffy look.

The hand lotion advertisements which caution women not to let their hands give their age away certainly are capitalizing on anxieties about aging; so are the fad diets which promote a "youthful figure" and the hair tint and dye slogans which promise that some product will cover up the gray or wash it away. Other types of cosmetics simply claim to make people of any age more attractive. However, implicit in this attractiveness may be the belief that coloring the face or hair through blushers, powders, and dyes conveys a sense of healthiness—and good health implies youth. "You're fifty and want to look forty. Your skin at this stage is losing its warm, vital color and becomes more neutral in tone. Now you must counteract this loss of color with a complexion prime coat in a rose or peach shade."[37]

Since certain signs of aging, such as wrinkles, baldness, and sagging skin, are not helped very much by adding color, some women and men who can afford it use plastic surgery to remove the years from their faces and sometimes from their bodies. While cosmetic surgery used to be the province of people in the public eye, recent reports in *Newsweek* and *The New York Times* disclose that more and more average people who have the money to spend are having cosmetic surgery.[38]

Hair transplant operations have also become popular among more affluent men. Hair has been associated with virility since Sampson and Delilah in biblical times. Because heredity as a cause of early balding was not understood until relatively recently, balding was generally regarded as the result of early aging and aging was associated with loss of sexual potency. With the exception of followers of Kojak, a bald television cop, some twenty- or thirty-year-old men become self-conscious about hair loss. These young men may become upset by their thinning hair because it makes them "look" older and, therefore, they may be regarded as less virile, less powerful. The stigma of baldness, however, affects even some older men who could be viewed as receiving sufficient power supplements from their careers. Both Senator Proxmire and Frank Sinatra, for example, underwent hair transplant operations to replace lost hair. In sum, because of the association of baldness and aging and the belief that significant loss of virility occurs in aging men, balding men of different ages are prone to quack remedies, as well as to those that work, such as hair transplants, but which are quite expensive.

For some middle-aged women, attention to clothing may serve the same function that their physical attractiveness once did—that is, to get them compliments. If they get compliments, they feel that perhaps they can't be so old. An article in *The New York Times* reported that many compulsive shoppers cite appearance as an important factor in their behavior.[39] In fact, some women may become clothesaholics because wearing something new to their jobs or to lunch with friends gets them the kind of attention that is spontaneously given to pretty young women.

The barriers which have prevented women from obtaining status through means other than their physical attractiveness have resulted in cosmetics usage, plastic surgery, and clothing purchases having become reasonable responses for aging women to make to a restrictive and nonsupportive environment. Until other avenues for status are as certain as youthful attractiveness, women will find it difficult to give up its pursuit entirely. As men age, they must dress, look, and have other accoutrements which are considered appropriate for men of a certain status, for men who have power. Although it may be difficult to prove that individuals are being exploited in a strict legal sense, it seems clear that advantage is sometimes taken of insecurities caused by aging changes.

SEXUAL PERFORMANCE AND AGING

There is little that has been regarded as a greater threat to a man's sexual power, to his sexual potency, than aging. Although Masters and Johnson have firmly refuted the notion that a man totally loses his sexual capacity with age, they and others, including Kinsey have established that there is a change in sexual performance with age.[40] Specifically, the frequency and speed of arousal and ejaculation are highest when a man is in his late teens and early twenties. While speediness of ejaculation may not be entirely positive for the men or their partners, the realization of the decline in speed of response may produce anxiety in some aging men. Like the female's fading beauty, the fifty-year-old man may feel that he is just a shadow of his former self.

In general, age affects different phases of the male sexual response in subsequent fashion: the length of time needed for erection to occur increases; a reduction in pre-ejaculatory fluid occurs; time between erection and orgasm lengthens; the force of ejaculation declines; loss of erection after ejaculation is rapid; and the length of time needed for erection after ejaculation increases.[41]

Women's sexual response is affected by age in the following ways: vaginal lubrication tends to occur more slowly; expansion capacity of the vaginal barrel decreases; contractions during orgasm are less frequent and less vigorous; occasional pain occurs as a result of uterine spasm; age-related atrophy of the body, and specifically of the genitalia and breast, are more profound in women than in men and are caused by the abrupt decline of estrogen and progesterone after menopause.

In spite of these changes, evidence of the continuing sexual activity of older people is provided by a study which compared the sexual activities of 250 married, single, and widowed men and women between the ages of sixty and ninety-three. Of the 149 married persons, 60 percent of the sixty- to seventy-four-year-olds were sexually active; 30 percent of those over age seventy-five were active.[42] Many of those in the oldest group, or their spouses, were afflicted with chronic illnesses which mitigated sexual activity. The married women reported less activity than the married men. Only 7 percent of the nonmarried people were sexually active.

The loss of sexual responsiveness in later life for those individuals who have a partner is thought to be primarily due to six factors: monotony, preoccupation with career or economic pursuits; physical or mental fatigue; overindulgence in food or drink; physical or mental infirmity of either spouse; and fear of failure associated with or resulting from these factors.[43]

For those individuals who are not married or whose spouses are dead or no longer interested in sex, an alternative form of activity may be practiced. Kinsey's data suggest that 25 percent of married and single men above age sixty masturbate regularly; 59 percent of unmarried women between the ages of fifty and seventy admit to masturbating; approximately 30 percent of older women supplant marital coitus with masturbation.[44] Other data suggest that 6 percent of a sample of 1700 men engaged in homosexual acts after age sixty.[45]

In summary, there are changes in sexual performance with age which may require sensitive understanding by the individuals involved.[46] For many people, motivation to continue a sexual life can outweigh physiological aging changes that reduce sexual capacity. An unwarranted assumption is that because an individual is older, he or she will neither desire nor find it possible to engage in sexual activity.[47]

ATTITUDES TOWARD OLDER AGE AND SEXUALITY

In spite of Kinsey's published evidence to the contrary, in 1959 a sample of college students aged seventeen to twenty-three expressed the belief that sexual activity was neither essential nor important for most old people.[48] More recently, one quarter of another college student sample expressed the belief that their parents, who were mostly in their forties, had intercourse an average of three times a month; another fourth believed their parents never had intercourse or had it less than once per year; and half of the sample of 646 students thought it must be about once a month or less.[49] Kinsey's data, however, suggest that the mode, the most frequently occurring category, of sexual response for married females was once per week by age forty and after.[50] In other words, it seems fairly likely that the college students were underestimating the frequency of their parents' sexual activity. The incest taboo may be at least partly responsible for children repressing the sexuality of their parents; if parents are seen as asexual, the danger of incest is greatly reduced. It is possible that young people may generalize the repression associated with the incest taboo to other adults who are as old as or older than their parents.

People involved in the field of gerontology and geriatrics have been devoting attention to this lack of acceptance by society of sex and sexuality among older people.[51] Even without their efforts, however, there have been a few "important" older people who have continued to maintain sexuality as part of their image long past the age when it was supposed to exist: examples are Pablo Casals, Picasso, Mae West, and Marlene Dietrich. Like the few women who have not been censured for marrying men much younger than themselves, society has been willing to make exceptions for a few high-status older persons. They have even been applauded for their sexual longevity.

However, the typical older person is assumed to be more neuter than either male or female. The idea of a sexual relationship between two older people is often considered by society to be either nonexistent or negative. A pornographic movie which showed two older people having sex would more likely be considered gross than erotic. Older people are not supposed to have sexual desires or needs, much less satisfy them.

In addition to the influence of the incest taboo, what are some of the other reasons that old age has come to be considered such a sexual desert? One possibility is that sexuality has been associated with perfect bodies, which only the young can have. Old age, with its bodily imperfections, may result in sexuality being devalued for older people.

Because of the uncertainty about the sexual appropriateness of a body not perfect according to societal standards, some individuals try to nudge or shove that body toward that standard through diets, pills, and fancy exercise equipment. While no one would deny the positive health value of keeping weight down and muscles toned, the denial of the sexuality of those individuals who violate the standard can be oppressive to them. The elderly, the handicapped, and the obese cannot meet the reference criterion for sexual attractiveness. Since sexual performance can be facilitated by sexual fantasies, the incongruence of the reality with the idealized fantasy may also cause performance decrements and, therefore, sexual avoidance in some older males and females.

The perceived asexuality of old age may be influenced by some facts pertinent to the present older generation. Individuals currently over sixty-five were raised by parents who were socialized during the Victorian era, with the result that some may continue to be influenced by Victorian notions about sex which were prevalent then. There may also be a need to protect male egos, which could be undermined if all aging men were expected to maintain their sexual performance in older age; if men are not expected to perform either by themselves or by their partners, they are protected from the risk of a power failure. At the same time, the present generation of older women may never have felt comfortable with their sexuality and may be just as happy not to have sex as an expectation. Society's denial of the need for sexual expression and even companionship in old age may also be inferred from data which suggest that some older people who become widowed may not be particularly encouraged to seek new spouses.[52] Sometimes the children of the older widowed person want to maintain the image of their parents as interested only in each other. The incest taboo may possibly preclude children from seeing their parents as sexual beings. Some other children may want the family inheritance to remain intact. If the older person were to remarry, both the image and the legacy might be affected. Some older widows may themselves hesitate to seek new partners because of their fear of having to nurse another spouse and then be left along again. Since females greatly outnumber males at older ages, removing sexuality as an area of involvement for them can serve a protective function. If sexuality were considered important for older people, older females would be even more disadvantaged and oppressed than at present.

CONCLUSION

The median age of the United States population will rise to thirty-seven by the year 2025. With the diminution of a youth-dominated society, the physical concomitants and the onset of aging may become less feared.

However, at the present time, some women and men seem to be anxious about the onset of the external signs of aging. Women have been found to be more expressive of that anxiety. Changes in appearance which occur as a result of the aging process have not been considered favorably by either men or women. Appearing youthful has been considered to be important in overall sexual attractiveness, particularly for women. As individuals age, compensations for their declining attractiveness are required. Status from employment and/or wages has been used to bolster sexual attractiveness for aging individuals. This avenue for status has in the past been available primarily to men.

The potential that employment offers as a status source for women is undermined by the need that both men and women have for men to be the high achievers. Before employment can substitute for youthful appearance, it will have to be acceptable for women to have more or as much status as their male partners. Both men and women will have to be comfortable with women determining the family's position, as almost all men in couple relationships have done up to the present.

Women, and men to a lesser extent, spend a considerable amount of money on cosmetics and clothing, at least partially in an attempt to look more attractive. The cosmetics and toiletries industry has directed much of its advertising at the anxieties of an aging public. Products are touted either as directly reducing the signs of aging or indirectly by increasing sexual attractiveness. The fear of losing sexual attractiveness with age may also be exploited by those marketing certain diets, fancy exercise equipment, hair restoration remedies, and "sexy" status objects such as automobiles and other luxuries.

The major conclusion of a number of studies of sexual activity and age is that sexual desire and activity are present in older people; reasons for individual variation in sexual responsiveness include not only differences in physiological aging, but also social, psychological, and cultural influences. Some of these social impediments to active sexuality in older age include: the lack of a partner; the desire that men may have to avoid performance failure; the generation currently old were raised with Victorian notions about sexuality and may have retained those ideas into their advanced age; and as a result of the incest taboo, many children may not encourage the sexual identities of their parents.

In general, advertising strategies are aimed at exploiting insecurities about the signs of aging. These insecurities, as well as the knowledge that a youth-oriented culture disregards the sexuality of its older population, may contribute to oppression in the later years for some older adults.

Notes

1. Particularly helpful suggestions for this chapter were received from Gretchen Batra, David Karp, and John Mogey.
2. See Kelly (1977) for details about this study as well as for references to other articles.

3. See Goffman (1963:2,3).

4. See Berscheid et al. (1973).

5. Way Bandy as told to Jean Libman Block (1978:163).

6. See Curtin (1972: 80). The interviewee is a woman in her seventies.

7. Sontag (1972) discusses the preoccupation that women have with their appearance. See also Bart (1975).

8. See Holter (1970:229).

9. An anthology of sexuality is presented by de Beauvoir (1973).

10. See Murstein (1972).

11. See Waller (1937).

12. See Elder (1969:520). Exchange theory is discussed by Homans (1961).

13. See de Beauvoir (1973) and also Strange (1976).

14. Robertson (1977: 190) notes currently that different cultures have used various standards for judging feminine attractiveness, but overlooks the universality of relative youth as the context within which that variability occurs.

15. See Schilder (1968).

16. See de Beauvoir (1973: 440).

17. See Back and Gergen (1960).

18. Way Bandy as told to Jean Libman Block (1978:163,253). He goes on to describe make-up and clothing useful for looking younger.

19. Kate Millet (1970:103) notes an effect of this socialization. She says, "The effect of male ascendancy upon human society in general and the masculine character (which governs society) in particular is such that it fosters notions of superiority and satisfaction over differential or prejudicial treatment from earliest youth." She notes that John Stuart Mill in *The Subjection of Women* considers" . . . the system of sexual dominance to be the very prototype of other abuses of power and other forms of egotism." Paula Johnson (1976) writes that women's access to concrete resources and competence, both in their expectations and in reality, is less than that of men. Their power influence is limited to indirect, personal, and helpless modes. She feels that this power style difference has negative consequences for women. David and Brannon (1976) feel that the need to evaluate men in terms of their power has led to the emphasis on judging success in terms of man's work.

20. See Robertson (1977:436). On pages 438–439 he notes people who held charismatic power; of the nine individuals represented, only one, Joan of Arc, is a woman.

21. See Treas and Van Hilst (1976).

22. Judith Bardwick (1975) discusses these ideas.

23. See Leo Simmons (1945:223).

24. See Martin for a biography of Jennie Churchill (1971).

25. In professional football, the inclusion in the program of young, attractive women cheerleaders may further increase the possibility for vicarious virility enhancement.

26. See Belknap and Friedsam (1958).

27. See Bart (1975). McKinlay and Jefferys (1974) report that depression was one symptom more often reported by women experiencing menopause, or who were in the period immediately following, than by women in earlier or later life stages. The depression did not seem to be directly related to menopause but to more general factors.

28. See Holter (1970:229).

29. Information reported by McEaddy (1976) and Hayghe (1976).

30. In 1963, the difference between the median real after-tax earning for "other male" family heads and women family heads in favor of men was $2,333, while in 1973, the difference in favor of men was $2,887. For a complete discussion, see Ryscavage (1975).

31. See Nancy Molinelli's article, "$5 Billion Industry Losing Personal Touch," pp. 29–38 and Robert Love's article, "Men's Lines Growing Fast, Expanding in Every Direction," pp. 38–40, both in *Chemical Marketing Reporter*, June 21, 1976.

32. However, see the article, "Older Woman Now Numerous, Better Educated, More Aware," by Alan S. Brown in *Chemical Marketing Reporter*, June 21, 1976: pp. 41–43. In it the potential lucrativeness of the older woman as a cosmetics consumer loyal to expensive name brands is described.
33. See *The Prime of Miss Jean Brodie* by Muriel Spark (1961).
34. Way Bandy as told to Jean Libman Block (1973:163).
35. See Terkel (1975: 324–325).
36. Mike Royko's article, "Fad Diet Hails Sardines but Nutritionists Can It," appeared in *The Boston Evening Globe* on November 30, 1976: 1, 8.
37. Way Bandy as told to Jean Libman Block (1978:253).
38. See "The Plastic-Surgery Boom," *Newsweek*, January 24, 1977: 73–74 and "Cosmetic Lib for Men" by James Kelly, in *The New York Times Magazine*, September 25, 1977: 118. *Newsweek* says, "They [plastic surgery customers] come from the growing ranks of United States middle-aged and elderly citizens who suddenly find themselves at odds with a culture that increasingly puts a premium on youth (p.73)."
39. See Lynn Ames' article, "Compulsive Shopping: The Buy-Now-And-Pay-Later Syndrome" in *The New York Times*, Wednesday, July 26, 1978, p. C9.
40. See Masters and Johnson (1970) and Kinsey *et al.* (1948).
41. See Masters and Johnson for aging changes in men and women (1970).
42. See Newman and Nichols (1960).
43. See Masters and Johnson (1970).
44. See Kinsey *et al.* (1948) for male sexual activity and Kinsey *et al.* (1953) for female sexual activity.
45. This study by Calleja is reported in McCary (1973a).
46. See Butler and Lewis (1976) for helpful information for older people.
47. See McCary (1973b) for other myths about sexuality.
48 See Golde and Kogan (1959).
49. See Pocs, Godow, Tolone, and Walsh (1977).
50. See Kinsey *et al.* (1953).
51. See Burnside (1975).
52. See Treas and Van Hilst (1976) for an interesting article about marriage and remarriage rates for older Americans.

References

Back, Kurt W., and Kenneth J. Gergen, "The Self Through the Latter Span of Life." In Chad Gordon and Kenneth J. Gergen (ed.), *The Self in Social Interaction Volume I*, pp. 241–250. New York: Wiley, 1960.

Bandy, Way, as told to Jean Libman Block, "How to Take 10 Years Off Your Face." *Good Housekeeping* 187(5), 1978: 162–163.

Bardwick, Judith, "Middle Age and a Sense of the Future." Paper presented at the Annual Meeting of the American Sociological Association. San Francisco, 1975.

Bart, Pauline B., "Emotional and Social Status of the Older Woman." In *No Longer Young: The Older Woman in America*, p. 3–22. Ann Arbor, Mich.: Occasional Papers in Gerontology, Institute of Gerontology, University of Michigan/Wayne State University, #11, 1975.

de Beauvoir, Simone, *The Coming of Age.* Translated by Patrick O'Brian. New York: Warner Paperback Library, 1973.

Belknap, Ivan, and Hiram J. Friedsam, "Age and Sex Categories as Sociological

Variables in the Mental Disorders of Later Maturity." In Herman D. Stein and Richard A. Cloward (ed.), *Social Perspectives on Behavior,* pp. 201–209. New York: Free Press, 1958.

Berscheid, Ellen, Elaine Walster, and George W. Bohrnstedt, "Body Image, Physical Appearance, and Self-Esteem." Paper presented at the Annual Meeting of the American Sociological Association, New York, 1973.

Burnside, Irene Mortenson (ed.), *Sexuality and Aging.* Los Angeles: University of Southern California Press, 1975.

Butler, Robert N., and Myrna I. Lewis, *Sex After 60: A Guide for Men and Women for their Later Years.* New York: Harper & Row, 1976.

Curtin, Sharon, *Nobody Ever Died of Old Age.* Boston: Little, Brown, 1972.

David, Deborah S., and Robert Brannon, "The Big Wheel: Success, Status, and the Need to be Looked Up to." In Deborah S. David and Robert Brannon (ed.), *The Forty-Nine Percent Majority,* pp. 89–92. Reading, Mass.: Addison-Wesley, 1976.

Elder, Glen H. Jr., "Appearance and Education in Marriage Mobility." *American Sociological Review* 34(4), 1969: 519–33.

Goffman, Erving, *Stigma.* Englewood Cliffs, N.J.: Prentice-Hall, 1963.

Golde, Peggy, and Nathan Kogan, "A Sentence Completion Procedure for Assessing Attitudes toward Old People." *Journal of Gerontology* 14, 1959: 355–363.

Hayghe, Howard, "Families and the Rise of Working Wives—An Overview." Special Labor Force Report 189. Washington, D.C.: United States Department of Labor, Bureau of Labor Statistics, 1976.

Holter, Harriet, *Sex Roles and Social Structure.* Box 142, Boston, Mass.: Universitet-forlaget, 1970.

Homans, George, *Social Behavior: Its Elementary Forms.* New York: Harcourt, 1961.

Johnson, Paula, "Women and Power: Toward a Theory of Effectiveness." *Journal of Social Issues* 32(3), 1976: 99–110.

Kelly, Jim, "The Aging Male Homosexual: Myth and Reality." *The Gerontologist* 17(4), 1977: 328–332.

Kinsey, Alfred C., Wardell B. Pomeroy, and Clyde E. Martin, *Sexual Behavior in the Human Male.* Philadelphia: Saunders, 1948.

Kinsey, Alfred C., Wardell B. Pomeroy, Clyde F. Martin, and Paul H. Gebhard, *Sexual Behavior in the Human Female.* Philadelphia: Saunders, 1953.

Martin, Ralph, *Jennie: The Life of Lady Randolph Churchill, Volume 2.* Englewood Cliffs, N.J.: Signet, 1971.

Masters, William H., and Virginia E. Johnson, *Human Sexual Inadequacy.* Boston: Little, Brown, 1970.

McCary, James Leslie, *Human Sexuality: Physiological, Psychological, and Sociological Factors,* 2nd ed. New York: Van Nostrand, 1973.

—*Sexual Myths and Fallacies.* New York: Schocken, 1973.

McEaddy, Beverly Johnson, "Women who Head Families: A Socioeconomic Analysis." Special Labor Force Report 190. Washington, D.C.: U.S. Department of Labor, Bureau of Labor Statistics, 1976.

McKinlay, Sonja M., and Margot Jefferys, "The Menopausal Syndrome." *British Journal of Preventive and Social Medicine* 28(2), 1974: 108–115.

Millet, Kate, *Sexual Politics.* Garden City, N.Y.: Doubleday, 1970.

Murstein, Bernard I., "Physical Attractiveness and Marital Choice." *Journal of Personality and Social Psychology* 22(1) 1972: 8–12.

Newman, Gustave, and Claude R. Nichols, "Sexual Activities and Attitudes in Older Persons." *Journal of the American Medical Association* 173, 1960: 30–35.

Pocs, Ollie, Annette Godow, William L. Tolone, and Robert H. Walsh, "Is there Sex after 40?" *Psychology Today* 11(1), 1977: 54–56.

Robertson, Ian, *Sociology.* New York: Worth, 1977.

Ryscavage, Paul M., "Annual Earnings of Household Heads." *Monthly Labor Review* 98(8), 1975: 14–25.

Schilder, Paul, "The Image and Appearance of the Human Body." In Chad Gordon and Kenneth Gergen (ed.). *The Self in Social Interaction Volume 1,* pp. 107–114. New York: Wiley, 1968.

Simmons, Leo, *The Role of the Aged in Primitive Society.* New Haven, Conn.: Yale University Press, 1945.

Sontag, Susan, "The Double Standard of Aging." *Saturday Review* 55 (Sept. 23, 1972): 29–38.

Spark, Muriel, *The Prime of Miss Jean Brodie.* Philadelphia: Lippincott, 1961.

Strange, Heather, "Patterns of Mate Selection and Marriage Ritual in a Malay Village." *Journal of Marriage and the Family* 38, 1976: 561–571.

Terkel, Studs, *Working.* New York: Avon, 1975.

Treas, Judith, and Anke Van Hilst, "Marriage and Remarriage Rates among Older Americans." *Gerontologist* 16(2), 1976: 132–137.

Waller, Willard, "The Rating and Dating Complex." *American Sociological Review* 2, 1937: 727–734.

CHAPTER **6**

Drugs, Doctors, And Hospitals

In this chapter, we will examine some of the ways in which the medical establishment profits from and sometimes exploits the health difficulties of the aging public. We will also discuss how attitudes of caregivers, and of society more generally, can oppress or decrease the quality of life of the older individual whose physical and/or mental health requires attention.

Often, it is not until we have come close to losing our health, after a brush with serious illness, that we realize that our life styles are very much influenced by our physical condition. As we grow older, we may adapt our way of life to reflect normal aging changes, changes which include lower reserve capacities and diminished strength. The focus may change for some from a goal of perfect physical fitness or perfect health to being healthier or more physically fit than others of similar age.

Aging is a natural phenomenon: it is the organism's irreversible loss of ability after maturity to function optimally in its environment.[1] This natural decline in optimal functioning should be differentiated from other declines which are due to disease processes. These disease processes are sometimes highly correlated with aging, but they are not one and the same thing. The goal of much research is to eliminate these diseases which are prevalent in advanced age. Their elimination would allow old age to be as healthy as possible.

At the present time, certain chronic health problems, among others arthritis and hypertension, are prevalent in old age. Over 80 percent of the older population report having some type of chronic condition. Many individuals have more than one. By their definition, chronic ailments are not quickly or easily stopped or reversed. Their natural course is to progressively worsen. While such health problems can affect people of any age, they are much more likely to be present in people in middle and old age. One of many results is that older people are more likely to have been hospitalized in the previous year than younger people. The health care system assumes greater salience for the lives of older people than for others.

Another issue which affects all ages, but which affects older people more heavily because of their greater use of the medical system, is the cost of care, including the price of drugs and the fragmentation of services. People with health problems are less likely to be in a position to question the cost of medical care. When mobility or life itself is at stake, cost often seems to be a trivial issue, at least at the moment. Illness, with all the goods and services that are devoted to its cure or containment, is an enormous source of profit and power for the manufacturers of the goods and the purveyors of the services.[2] The potential for exploitation of sick people and their families is tremendous.

In addition to the greater importance that the health care system has for the lives of older people because of greater frequency of use, there are other aspects of the medical establishment that more heavily affect the older individual; for example, the sometimes negative attitude of caregivers toward older people.

HEALTH IN OLDER AGE

Although most older people have at least one chronic health problem, two-thirds of the noninstitutionalized aged, the overwhelming majority of the elderly, reported their health as good or excellent, if they compared themselves to others their own age.[3] In the same survey only 9 percent said their health was poor, but proportionally twice as many elderly with poor health were minority group members. This relatively higher incidence of poor health among minority elderly also applied to residents of the South, of nonmetropolitan areas, and to those with low incomes. There were no differences between men and women regarding the incidence of poor health. However, proportionally five times as many men as women said that they were unable to carry out a major activity.

In contrast to the small percent who reported their health as poor in the preceding survey, a nation-wide sample of participants age fifty and over in a Louis Harris poll on aging most often volunteered poor health or poor physical condition when they were asked what was the worst thing about being over sixty-five years of age. The 70 percent who offered this as a problem area outnumbered by more than three to one the second highest percent, who gave loneliness as a problem. When asked what life areas created very serious or somewhat serious problems for them personally,

50 percent of these older Americans said health.[4] While the first survey discussed found only 9 percent of older people who gave their health as poor, it is evident that one's health condition can be considered a serious personal problem much more often. Although the variation in health conditions is as broad among the elderly as in other age groups, any illness tends to be more serious, to last longer, and perhaps be more feared in old age.[5] As a result, health care for the elderly is a very salient life dimension.

As greater proportions of the population live to advanced age—in 1900, 4 percent lived to age sixty-five, while in 1975 slightly more than 10 percent did—diseases which are more likely to occur in those who are older have become more prevalent.[6] Robert Butler, in his Pulitzer-Prize-winning book, *Why Survive?,* writes that "the exciting aspect of medical care for the elderly is that much of what has long been considered to be aging is disease."[7] The high incidence of certain chronic conditions facilitated the view that such diseases were an inherent part of the aging process. As a result, even now when older people see a physician for a problem, they are labelled "old and frail" and sometimes (too frequently?) told that, at their age, they should not expect to be in perfect shape. The care they are given may be less than adequate.

The story was told to one of the authors of an eighty-year-old woman who presented certain symptoms, including weight gain, skin changes, dulled mental processes, and confusion. These symptoms can be associated with hypothyroidism, but in her case they were diagnosed as "what you can expect in old age." The lady later experienced congestive heart failure, one result of hypothyroidism. Her daughter then remembered that when her mother was younger she had taken daily thyroid medication. She had stopped taking it, and had also changed physicians to one closer to her residence. She neglected to mention her thyroid condition, and her doctor failed to diagnose her symptoms as anything other than old age. The cardiac condition might not have occurred if the hypothyroidism had been corrected in time. Had the woman been younger and viewed as a productive member of society, more effort might have been directed toward finding a specific cause for her symptoms. Because she had no real role to play, she may have been less effectively treated.

On the other hand, social critic Ivan Illich suggests that medical treatment can increase discomfort and lengthen a life much reduced in quality.[8] In an opinion different in tone from Butler's he writes, "Old age . . . which has been variously considered a doubtful privilege or a pitiful ending but never a disease, has recently been put under doctor's orders. The demand for old-age care has increased, not just because there are more old people who survive, but also because there are more people who state their claim that old age should be cured." He goes on to say that "the transformation of old age into a condition calling for professional services has cast the elderly in the role of a minority who will feel painfully deprived at any relative level of tax-supported privilege. From weak old people who are sometimes miserable and bitterly disappointed by neglect, they are turned into certified members of the saddest of consumer groups, that of the aged programmed never to get enough." On the one hand, older people may be viewed as expendable and given less than adequate care; at the same time, the salience of their health to them lends itself to exploitation by those industries offering quick, sometimes quack, remedies for almost any ailment. However we feel about the implications, as we move from the view that bad health comes with old age to the view that disease and aging are not synonymous, but that certain diseases are more prevalent in old age, more and more older people can be expected to seek treatment for conditions which were once considered inherent components of old age. One direct result of the greater use of health services by the elderly is the greater expenditure for health care for and by older people.

MEDICAL COSTS

The amount of medical expense attributable to those sixty-five and over is much out of proportion to their numbers in the population: 29 percent of medical expenses are for the 10 percent elderly population.[9] In the United States, Medicare payments covered only 42 percent of the total health costs of the elderly in 1975.[10] Although the absolute amount of money spent for Medicare continues to increase and is high, the percent of total health care costs which are paid by Medicare continues to decline. Medicare does not cover prescription drugs outside of an institution, eyeglasses, hearing aids, certain out-patient, and in-home services even though such services and appliances are believed to delay institutionalization. But then Medicare does not pay for institutionalization for any extended period of time. Because of the fragmentation of Medicare services, older health care consumers can be forced to buy expensive additional insurance for uncovered goods and services. The hearing aid field has been a prime example of the hard-sell opportunism that has existed.

However, in 1977 the Federal Drug Administration finally published regulations regarding the sale of hearing aids. These regulations require that certain types of information about the aids be made available to the dispensing professionals as well as to the client. They also require that the client have a full medical evaluation in the six months prior to the sale unless a fully informed adult waives the requirements. Until the establishment of these regulations, older individuals not only have had to pay the full cost of the hearing aids themselves, but have been able to receive appliances unsuited to their hearing problems.[11] Along with the new regulations, a proposal was advanced by the Federal Trade Commission to enable a hearing aid purchaser to cancel a sale within a thirty-day period and receive an almost complete refund. The proposal also requires the disclosure of information to the effect that many individuals with hearing loss cannot be helped by a hearing aid.

Although there are certain goods and services which Medicare and Medicaid do not cover, government funds paid 61 percent of the total health costs of the elderly in 1975.[12] This is in contrast to 1966, before the implementation of Medicare and Medicaid, when public funds paid only 30 percent of the health costs of the elderly. While the benefits that these programs have provided are large, there are also some problems. As the costs of the programs have risen, the amount that the older person must spend each year before Medicare will pay for hospital bills increased to $124 in 1977. The annual deductible was $40 in 1966. The higher deductibles are mandated by the legislation for the Medicare bill; there are automatic rises when hospital costs increase. In addition, many older people pay coinsurance premiums in order to be covered for services that are limited under Medicare. Consequently, while the elderly were the most advantaged group in 1978 when it came to national health insurance, medical care for those sixty-five and over was by no means free. The program has allowed the expenses of the elderly to be better anticipated rather than eliminated altogether.[13]

One of the more serious deficiencies of the Medicare program has been its inability to pay for long-term institutional care. Only a small percentage, about 5 percent, of the elderly are institutionalized at any given time, however, the fear that many older people and their families have of the financial catastrophe associated with nursing home placement plainly exacerbates the difficulties of growing old. Although Medicaid will cover the expenses of "needy" individuals who require nursing home care, the necessity to plead poverty, not only by the person who is to receive the care, but also by any spouse, makes it clear that certain types of expensive health services are a privilege and not a right in this society. *The New York Times* reported an incident probably not uncommon for older married couples when they are forced to seek institutional care for one of their members.[14] In the particular case discussed in the article, the wife in the forty-nine-year marriage had Huntington's Chorea and required total care. Because the couple had assets of $2,715, or about $500 more than allowed in order to be eligible for Medicaid at that time in their state, they had a choice of either bringing their assets below the allowable level or of seeking a divorce. We might ask what kind of a society is it that sets up such crazy choices for its members, choices that force either near destitution or divorce. Clearly, it is a society that sees health care as a privilege and not a right for its citizens.

Sometimes the high cost of medical treatment discourages older people, as well as people of other ages, from seeking care which is preventative.

Even older people who have Medicare Part B, which pays doctors' bills, may avoid having routine checkups as long as possible, waiting until a condition has become acute because they want to avoid paying the deductible. A strong relationship between income and receiving preventative treatment for older people was found in a sample of New York City residents. Lack of money was given most often for not seeing a physician.[15]

Unfortunately, the amount of money spent on health care for the elderly is not necessarily related to the quality of care received. As with other businesses, where competition and alternatives are lacking, the consumer pays a high cost regardless of the quality of care offered. The money is being accumulated by a medical establishment which often offers fragmented care, care which lacks empathy and support for the special problems of the elderly, and which ignores the social environment of the older person. In addition to being fragmented and expensive, medical care for everyone including the elderly is often offered in an atmosphere which is intimidating and which discourages questioning.

If health care is the goal of the medical establishment, why is it not better done? One reason may be that in addition to patient care, an obvious function of the American health care system is profitmaking. Even nonprofit institutions want to accumulate money which can be spent for expensive equipment and "nice" facilities with which to attract doctors who are accustomed to having only the best. It has been suggested by some that the money-making aspect is more organized than the patient care function. Barbara and John Ehrenreich in *The American Health Empire* write,

> It was Medicare that transformed the old bogeyman of government interference into a Santa Claus for the health industry. The drug industry and even the commercial insurance industry have found that they can live more than comfortably with Medicare and Medicaid. And of course, it was Medicare that sent the hospital supply, equipment, [and other related] industries spiraling into a boom.[16]

Medicare and Medicaid, which together amount to a multibillion dollar industry, use private insurance programs to handle billing and payments. Blue Shield in 1978 held thirty-two of the forty-seven contracts awarded to private insurees to handle doctor payments under Medicare. Even more importantly Blue Shield, which pays doctors' bills, until recently had boards made up largely of physicians. Although physicians no longer hold a majority of positions on the boards of directors of the seventy Blue Shield health insurance plans, they still fill slightly less than half of those positions.[17] Blue Shield's sister organization, Blue Cross, also one of the largest health insurers, attempted to exercise little cost control over the hospitals. Reimbursement, until the mid 1970s when hospital costs skyrocketed, was on a cost-plus basis. The effect was ever-increasing fees to subscribers. Blue Cross has traditionally been controlled by the hospital establishment which created it during the Depression to insure that they, the hospitals, got paid.

In recent years, the drug industry, physicians, the hospital supply business, health insurance, and the nursing home industry have been top money makers. In fact, physicians are the highest paid professionals in the United States. Their fees have risen a minimum of 43 percent faster than the cost of living since 1950, and faster than their expenses.[18] In spite of the legal potential for large income accumulation that physicians have, illegal aggrandizement of income, particularly through the Medicaid and Medicare programs, is utilized by some. An interesting case surfaced in the Boston area where two well-respected physicians, who were on the faculties of Harvard and Tufts Medical Schools and who practiced jointly, pleaded guilty to fraudulent Medicare claims (one of the physicians later withdrew his guilty plea).[19] In the initial guilty plea the only discrepancy between the physicians' and the government's case was over the number of falsified claims. The doctors' estimate, lower than the government's, was that 33,000 were fraudulent. Why would these physicians, who it is estimated earned $150,000 per year, have indulged in Medicare fraud, which it is estimated would have contributed only about $5,000 to each of their net incomes? A neighbor interviewed by a newspaper reporter said,

> Some doctors get to feeling they're gods and can do no wrong. In his own little way [Dr. A] was like that. He came to see himself as the "perfect doctor, the perfect human being." If he did something, it had to be all right, like Nixon and the presidency. In his own eyes, [Dr. A] could do no wrong.

Power and profit are themes that run strongly through the story of the health care system.

Although in the history of the Medicare/Medicaid program fewer than 1 percent of physicians have been convicted of fraud, the case described suggests that such fraud may be more widespread than anyone would like to believe. In the particular case cited, the physicians were described as being frustrated by the delays in Medicare/Medicaid reimbursement and also by the fact that Medicare paid only 50 cents on the dollar. Since Medicare pays less than the full amount, doctors may add a few imaginary items in order to assure themselves of getting reimbursed at the rate to which they feel entitled. The practice is referred to as defensive billing. Once again, without competition or regulation, consumer and taxpayer costs cannot be controlled.

The abuse of Medicaid by clinical laboratories was noted by the Senate Special Committee on Aging.[20] They estimated that at least $45 million out of $213 million in Medicare and Medicaid payments for clinical laboratories could be fraudulent or unnecessary. A six-month survey sponsored by the Committee and conducted in five states concluded that a laboratory could bill Medicaid for a patient who had not been seen by a physician, for lab tests never performed, at a rate exceeding four times the cost and twice the going rate for a privately paying patient and be virtually assured that they would not get caught or prosecuted. The real victims of Medicare and Medicaid fraud are not the abstract government, but the people whose taxes pay the bills, primarily the adult population of the country, and those people who are Medicaid or Medicare recipients, who eventually stand to have fewer costs covered. Those who are making the money may not be intentionally exploiting the aging, but by virtue of the fact that older people tend to see physicians and stay in hospitals more frequently, the aging are indirect victims. As the exploitation produces more need for cost control, cost control measures frequently reduce services and may lead to ethical choices concerning who deserves care. Those who are not productive, those who have lost the right or ability to be productive, may be seen as less deserving.

Even if most laboratories and physicians do not indulge in overbilling, the cosy relationship of the various components of the medical establishment is evident from the cross-fertilization of their boards of directors.[21] Doctors, once practicing singly, now depend on their affiliations with hospitals and health systems for the type of technological equipment which is increasingly necessary or desired in the medical world. The hospitals depend on insurance companies like Blue Cross, who find it more cost effective to have fancy equipment concentrated in large health centers. The insurers eagerly support the growth of certain hospital-medical empires.

But how does this corporate intermingling affect the aging? Older people use health service more than other age groups. They tend to be poorer risks for the insurance companies. When Medicare was established in 1966, it allowed the insurance companies to get rid of their riskiest customers. At the same time, the insurance companies became the intermediaries for Medicare (Blue Cross is the major Medicare intermediary), but the policies were underwritten by the Federal Government. The private companies in effect gave up some of the disadvantages of insuring older people while retaining some of the advantages when Medicare was adopted.

Both the federal government and the private insurers have more recently begun to recognize the financial desirability of keeping people out of institutions. While keeping people out of institutions may be in everyone's best interests, it is important to assure the availability of appropriate health care in the community. Unfortunately, many out-patient services and programs remain unreimbursable through Medicare. Medicare costs are kept down without profit or management controls by encouraging or requiring the use of services for which reimbursement is not available or by forcing people to reach the poverty level before they are eligible for third-party payments through the Medicaid program.

The inadequacy of community facilities for adults of all ages who have been discharged from mental hospitals, those discharges a result of greater reliance on drug control and greater interest in lowering costs, is illustrated in a report issued by former Senator Frank Moss who was a member of the Senate Special Committee on Aging.[22] He wrote,

> I have visited the psychiatric ghettos of Long Beach and Far Rockaway, N.Y. I have toured several of the old hotels and boarding homes where thousands of former mental patients live. I have seen their world of cockroaches and peeling wallpaper, of flaking paint and falling plaster . . . It became apparent to me that operators were cutting corners in order to be able to maximize profits.

The negative effects are two-fold. The individuals living in those places are victims of a system which regards mental handicaps, advancing age, and poverty as dehumanizing conditions; by virtue of which, persons with such characteristics are not deserving of more adequate treatment. The operators are ripping off the taxpayers, who in turn decry the highest cost of Medicaid payments. The cycle begins anew with the government seeking ways to reduce Medicaid costs—reducing benefits is a tried and true approach.

Although defrauding or exploiting the Medicare and Medicaid systems does not always directly affect the aging and aged, the attitude that is created toward the programs can contribute to the elderly's less than adequate care.

OTHER PROBLEMS WITH HEALTH CARE PROVIDERS

The turn by aging individuals with health problems to practitioners who are not licensed physicians can sometimes be a result of their impression that the medical establishment is only interested in making money and is not sensitive to the patient's anxiety. In some cases a physician, often an "expert" in the field, has correctly diagnosed an ailment but has failed to address the psychological difficulties that the patient may have in accepting such a diagnosis. Unwilling or unable to treat more than the physiological symptoms, the physician loses the patient's confidence and is, in effect, responsible for the patient's decision to turn to a less reputable type. Elisabeth Kübler-Ross emphasizes the necessity to offer hope to the distressed patient; not necessarily hope for a full recovery, but hope that the physician will be available to the patient, that pain will be controlled, that miracles are possible, and so on.[23] For the person who frantically searches for the health professional who will help, at least by being available, the search can be expensive and exhausting for both the individual and the family. The quest can include not only visits to various health care providers, but also purchases of any type of medication which it is hoped will help. A greater percentage of older individuals who have perceived their medical care as poor or fair have been found to purchase over-the-counter drugs.[24] In many cases, more attention to the social and psychological needs of the patient, who if elderly may be relatively alone and afraid of debilitating illness, might be the type of response that would give people their money's worth.

The kind of care that many doctors and hospital clinics are designed to offer, that is treatment for a specific condition, may not be appropriate for many of the elderly. Their multi-symptoms and their anxieties regarding the seriousness of various problems may lead older people to desire reassurance that their conditions are not life-threatening. Their needs may result in their being considered nuisances and being given little attention or patience. The benefit of services designed to meet their needs is illustrated by a study carried out in a Boston area hospital.[25] In that situation, outpatients who were considered troublesome, the chronic complainers, those patients viewed unfavorably by physicians, were referred to a special clinic. Half of all of the referred patients were over fifty years of age. These patients were told that they would be seen as often as they wished regardless of the severity of their symptoms. As a result of their increased control in the situation, the frequency of appointments decreased. It appears that if the psychological needs of patients are considered, and services offered in a treatment milieu felt to be appropriate by the patients, that is, one not labelled "psychiatric," then the fear and anxiety of decreased physical functioning in older age might be lessened.

The lack of sensitivity to the older patient's needs may be at least partially a result of the fact that the speciality of geriatrics has received very little attention by medical schools in this country. Only ten medical schools out of a total of eighty-seven responded affirmatively to a survey questionnaire which asked whether they offered or planned to offer a training specialty in geriatric medicine.[26] In contrast to the limited amount of geriatric training in medical schools, 40 percent of internists' patients are older people with whom they spend 60 percent of their time.[27] An obvious need is for specialists in internal medicine to have training in geriatric medicine.

In conclusion, physicians not only influence the high cost of medical care, but they also can intimidate the patient who does not feel comfortable taking up the busy physician's time. The result can be misunderstood diagnoses and incomplete understanding of medication schedules and drug side-effects. Dr. Edgar F. Berman, a physician who has worked with

Drs. Schweitzer and Dooley, was quoted to the effect that "most doctors go into the profession to make money, and doctors practically run Blue Cross, dictate policy, determine who goes into a hospital, and when they can leave."[28]

Physicians are also the agents by which a patient can obtain other services or goods, such as prescription drugs or nursing services in some cases. Visiting Nurses and the aides who work with them provide many health-related services to home-bound or frail elderly, but are only available on "doctor's" orders. Many physicians are fully involved with the VNA; however, others may refuse to refer patients, perhaps in the belief that the nurses are a threat to their livelihood and status. When the nurses make home visits, administer medications, and change dressings, some doctors may feel threatened that their own positions are being unsurped.

In addition, although physicians currently complain about the extent of paperwork involved in seeking reimbursement through Medicare, defensive billing or fraud by members of their profession and other agents of the health care system can only serve to increase the paper work and regulations that accompany the program.[29] Attempts to reduce fraud have been stepped up with the passage of regulations which would change the penalty for fraud under Medicare or Medicaid from a misdemeanor to a felony, with increases in the maximum fine and jail sentence.

The halfhearted attempts at government regulation are exemplified by an incident which occurred in 1977. At that time, a list of physicians and group practice units that had received large Medicare reimbursements was published. It was later found that the list was full of errors. The confidence of the public in the medical establishment and in the government's ability to prevent and detect fraud must surely be shaken by such events. The result may be increasing criticism by the public of the programs which are associated with such problems.[30]

In conclusion, it should be noted that there are sensitive doctors just as there are good nursing homes. Their high salaries and overcrowded schedules are at least partly the result of a desire and a demand by the public that illness be cured. Perhaps the time has come for both the public and the medical profession to become more realistic regarding the available technology.

HOSPITALS

People see hospitals as money first and health second. On our admitting forms we ask all these questions—next of kin, who's gonna pay the bill? . . . The *last* question is: "What is wrong with you, sir?"[31]

The elderly use hospitals more than their numbers in the population suggest; therefore, negative characteristics of hospitals affect the quality of their lives more heavily. In addition to the priority given to how the bill will be paid, several other characteristics of hospitals which can negatively affect the quality of patient care include: the emergency room treatment of symptoms which often ignores associated social problems such as loneliness; the transfer between hospitals of poor patients of whom a disproportionate number are elderly; the practice of one standard of medicine for the young or rich and another for the old or poor; and the lack of sensitivity shown to dying patients.[32]

Another type of problem is evidenced by the following situation described in a newspaper account.[33] An outpatient clinic, which in many ways functioned as a public hospital, planned to build a new facility in the suburbs. Among the reasons that the move had been opposed by some area residents was the effect that such a relocation would have on the city's elderly. The move's opponents noted that 76 percent of the elderly lived in the city and accounted for 33 percent of the patient days at the medical center even though they comprised only 8 percent of the city's population. The services which would have continued at the inner city facility would have been inadequate for the needs of the elderly and inferior to those available prior to the move. The move to the suburbs was initially challenged by H.E.W.; it has been suggested that political pressure resulted in a reversal of their opposition. In general, the effect is for inner city elderly to lose out on services when hospitals move to the suburbs. Emergency care which is needed in three fourths of the leading causes of death—heart disease, stroke, and accidents—is often not readily available, particularly for the elderly, because of the inadequacy of the facilities which are located near them.[34] These problems for the elderly exist in spite of the fact that total expenditures for short-term care in hospitals has tripled in the years between 1969 and 1977. Most of the increase is attributable to inflation and poor management rather than to improved service.[35]

In addition to the types of problems already mentioned, there is some feeling that hospital emergency rooms in many cities and towns do not attract the best-trained staff. Many doctors who practice in public hospitals are foreign trained. In fact, in 1975, 24 percent of all United States doctors were educated in other countries.[36] While medical school policies restrict the number of Americans who can be trained in the United States, the need for doctors' services at public institutions requires recruitment of foreign-trained physicians. These physicians have consistently scored lower on medical certification tests than those locally trained. While it is not clear whether it is their medical training or their lack of facility with the English language that influences the test scores, either factor may result in inadequate patient care, particularly for those patients whose native language is neither English nor the doctor's. Minority elderly account for a high proportion of patrons at public hospitals in urban areas.[37]

The health care they receive may be less than optimal for many reasons, not the least of which is the lack of expertise and language fluency of the staffing physicians.

ATTITUDES TOWARD AGING AND THE AGED

She flicked her wrist nearly out of Doctor's Harry's pudgy careful fingers and pulled the sheet up to her chin. The brat ought to be in knee breeches. Doctoring around the country with spectacles on his nose! "Get along now, take your schoolbooks and go. There's nothing wrong with me."

Doctor Harry spread a warm paw like a cushion on her forehead where the forked green vein danced and made her eyelids twitch. "Now, now, be a good girl and we'll have you up in no time."

"That's no way to speak to a woman nearly eighty years old just because she's down. I'd have you respect your elders, young man." ... Cornelia and Doctor Harry were whispering together. She leaped broad awake, thinking they whispered in her ear.

"She was never like this, *never* like this!" "Well, what can we expect?" "Yes, eighty years old ..."[38]

This vignette succinctly illustrates the attitudes of some members of the health profession toward the elderly. Individuals in the medical and other health care fields share the attitudes toward the elderly that are part of their society. To the extent that society's attitudes toward aging and the aged are negative, the attitudes of the health care providers will also be somewhat negative unless training programs are designed to combat those stereotypes. Sadly, the medical establishment is organized in such a way as to exacerbate already existing negative stereotypes toward the elderly. The medical profession is geared toward diagnosing and treating acute illness; quick return on effort is desired.[39] Chronic conditions, by definition are not easily cured and do not offer that immediate reinforcement potential to the treating physician. Consequently, the elderly, who often have chronic rather than acute conditions, have less to offer physicians as compared to younger patients. Other conditions which may contribute to the less than preferred status among physicians for the elderly are: the substantial paperwork that is required by Medicare and Medicaid for reimbursement; the lack of a payment mechanism under Medicare for out-of-institution prescriptions (this lack causes some older patients not to follow doctor's orders when they involve a costly prescription); the complexity of symptoms among the elderly; the reinforcement of prejudice against the elderly that occurs in medical schools, that is, medical education has not strived to alleviate the stereotypes that entering medical students hold toward the elderly; and the need for house calls for elderly patients.[40]

The question that remains is, do attitudes affect behavior? One study found that in spite of the negative attitudes toward caring for the elderly, the care that was given was not affected, nor did the elderly report perceiving negative attitudes directed toward them.[41] However, certain medical conditions of the elderly are reportedly misdiagnosed, not properly treated, or ignored.[42] Since doctors are the agents in our society who are trained in diagnosis, the burden of responsibility for misdiagnosis remains in part with their training institutions, which too infrequently offer specialized training in geriatric medicine.

Some conditions misdiagnosed because of stereotypes about the elderly include: reversible brain syndrome, which becomes irreversible if not treated properly and promptly; chronic brain disorder, which is often used as a catch-all diagnosis; stroke, which even when identified properly may not result in adequate therapy in the recovery phase; the absence of sexual function, a lack of which is viewed as normal; and sensory impairments, which contribute to mental disorders such as paranoia. Another type of misdiagnosis is illustrated in the following example. The patient, who is over sixty-five, told the story of her physician's incorrect diagnosis of pain in her jaw. He attributed the pain to arthritis, a common ailment in older age. She was not satisfied and went to her dentist, who filed her teeth, with the result that the pain disappeared. The pain was the effect of the misalignment of her teeth caused when she received an injury in a rafting accident on the Colorado River.[43]

Although the therapy goals for older people often mean stabilization rather than complete recovery, and are less than perfect objectives by medical school standards, the effect of stabilization on an individual's life quality may be large. Unfortunately, stabilization is not felt to be as challenging or worthwhile for the health care specialist to pursue. As a result, older people may receive less than adequate rehabilitation services; older stroke patients, for example, are sometimes offered less than vigorous follow-up care.

Health care personnel other than physicians also hold stereotypical attitudes, often negative, about the elderly. Nurses have been found to view working with the elderly as less than desirable. Only small numbers of graduating nurses enter geriatric nursing and those who do enter sometimes offer minimally adequate care.[44]

On the other hand, general attitudes toward the elderly by health care professionals who work with them have at times been found to be more positive than those of professionals who work with other groups.[45] However, in one such case, where the responses of therapists who worked with the elderly were very positive on an attitude questionnaire, the therapists also said that they found their work with elderly clients less than satisfying.[46]

In summary, the literature on attitudes of professionals toward the elderly, particularly the way that those attitudes affect the behavior of the professionals, is not always consistent. Beliefs that greater understanding of the elderly by psychiatrists would be beneficial to the elderly in terms of the treatment received coexist with contrary findings. In one instance, medical students who were exposed to a social medicine course which focused on the elderly, increased their factual knowledge but did not change their attitudes very much, particularly their lack of desire to practice geriatric medicine.[47] Others have found that while physicians who were surveyed held a negative attitude toward aging and toward the elderly person's adaptability, the extent of diagnostic tests and procedures used with an older person was more a function of the physician's atttitude toward preventative medicine in general than of the physician's attitude toward aging.[48] Physicians and other health care professionals have been found to have inadequate knowledge of the behavior potential that older people have if the environment is supportive. One unfortunate application of this lack of knowledge is the overuse of medications on nursing home patients. If knowledge of the benefits of a therapeutic, adequately staffed environment on the behavior of the elderly person were better understood, there might be less use of restraints and overmedication, and more pressure placed on nursing home administrators to provide a supportive setting. Without a therapeutic setting, drugs are overused to control agitated or depressed residents, residents who might be less agitated and depressed if their quality of life were higher.

DRUGS

Samuel Lee, jun., of Windham, Connecticut, got the first drug patent in 1796. The specifications for his 'Bilious Pills' were burned in a Patent Office fire, but a later dispensatory gave the ingredients as gamboge, aloes, soap, and nitrate of potassa. Guarded by an American eagle, Lee's remedy went forth to battle bilious and yellow fevers, jaundice, dysentery, dropsy, worms, and female complaints.

This pioneering nostrum maker is a shadowy figure, but some of Lee's character may be deduced. He had ingenuity, as the priority of his patent attests. He possessed vigor, for he made a success of his patent by marketing techniques scarcely yet exploited by American entrepreneurs. He was equipped with imagination, as the cleverness of his advertising attests.[49]

It is no secret that drug companies, in Samuel Lee's tradition, are in operation to make a profit. In order to stimulate business, new products are developed and marketed almost daily. Sometimes the new drugs are only slight modifications of old drugs. The new products may attract buyers who had been using products manufactured by other companies. At the same time, the promotion of established brands in physicians' journals helps to develop a familiarity with particular names, an advantage when the exclusive patenting rights to the drug expire.

The sale of goods for profit is a basic component of our economic system. Profit need not be a four-letter word. However, taking economic advantage of vulnerable people is considered exploitative. By some standards, the drug companies have been making very large profits off of people who are sick or afraid of becoming sick. During the 1960s and into the 1970s, the drug industry was either first, second, or third in profit among all United States companies including such moneymakers as cosmetics, recreation, and entertainment.[50] The continuing quest for large profits has led the drug industry into such diversified fields as cosmetics, hospital supplies, and pet food, as the regulation of the federal government over the industry has increased. With the successful challenge in 1976 of the ban on advertising drug prices, consumers were given hope that the cost to them for drugs would be lower. Since Americans spent over $10 billion for drugs and sundries in 1975, the impact on the consumer could be substantial.[51] The impact on the elderly consumer could be even more significant, since those sixty-five and over spent an average of $118 for drugs in 1975 while those younger spent only $41. Educational efforts aimed at increasing the use of generic drugs rather than drugs known by their trade names should also help consumers.

Although all age groups, from infants to the elderly, use drugs and all are exploited by the high profit margins on many drugs, the elderly are more heavily burdened by high drug costs: 25 percent of drug expenses are associated with the elderly, or 10 percent of the population. Furthermore, 87 percent of the drug expenses of the elderly are paid out of pocket since Medicare does not pay for outpatient drug bills. The high cost of drugs may also influence physician visits; an elderly woman whom we know says that she has cut down on her visits to her doctor because all the doctor does is give her a prescription which usually costs $10 or more to have filled.

In addition to being exploited by high drug prices, the elderly are sometimes victims of unintentional drug abuse. In one study, 5 percent of the patients admitted to a Miami hospital who were suffering from an acute drug crisis were fifty to eighty years old.[52] The abuse of drugs can be a result of too great a reliance on drugs by physicians, the specialization in health care which results in poor coordination of patient care, the multiple use of drugs sometimes obtained from more than one pharmacy, or confusion by the patient of medication schedules.[53] The elderly are of course not the only age group who are subject to adverse drug effects; however, because of their disproportionate use of drugs, their opportunities for problems are increased.

For much the same reason any claims made for a drug which are fraudulent can also potentially create more problems for the elderly. One case of fraud involved the testing of a new drug designed to treat senility.[54] The subjects were said to be residents of a Florida nursing home. Some of those to whom the drug had supposedly been given were not residing in the nursing home on the testing days. The results of the study were apparently fabricated in order to try to win the Federal Drug Administration's approval to market the drug.

Another way in which drugs can have negative affects on the lives of the elderly is when they are used not simply to alleviate pain and suffering, but to control human behavior. If passive behavior in nursing homes and other institutions can be facilitated through drug therapy, there is less need for employing sufficient staff to provide more beneficial therapy. Visitors to a nursing home may receive the impression that all old people are spaced out. Visitors do not know that the residents may be strung out on drugs. The development of tranquillizers and other psychoactive drugs has allowed the nursing home industry to rely on drugs rather than staff to influence patient behavior.[55] Drugs which are dispensed in an institution, such as a nursing home, will be billed either to the patient, to Medicaid, or to Medicare. A nurse in a nursing home, which did not have its own on-premise pharmacy, reported to one of the authors that she was aware that the unused portion of a drug supply was returned to the druggist, undoubtedly to be redispensed and billed a second time. The legal alternative, which requires that unused portions of drugs given to patients in institutions without their own pharmacy be thrown away even though they have been paid for, is hardly preferable. The expense to the federal government, to the taxpayers, and to the elderly because of the government's own wasteful regulations could be significant.

The increasing reliance on drugs, rather than on other methods of health care, may be a far more significant feature of the oppression of the aging which has been fostered by the drug industry. Wherever one looks, there is advertising for prescription and nonprescription drugs which encourages people to believe that there is a pill for every discomfort. Overweight? Take a pill to curb your appetite. Can't sleep? Take a pill. Tense, overwrought? Take a pill. Irregularity? Take a pill. The television advertising for irregularity medications fails to stress the importance of diet in maintaining normal bowel function. Once again, the "simple" solution, though one more prone to side-effects, is advocated. The strategy, which is aimed at adults of all ages, and particularly at those entering middle and old age, leads us to believe that there is a pill that can cure any problem, even those which are not minor. The disbelief when we find that there is no pill for some particular ailment may lead us to spend substantial time and money in continuing the search. The drug use of those younger, teenagers and young adults, may also be an outgrowth of their perception that psychological discomforts can be lessened with a pill. Got an identity problem? Pop a pill.

In spite of the problems that drugs can cause, most of us would not want to return to an era when drug technology were less advanced, especially when we consider the benefits of drugs such as polio vaccine, cortisone, and penicillin. However, we should recognize that we have paid a high price, in terms of our psychological independence, for drug treatment in life areas which are not seriously life-threatening. The drug companies, which have fostered this dependence, are able to reap the profits of their advertising strategies. Drug advertising for over-the-counter products attempts to capitalize on diseases which are particularly prevalent among the elderly and which are chronic, therefore requiring ongoing medication. One such condition, arthritis, has spawned many remedies. Aspirin, which is an effective pain reliever for many people who have arthritis, is the basic ingredient in other more expensive "special arthritis preparations."

Legislation which was introduced in 1978, if passed, would bring about the biggest change that has occurred in the drug regulation field since the 1930s, and would increase the federal government's power over prescription and nonprescription drugs. The effect of passage of the legislation would be a requirement that more information be given to patients regarding side-effects, an increasing use of generic rather than trade name drugs, and the opening of records regarding research that has been carried out with drugs. The drug industry is strongly opposed to the legislation, which they claim would allow foreign drug companies to steal formulas and market the drugs outside of the United States. The bill would offer more consumer protection and lower drug costs, two functions to which the drug industry and the medical establishment have paid limited attention.[56]

CONCLUSION

Because good health is so important to everyone, the potential for economic exploitation, as well as psychological oppression, exists within the health care field. The higher incidence of chronic conditions in old age results in greater dependence by the older individual on the health care system, which includes drugs, insurance, doctors, and hospitals.

At the present time, medical expenditures for the elderly are high and proportionally greater than the elderly's representation in the population. Unfortunately, high cost does not necessarily mean high quality. Fragmentation of services, a lack of sympathy for the situation of the elderly individual, and even a lack of reimbursement ability for high cost items, such as glasses, hearing aids, and prescriptions, are aspects of Medicare and the noncompetitive health care system which disproportionally oppress or exploit the elderly. Medical expenditures are higher than they otherwise might be because of the cosy relationship that exists between drug companies, doctors, insurance companies, and hospitals. One result of the limited control of the insurance companies and government over expenses for drugs, doctors, and hospitals is reduction in benefits and services as a method of cost cutting. The older public is affected by the high cost of medical care either because of higher out-of-pocket expenses, as for drugs, or higher premiums for Medicare and co-insurance. On the other hand, the elderly are advantaged because they do have a national health insurance program (Medicare), even if it is by no means free or all-inclusive.

Hospitals can be inhospitable and insensitive to the life situations of the elderly, often minority members in the cities, who use their outpatient and emergency facilities. The physicians who staff hospitals and those who practice outside of such institutions often have little formal geriatric training. Research has shown that the psychological needs of the older patient are important considerations, which are sometimes ignored by the physician who often spends only the minimum amount of time necessary with each patient. The turn to nonphysicians, including quacks, can be a direct result of the inadequate attention paid by the physician to the total needs of the patient, including the need for reassurance of the physician's availability.

The drug companies who advertise that your best interests are their interests are often more interested in maximizing their profits, which have consistently ranked at the top of all industries in this country. The elderly are disproportionally affected by high drug prices; as a group, they account for 25 percent of all drug expenses.

Negative attitudes toward the care of the elderly is facilitated by current medical training. Once the physician encounters elderly patients in his or her practice, the paperwork required by Medicare or Medicaid for reimbursement, as well as Medicare's inability to pay for out-of-institution prescriptions, may further increase the elderly's lack of appeal to physicians. Personal characteristics of the elderly, which include symptom complexity, a need for house calls, and their average longer time to respond to treatment, all operate to continue the physician's negative attitude toward caring for the elderly. However, the evidence is not completely consistent regarding the influence that negative attitudes toward care of the elderly have on the care actually received.

In summary, there are individuals and industries in the health care field that have taken economic advantage of the vulnerability of sick people or people who are experiencing age-related health problems. The public, however, has allowed this to occur, and has even facilitated the rise of the physician from a technician to a god-like figure. In a culture where youth is venerated and old age discredited, the elevation of the health care profession is almost unavoidable. Until aging becomes a psychologically more comfortable phenomenon, the potential for exploitation of aging and the aged by the health care system will be likely to continue.

Notes

1. See Robert Butler (1977).
2. For a treatise on the exploitation of illness in capitalistic societies see Waitzkin and Waterman (1974).
3. See Mary Grace Kovar (1977).
4. See the results of the Louis Harris (1975) survey of Americans' beliefs about health. The statistics are from p. 20.
5. Kovar (1977) among others mentions this fact.
6. See U.S. Senate Special Committee on Aging report, "Every Tenth American" (1977: xvii–xxvi).
7. Butler's chapter on health, "The Unfulfilled Prescription" (1975: 174–224), is particularly interesting. The quotation is from p. 174.
8. See Ivan Illich's, *Medical Nemesis,* for a thought-provoking analysis of health care (1977). The quotations which follow are from pages 76 and 78, respectively.
9. See the U.S. Senate Special Subcommittee on Aging's report, "Every Tenth American" (1977).
10. See the U.S. Senate Special Subcommittee on Aging's report, "Areas of Continuing or Emerging Concern" (1977).
11. See the U.S. Senate Special Subcommittee on Aging's report, "Areas of Continuing or Emerging Concern" (1977).
12. These figures are from the U.S. Senate Special Subcommittee on Aging's report, "Health Costs and Problems in Medicaid and Medicare" (1977).
13. For a useful analysis of the situation see James Schulz (1976).
14. See "Texas Man, 76, Seeks Divorce So Wife Can Receive Medicaid" in *The New York Times,* July 6, 1978, p. A16.
15. See Marjorie Cantor and Mary Mayer for a health survey of New York City's elderly residents (1976).
16. See Ehrenreich and Ehrenreich (1971) for an analysis of the money-oriented functions of the health care system. The quotation is from p. 119.
17. See the *Boston Evening Globe,* Wednesday, March 22, 1978, p. 6.
18. See "Soaring doctors' fees lead all price hikes" in the *Boston Evening Globe,* Thursday, March 23, 1978, pp. 1, 21.
19. See Loretta McLaughlin, "A Medicare Fraud and Two Beloved Doctors" in the *Boston Sunday Globe,* May 7, 1978, pp. 1, 19, 20. The quotation is from p. 20.
20. See the U.S. Senate Special Subcommittee on Aging's report, "Health Costs and Problems in Medicare and Medicaid" (1977).
21. See Loretta McLaughlin's newspaper article noted in footnote 18.
22. See former Senator Moss's statement in the U.S. Senate Special Subcommittee on Aging's report, "Health Costs and Problems in Medicaid and Medicare" (1977). The quotation is from p. 27.
23. See Elisabeth Kübler-Ross (1969).
24. See Pearl German (1975).
25. See Don Lipsitt's interesting account of an innovative service delivery system (1977).
26. These unfortunate findings were reported by the U.S. Senate Special Subcommittee on Aging's report, "Steps toward an Aging Research and Training Strategy" (1977).
27. See Butler and Lewis (1977).
28. See "High Medicaid Costs Blamed on Physicians," UPI *Boston Sunday Globe,* October 30, 1977, p. 40.
29. At the present time only about half of all physicians will accept Medicare payments according to the U.S. Senate Special Subcommittee on Aging's report, "Health Costs and Problems in Medicaid and Medicare" (1977).

30. United Press International published a report of the problems with regulation in *The New York Times*, Wednesday, March 15, 1978, p. 48.
31. See Betsy Delacy's account in Studs Terkel's, *Working* (1975: 646–650). She is a "patient's representative" in a hospital. The quotation is from p. 649.
32. Butler (1975).
33. See Roger Wilkins' "Flight of Hospitals to Suburbs: Another Sign of Cities' Plight" in *The New York Times*, February 24, 1978, p. A14.
34. Butler (1975: 175).
35. See Kovar (1977).
36. See John Gunther, *Boston Evening Globe*, Wednesday, March 8, 1978, p. 19, "Foreign Doctors in the U.S."
37. See Kovar (1977).
38. Katherine Anne Porter's short story "The Jilting of Granny Weatherall" is reprinted in Bradley, Beatty, and Long (1956: 1483–1490).
39. See Butler (1975).
40. See Spence *et al.* (1968) for a discussion of the lack of effect of medical education on negative attitudes toward the elderly.
41. See German (1975).
42. Butler (1975).
43. Eleanor Slater, former Chief, Division of Aging in R.I., told this autobiographical account to an undergraduate aging class at U.R.I.
44. See Brock and Madison (1977).
45. See Wolk and Wolk (1971).
46. See Garfinkel (1975).
47. See Berezin (1972) and Cicchetti *et al.* (1973).
48. See Coe and Brehm (1972).
49. See *The Medical Messiahs* by James Young (1967) for a history of the drug industry. The quote is from pp. 16–17.
50. See Ehrenreich and Ehrenreich (1971).
51. See U.S. Senate Special Subcommittee on Aging's report, "Areas of Continuing or Emerging Concern," (1977) for information on drugs and the elderly. The figures cited in this and the subsequent paragraph are from that source.
52. See Peterson and Thomas (1975).
53. See Basen (1977).
54. This report was written by Richard D. Lyons, "Cases of Fraud Found in Testing Drugs on Humans" and published in *The New York Times*, March, 8, 1978, p. A11.
55. See an interesting article by Bernstein and Lennard (1973).
56. See Richard K. Lyons' article "Administration Unveils Its Plan To Revise Pharmaceutical Law" in *The New York Times*, Friday, March 17, 1978, page A14.

References

Basen, Michele M., "The Elderly and Drugs—Problem Overview and Program Strategy," *Public Health Reports* 92 (1), 1977: 43–48.
Berezin, Martin A., "Psychodynamic Considerations of Aging and the Aged: An Overview." *American Journal of Psychiatry* 128 (12), 1972: 1483–1491.
Bernstein, Arnold, and Henry L. Lennard, "Drugs, Doctors, and Junkies." *Society* 10 (4), 1973: 14–25.
Bradley, Sculley, Richmond C. Beatty, and E. Hudson Long (ed.), *The American Tradition in Literature: Shorter Edition Revised.* New York: Norton, 1956.

Brock, Anna M., and Ann S. Madison, "The Challenges in Gerontological Nursing." *Nursing Forum* 16 (1), 1977: 95–105.

Butler, Robert N., "Research Programs of the National Institute on Aging." *Public Health Reports* 92 (1), 1977: 3–8.

Butler, Robert N., *Why Survive? Being Old in America.* New York: Harper & Row, 1975.

Butler, Robert N., and Myrna I. Lewis, *Aging and Mental Health, 2nd ed.* St. Louis: Mosby, 1977.

Cantor, Marjorie, and Mary Mayer, "Health and the Inner City Elderly." *Gerontologist* 16 (1), Part I, 1976: 17–25.

Cicchetti, Domenic V., C. Richard Fletcher, Emanuel Lerner, and Jules V. Coleman, "Effects of a Social Medicine Course on the Attitudes of Medical Students toward the Elderly: A Controlled Study." *Journal of Gerontology* 28 (3), 1973: 370–373.

Coe, Rodney M., and Henry P. Brehm, *Preventative Health Care for Adults: A Study of Medical Practice.* New Haven: College and University Press, 1972, pp. 88–108.

Ehrenreich, Barbara, and John Ehrenreich, *The American Health Empire: Power, Profits and Politics. A Report from the Health Policy Advisory Center (Health PAC).* New York: Vintage, 1971.

Garfinkel, Renee, "The Reluctant Therapist (1975)" *Gerontologist* 15 (2), 1975: 136–137.

German, Pearl S., "Characteristics and Health Behavior of the Aged Population." *Gerontologist* 15 (4), 1975: 327–332.

Harris, Louis and Associates, *The Myth and Reality of Aging in America.* Washington, D.C.: National Council on the Aging, 1975.

Illich, Ivan, *Medical Nemesis.* New York: Bantam, 1977.

Kovar, Mary Grace, "Health of the Elderly and Use of Health Services." *Public Health Reports* 92 (1), 1977: 9–19.

Kübler-Ross, Elisabeth, *On Death and Dying.* New York: Macmillan, 1969.

Lipsitt, Don R., "Psychological Barriers to Getting Well." In Richard Kalish (ed.), *The Later Years,* pp. 332–337. Monterey, Calif.: Brooks/Cole, 1977.

Peterson, David M., and Charles W. Thomas, "Acute Drug Reactions among the Elderly." *Journal of Gerontology* 30 (5), 1975: 552–556.

Schulz, James, *The Economics of Aging.* Belmont, Calif.: Wadsworth, 1976.

Spence, Donald L., Elliott Feigenbaum, Faith Fitzgerald, and Janet Roth, "Medical Student Attitudes toward the Geriatric Patient." *Journal of the American Geriatrics Society* 16 (9), 1968: 976–983.

Terkel, Studs, *Working.* New York: Avon, 1975.

United States Senate Special Subcommittee on Aging, "Areas of Continuing or Emerging Concern." In *Developments in Aging—Part I: 1976,* pp. 132–177. Washington, D.C.: United States Government Printing Office, 1977.

———,"Every Tenth American." In *Developments in Aging—Part I: 1976,* pp. xvii–xxvi. Washington, D.C.: United States Government Printing Office, 1977.

———,"Health Costs and Problems in Medicaid and Medicare." In *Developments in Aging—Part I: 1976,* pp. 23–42. Washington, D.C.: United States Government Printing Office, 1977.

————,"Steps toward an Aging Research and Training Strategy." In *Developments in Aging—Part I: 1976,* pp. 102–117. Washington, D.C.: United States Government Printing Office, 1977.

Waitzkin, Howard B., and Barbara Waterman, *The Exploitation of Illness in Capitalist Society.* Indianapolis: Bobbs-Merrill, 1974.

Wolk, Robert L., and Rochelle B. Wolk, "Professional Workers' Attitudes toward the Aged." *Journal of the American Geriatrics Society 19* (7) 1971: 624–639.

Young, James Harvey, *The Medical Messiahs.* Princeton, N.J.: Princeton University Press, 1967.

7

Nursing Homes As Total Institutions

In this chapter, we describe and attempt to explain the oppression that many present-day nursing home residents experience. We will concern ourselves with whether the negative characteristics of nursing homes are due primarily to exploitation by operators—although some homes are nonprofit, the vast majority are run as profit-making, or proprietary, homes—or to more fundamental aspects of the social and economic structure of our society and the values linked to that structure.[1]

A BRIEF BACKGROUND

Institutional homes for the aged have been in existence for many centuries. Some of the earliest were established in Constantinople by Helen, the mother of the Roman Emperor Constantine the Great. These institutions, referred to as the "gerocomcia," were supported by private funds and were favored by both the Church and the Emperor. During the Middle Ages, the destitute aged were cared for in "hospitals" attached to monasteries. In America, during the Colonial period, there were very few institutional alternatives for the dependent elderly. It was not uncommon for the physically dependent aged who had no family to be auctioned off following a town meeting to whoever would offer the lowest bid to provide for them. During the nineteenth century a number of mental hospitals and poor houses were constructed.[2] By 1960, some 9,582 nursing homes had been opened; in 1976, there were 23,000, an increase of 140 percent.[3] This increase in numbers was largely the result of the social programs of the 1930s, and especially of the Medicare and Medicaid legislation enacted in the mid 1960s.

Homes for the aged, sometimes incorrectly referred to as nursing homes, in fact usually offer no supervisory care. Residents are expected to monitor their own medication. Meals and linen are provided. Medicaid payments per resident are the lowest for this type of care. Today's nursing home is a highly structured environment where as one staff member put it: "We know everything about these people: who visits them, what kind of pills they take, even when they have a bowel movement." As in most institutions, those higher in the hierarchy often make the decisions. Nursing homes may be the most frequent places where white middle- and working-class elderly live in environments that can be considered deprived, at least with respect to the autonomy and status of the residents.

CHARACTERISTICS OF RESIDENTS

Although only 5 percent of people sixty-five and over live in institutions at any given time, individuals have a 20 to 25 percent chance of being institutionalized at some point during their later years.[4] Predisposing factors to institutionalization of older people have been found to include: (1) disturbances in thinking and feeling, such as delusions or depressions; (2) physical illness; (3) potentially harmful behavior to self or others as evidenced in confusion or depression; (4) actual harmful behavior, such as refusing necessary medical care or doing violence to others; and (5) environmental factors, such as the inability of a responsible other to care for the person.[5] The importance of environmental factors is reinforced by data from a survey in England which found that half of the residential care applicants were not only incapacitated, but also had housing problems, difficulties with household relations, or were lonely. Twenty-eight percent had no or only slight physical disability.[6] Other surveys have found that the actual medical diagnoses attached to nursing home residents often include chronic brain syndrome, disorientation, and incontinence, as well as the need for extensive nursing care.[7] Whatever the diagnosis, underlying the reason given for admission to a nursing home is the fact that the individual has not been able to take adequate care of him or herself at home. This inability is not necessarily the result of the older person's physical condition alone; it is often the result of a deficiency of societal resources which, if available, could have supported continued residence in the community.

The inadequacy of the environment in meeting the needs of some of the elderly is a consideration to keep in mind when reviewing the characteristics of those who live in nursing homes.[8] Residents are primarily very old: in 1974, 17 percent were age sixty-five to seventy-four, 40 percent were seventy-five to eighty-four, and 43 percent eighty-five plus; 72 percent were women; 69 percent were widowed, 15 percent were single, and only 12 percent were married; most were white. Minorities have not been well represented for the following reasons: family bonds may be stronger for some minority members; the life expectancy of minorities is shorter than for the majority—for black women it is about sixty-nine years in contrast to seventy-five years for white women—consequently, the chronic conditions associated with old age do not have a chance to seriously disable those who die younger; in addition, when minorities do require institutionalization, they are sometimes confronted by informal segregation policies. Family members may be told by the nursing home administrator that their relative "would not be happy here."

Another characteristic of nursing home residents is that at least half of them are poor people, as evidenced from the fact that 50 percent of nursing home revenues come from the Medicaid program.[9] Some residents may have been poor before they entered, while others may have become poor as a result of using their assets to pay for their nursing home care.

Estimates vary as to the number of the elderly who are institutionalized who could have remained in the community if adequate supports had been available. There is consensus that at least some of those who are institutionalized could have avoided nursing home placement. If environmental conditions contribute to the probability of older people entering nursing homes, why are those conditions allowed to exist? One reason may be that society has attached little value to those elderly, whether male or female, who have become sick and dependent and who have limited financial assets. One result has been the development of "hiding places to die."[10] (Another result is differential care within the nursing home for those residents who are economically advantaged versus those who are not.[11])

Although the supervised personal care which nursing homes offer is theoretically available in the individual's own home, the cost of locating and employing qualified help limits the opportunity that many people can make of private home care. For old as well as young, there are more choices in living situations available to the economically advantaged. In addition to the cost of home care, there are difficulties in finding qualified help. Because of limited funding, community-based care programs are often available to only a proportion of those who need them. Recruitment of qualified staff can be difficult because of society's negative attitudes toward the handicapped elderly. As middle-aged women, the traditional caretakers of older parents, turn to the labor force in greater numbers, the probability that older people will be cared for in their families' homes further decreases.[12] The wealthy, who still have some control over their finances and their legacies, may be more able to choose between care at home or care in an institution. Individuals who belong to certain ethnic groups which expect families to care for their older, less able members may also be cared for in their families' homes. However, if ethnic ties continue to loosen, only the rich may eventually have the option of private care at home when more than occasional care is required.

The simpler, more feasible, though less preferred solution for many handicapped elderly is for themselves, their families, or social workers to look to nursing homes for the type of care that is required. For some older women, and for those minorities who are admitted, ending their lives in nursing homes may be an intensification of the inequality with which they may have been confronted throughout their lives. By the same token, because of societal pressures that they be independent and strong, the placement of older men in nursing homes may be even more difficult for them than for the older women.

Nursing homes serve necessary functions when other resources are lacking. It is sometimes difficult to avoid the impression that nursing homes are a very bad choice for all people. In truth, few families would be physically or emotionally able to take full time care of a disoriented, incontinent relative, so the availablity of some type of custodial care is necessary as part of a continuum of health care services. However, there may be better models of custodial care than that which present-day nursing homes offer. We will examine some of these alternatives after we discuss the characteristics of today's nursing homes.

NURSING HOME CHARACTERISTICS

Upon entry into the nursing home, the new resident is confronted by certain features of total institutions that can be oppressive. Sociologist Erving Goffman has referred to nursing homes as one type of institution developed to care for incapable and harmless people.[13] He writes that a total institution, of which a nursing home is one type, is ". . . a place of residence and work where a large number of like-situated individuals, cut off from the wider society for an appreciable length of time, together lead an enclosed, formally administered round of life." The oppressive aspects of institutionalization, according to Goffman, include: a barrier to easy interaction with the outside, the loss of identity, a need for conformity to rules which are the same for everyone, and indignities that are experienced at the hands of staff and others who are more powerful.

By virtue of entry into the nursing home, a barrier is placed between the individual and the greater society. Going and coming are no longer personal decisions; they must be discussed with and permitted by the staff. Nursing home residents as a result are set apart from the rest of society even more so than old people in general. Individual nursing homes may also have practices that further strengthen the barriers to interaction with the outside. For example, in one home, residents were issued identification bracelets similar to those worn by hospital patients.[14] Those who ventured outside of the home felt that because of the bracelets, they were treated differently by people with whom they came in contact. The barriers that keep residents from interacting with outsiders may also influence the visiting patterns of family and friends to the home. Reduced interaction with residents may be a way of avoiding the stigma that is associated with life in a nursing home. Such avoidance may have important consequences, not only for the residents' feelings of alienation from the larger society, but also for the quality of their lives. As a result of reduced interaction between the residents and the outside world, inside standards of care may be reduced. However, even when the barriers are lowered, that is, when family, friends, or social workers visit, the lack of realistic alternatives to nursing home placement may limit the effectiveness of these outsiders as advocates for change.

After entry, nursing homes do not require the stripping, showering, and issuance of institutional garb that are usual upon entry into prisons and some mental hospital facilities and which are part of the self-mortification process that contributes to the loss of identity. However, residents may have some of their clothing lost in the wash, misplaced, or mistakenly appropriated by others so that the appearance of residents several weeks or months after entry may become quite different from when they lived at home. Their appearance may approximate that of people in other types of institutions who must, in fact, wear institutional garb.

The tendency to infantilize elderly nursing home residents is another way in which adult identity is undermined in some nursing homes. The following story illustrates the destructive form such infantilization can take. A woman resident of a "good" nursing home was to begin stroke rehabilitation therapy. On her first day, she was nervous and wet her pants. The "therapist" told her that because she had been "naughty" she would not receive therapy that day.[15]

Another type of infantilization was noted with much chagrin by a head nurse.[16] She reported that, while accompanying a visitor who had a professional interest in the quality of nursing home life, she introduced one of the residents as a "cute" lady. The visitor pointed out that the resident was not "cute," that she had had a full life before entering the nursing home, and that she should be given the respect that was due her. A poem given to us by a nursing home administrator elaborates on the point made by that anecdote:

What do you see nurse, what do you see?
What are you thinking when you look at me?
A crabbit old woman, not very wise,

Uncertain of habit, with far away eyes,
Who dribbles her food, and makes not reply,
When you say in a loud voice, "I do wish you'd try,"
Who seems not to notice the things that you do,
And forever is losing a stocking or shoe,
Who, unresisting or not, lets you do as you will
With bathing and feeding, the long day to fill.
Is that what you're thinking, is that what you see?
Then open your eyes, you're not looking at me.
I'll tell you who I am as I sit here so still,
As I move at your bidding, as I eat at your will,
I am a small child of ten with a father and mother,
Brothers and sisters who love one another.
A young girl at sixteen with wings on her feet
Dreaming that soon now a lover she'll meet.
A bride soon at twenty, my heart gives a leap,
Remembering the vows that I promised to keep.
At twenty-five now I have young of my own
Who need me to build a secure happy home.
A woman of thirty, my young now grow fast,
Bound to each other with ties that should last.
At forty my young now soon will be gone,
But my man stays beside me to see I don't mourn.
At fifty once more babies play around my knees,
Again we know children, my loved one and me.
Dark days are upon me, my husband is dead,
I look at the future, I shudder with dread,
For my young are all busy rearing young of their own
And I think of the years and the love I have known.
I'm an old lady now and nature is cruel,
'Tis her jest to make old age look like a fool.
The body it crumbles, grace and vigor depart,
And now there is a stone where I once had a heart.
But inside this old carcass a young girl still dwells,
And now and again my battered heart swells.
I remember the joys, I remember the pain,
And I am loving and living life over again.
I think of the years all too few, gone so fast,
And accept the stark fact that nothing can last.
So open your eyes, nurse, open and see,
Not a crabbit old woman, look closer, see Me.[17]

In addition to the loss of a life history and the increase in infantilization which contribute to a lessening of self-identity, entering a nursing home usually means that the resident has had to give up his or her home or apartment and cannot move back to the community unless someone is willing to help locate new housing. Since where we live is often an important component of adult identity, the awareness that residence in the nursing home is the final place of a lifetime can be both a problem for one's identity and traumatic in its own right.

Nursing home life can remove many personal choices both large and small. Feelings of emptiness and a lack of control over one's life may increase as others make most important and even unimportant decisions. The lack of control includes difficulties that residents may have in obtaining goods, services, and even food which previously contributed to their self-identities. A feeling may develop in some residents that the institution is not concerned with their personal integrity. Such a feeling can be very threatening, since they are dependent almost entirely on the institution.

Several studies have shown the importance of allowing nursing home residents some control over their lives and in that way enabling them to maintain their sense of integrity and identity as competent people. In one study, residents who were given plants for which they were responsible showed higher morale than a control group whose plants were cared for by the staff.[18] In another study, nursing home residents were given differing amounts of control over the scheduling of visitors.[19] Those residents who were allowed to set appointment times themselves and therefore knew when visitors were coming showed the highest morale. The availability of what may appear to be trivial choices is evidently not trivial to those participating in them. Maggie Kuhn, leader of the Gray Panthers, goes even further; she advocates that control of the nursing home environment be given to the residents.[20] She asks for full membership on the boards of directors of nursing homes for older persons who are residents and who are interested and able to participate.

The bureaucratic structure of nursing homes that does not facilitate the participation of residents in decision making can also contribute to the alienation of lower level staff. To the extent that aides, in particular, see their jobs as custodial and janitorial and feel that they deserve better, they may feel oppressed. Aides are often paid the minimum wage for work that is considered to be menial by the rest of society. Sometimes aides are recruited from the ranks of young people whose lack of job skills precludes their finding other employment in a tight job market. Evidence for their lack of job commitment is provided by statistics which indicate that the annual turnover rate for nursing home employees is around 75 percent.[21]

Societal attitudes, often negative toward the aged, may also contribute to staff feelings of oppression and exploitation from their employment. Nursing home employees may have to bear the brunt of remarks which indicate great amazement at their tolerance for working with "dirty old people."[22] One of the more evident ways in which these societal attitudes are reflected is in training programs for nursing home employees. Although there are many programs to train people who work with other dependent groups, such as children, there are not many to train geriatric workers. Often the people hired to work in nursing homes as aides, the workers who provide 80 to 90 percent of the direct care of residents, are untrained persons. Other personnel are sometimes employed in nursing homes not because they particularly want to work with the handicapped elderly but because the hours are convenient or the jobs not very demanding. Within medicine there are pediatric specialties in virtually every medical school; in 1974 only about 13 percent of all medical schools were planning to develop or actually had geriatric specialities.[23]

The fact that many nursing homes pay low wages may result in little ability on their part to screen out job applicants unsuited to nursing home work. Homes that are inferior continually stand to reinforce that status by having few dedicated people who want to work there for any length of time. In better homes, new workers may be observed more carefully in order to retain more suitable workers and screen out others.

With societal attitudes and low wages working against their job enjoyment, it is surprising to find as many responsible and dedicated workers as there seem to be. Unfortunately, the feelings of those who are oppressed by their jobs may affect the quality of care that the residents experience. They may take out their frustrations on the only people lower in status than themselves, the residents.

What is the reason that as a society we allow individuals untrained in geriatrics or gerontology to work with the handicapped elderly? One reason may be that we place little value on the quality of the lives of people who are no longer productive. Although many positive changes are evolving in regulations for nursing homes, there are still no established standards set by the government or by the industry itself as to the types of people that are most appropriate to work with the elderly. In contrast to other fields which have established standards for personnel training, work with the elderly has not yet achieved that degree of professionalism.

THE QUALITY OF CARE

If societal conditions, including the profit motive and status of staff in the nursing home, ultimately influence the quality of care nursing home residents receive, would more money for nursing homes result in better care? The answer is both yes and no. More money, if it were actually used to benefit the residents, might provide more services, better food, higher pay for employees, and more desirable staffing patterns. However, in even the best-equipped homes the quality of care is dependent on people. Money cannot always buy staff commitment, particularly when that commitment involves direct service to people considered unattractive by much of society.

In a recent review of the quality of nursing home care, five correlates were identified. They were: the home be nonproprietary, relatively small in size, wealthy in resources, sociable, and that it have a staff with positive attitudes toward the residents.[24] Although money can reward people and grant them the appreciation that is their due, it cannot always attract people with values attuned to the needs of the elderly. More money would not in itself lead to better care, although it might allow training programs to be developed for geriatric workers which could screen out those unsuited for work with the elderly and enable those who are appropriate to be adequately compensated for their work, thus raising their status in our income-conscious society. As a result, motivation to provide quality care might be increased.

The importance of staff personalities and not formal training is illustrated by the following case study of two similar homes.[25] Both of these homes are located in the same working-class community within a larger metropolitan area. They are administered by the same person and share a dietician and other professionals. The buildings are similar in appearance, which is slightly run-down. Both care for retarded people who have grown old. Both are proprietary (profit-making) homes. Their administrator delegates much of the day-to-day responsibility to the head nurses. Cleanliness standards are similar. People familiar with both settings are, however, quick to point out that one of the homes is "good," the other not so good.

The head nurse in the better home is an assertive woman in her early thirties who holds a hospital diploma. She is committed to her work, as evidenced by her frequent visits to residents' rooms, her expression of affection and support through physical contact, and her vigilance that other staff interact with residents in a similar manner. Because of her awareness of the type of behavior that is important, and her willingness to assert her views, she has managed to prune and cultivate her staff so that they have positive feelings, attitudes, and behavior similar to hers. Her interest in humane treatment does not rely only on staff selection, but includes appropriate in-service training sessions with consultants brought in from the outside with rewards for workers who meet her standards. In order to increase her knowledge of the aging process, she has taken university courses in gerontology on her own time.

The head nurse in the second home is more distant and spends most of her time behind her desk. She interacts less with the residents. Staff members are less interested in the in-service training required by the state because they are aware that they will not be rewarded for their interest or learning.

The individual values of the person in charge may strongly influence the values of others lower in the hierarchy. As in Ken Kesey's *One Flew Over the Cuckoo's Nest,* it is often the head nurse who sets the tone in an institution.[26] Until social conditions change, the quality of nursing home care may remain somewhat random and be ultimately dependent on the values and other personality characteristics of the head nurse or occasionally the administrator.

THE PROFITABILITY OF NURSING HOMES

Mary Mendelson suggests in *Tender Loving Greed* that the administration of any increased funding for nursing homes should be carefully monitored.[27] She quotes a nursing home operator regarding the need to increase payments to homes. She reports that he " . . . scoffed at the notion that other operators were losing money in the business. He himself was making plenty of money he boasted, even though almost all of his patients were on welfare. If the government raised its rates he told [Mendelson], the money would stay in the operators' pockets."

Conflicting reports, however, exist regarding the profitability of nursing home ownership. In one account, 106 corporations that controlled 18 percent of nursing home beds were recipients of one third of the $3.2 billion in nursing home revenues in 1972. Between 1969 and 1972 the same corporations had *growth* in assets, gross revenues, and net incomes of well over 100 percent. In another more recent HEW survey, a sample of nursing home profits showed a more limited return.[28] However, in 1976 almost $6 billion in Medicaid and Medicare were paid to nursing home operators.[29]

If more money does not necessarily mean better care, why does poor care cost so much? One reason for the high cost of care may be that current federal and state regulations facilitate financial manipulations by operators. While many of the profit making schemes are not unique to nursing home operations, there are conditions within the field which encourage fraud, or more legally and more unfortunately, facilitate less than appropriate care for older people. There are some who estimate that a high proportion of nursing home drug bills are inflated in order to allow for kickback systems between druggists, doctors, and nursing homes. [30]

In addition, nursing homes have been cited for allowing life-threatening situations to exist because of administrative concern for profits. One example of such a situation is the failure of some homes to conform to fire regulations. High staff turnover, because of poor working conditions, may result in staff not being well trained in evacuation procedures. In 1973, 6400 nursing home fires occurred, killing 551 persons. This was a sharp increase from 1971. A January 1974 study found that 59 percent of skilled nursing homes, those which have the more seriously incapacitated patients, had fire code deficiencies.[31]

Another oppressive practice related to profit making includes overuse of medication on residents, so that they remain in a subdued drugged state much of the time, requiring fewer staff to supervise them. It is ironic that nursing homes may try to prevent suicides by controlling drug availability, and then proceed to administer those same drugs to such a degree that the resident "might as well be dead." But then care of a live, sedated patient continues to be reimbursable for the nursing home.[32] In all fairness, the blame for overdruggings must be shared with the physicians who allow the overmedicating, partially out of ignorance of what even handicapped older people can do if environmental resources exist.

Another area where nursing homes can effectively increase their profits while reducing the quality of life of the residents is related to nutrition. Since it is not unusual to find that meal times are the organizing focus for residents' lives, penny-pinching on food may directly contribute to the oppression of the residents. A nursing home activity director told one of the authors that she had organized a cooking group in the home. The residents enjoyed it and were able to cook some of their favorite dishes. When she broached the possibility of having such meals one day a week for all the residents, the administrator said that the cost per person for such a meal would be well over one dollar and therefore, would not be financially feasible.

While "business is business," there is virtually no other profit-making industry which is subsidized with as much public money. Nor is there any other business which has been given the job of taking care of incapacitated people and which actually receives such limited supervision. Most nursing homes get paid through third-party payments with the result that the consumer (resident) has little control. Only when nursing homes repeatedly violate procedures, and/or manage to attract attention to themselves, do they not get paid. Industries in this country theoretically operate on a competitive basis which assumes that those whose goods or services are inferior will go out of business. Underlying this system are the assumptions that there is a limit to the price that can be asked for a given good or service, after which people will not pay the price, and that there are alternatives for the consumer. Without choices consumers are forced to accept whatever is provided, at whatever price.

Most elderly are not seriously limited in their functioning. However, the elderly population is increasing in size and as a proportion of the total population. We will likely see a greater number of people afflicted by a handicap as they grow older. Society is now, and will continue to be, pressed to deal with the issue of providing special living environments for those who need them. In the present and in the future we need to work toward a greater emphasis along the line of alternatives to, or new models of, institutionalization, because the number of people who will require specialized living environments probably will not decrease.

ALTERNATIVES

Consider for a moment the philosophy and tradition regarding the care of children with whom frail, older people have sometimes been compared in terms of their dependency. There is probably no area where a more clearly defined double standard exists than for public policy regarding the removal of children from their homes and the removal of older people from theirs. Public policy regarding the removal of children from their homes, even when the parents are potentially or actually abusive, is very conservative. In addition, day-care facilities for children have not yet developed in correspondence to the numbers of employed mothers of preschool children. This negative policy toward out-of-home care for children exists, in part, because of strong feelings about the need to keep them in their own homes. On the other hand, public policy regarding care for older people has resulted in enormous sums of money for the development of nursing homes to which older people are not only removed from their homes but, too often, from their communities. In addition to the effect on the individual of such a policy, the cost to the governemnt is also significant: the average daily reimbursement to the nursing home under the Medicaid program was thirty-one dollars per patient in 1976.[33]

Children have benefited from studies which have described the negative effects of orphanages.[34] Older people have not yet reaped the same kind of benefits as a result of studies which have shown that elderly individuals who were institutionalized died sooner than an equally handicapped, but noninstitutionalized, control group.[35]

Society is also prepared to accept the limitations that children have and structure their environments in such a way as to increase their safety, their self-confidence, and their general well-being. The lead poisoning regulations in some states, which require the removal of lead paint from the walls wherever children under six years old spend a great deal of time, are an example of such safety requirements. Many elderly have yet to benefit from environmental supports outside or inside nursing homes. For example, constructing nursing homes to meet the needs of some of the residents, such as having the corridors form a continuous loop to insure that wandering residents would eventually come back to where they started, might lessen the need for drug control.[36] Such a design has had limited implementation. Too often nursing homes, like other institutions, may be constructed and run for the convenience and cost-saving of the owners and subsidizers. Inside or outside of the nursing home, we may be quick to label a forgetful, older person as senile; however, we do not follow through on our diagnosis and provide a really supportive environment. At the same time that we use the label "senile," we often irritatedly blame the same person for his or her behavior and/or ignore the usefulness of environmental modifications.

One possible reason for the inadequacy of environmental supports for older people is a result of the need not only to be cost-effective, but downright cheap when caring for handicapped older people. Proponents of alternatives to institutionalization sometimes argue that it is cheaper to maintain people in their own homes, with a combination of home care, day care, and meals on wheels. However, when the total expenses of the individual are considered, that is, when all forms of third party payments are included, it can be more expensive to the government to maintain a person at home, particularly if the person is receiving Medicaid and is living in subsidized housing.[37] However, the real issue is that there is no way for most of us to attach a value to remaining in the community; it is priceless. One solution is to keep costs of alternatives as low as possible and encourage their development on a humane basis, not simply because they may be substantially cheaper than nursing homes.

Alternatives to institutionalization have begun to develop. Their growth in the future may indicate that society's attitude toward the handicapped elderly has started to change. The development of community programs, such as meals on wheels, day care, home care, and congregate living, aid the elderly to remain in their communities; however, the continued funding of these programs, in the past, has often been predicated on a demonstration that they cost *less* than nursing home care. While one cannot expect unlimited financial resources to be made available for programs for the elderly, it is also unreasonable, at a basic humanistic level, to warehouse people who could be reasonably maintained in a more personalized living situation with an equal expenditure.

In the United States, elderly day care is just in the developmental stages, although similar facilities have been in existence in other countries, such as England, for a longer time. While some programs in this country are designed to offer working families a viable solution for an incapacitated parent who cannot be left alone, they are also useful for those elderly who do not and cannot live with their families, but who find it increasingly difficult to care for themselves adequately. One drawback to the establishment of day-care programs has been their high cost to the client. Until recently there has been no or only limited insurance coverage. In 1976, the cost of a good day-care program ranged anywhere from $3.50 to $33 per person per day, and this was superimposed on the costs to the client of rent, utilities, medical expenses, and food used away from the day-care site.[38] Medicaid payments have been allowed in some states such as Massachusetts; however, rates are set at levels which have to be less than those of nursing homes. The bureaucratic reimbursement structure encourages practices such as longer days and more days for clients because the payments are higher, even though such concerns may not always be in the client's best interest.

Home care corporations, which provide home health aides, transportation, nursing, and chore services, are another growing alternative to nursing home placement for some older people. Home care appears to be a particularly viable alternative for those people who can manage with some help.

One new interesting alternative is the congregate living situation in which older people, who require some support in maintaining their independence, have their own one- or two-room apartments, have meals provided in a dining area, and have housekeeping and chore services furnished. Kitchen areas are also available for those who prefer to do their own cooking. Unlike the single room occupancy hotels, there is an administrator in charge who has responsibility for the well-being of the residents. Some congregate living situations have housed senior nutrition centers on the premises and have also located child day-care centers within the building. In this way the complex remains integrated with the greater community. The congregate housing model appears to incorporate some of the best features of the older style boarding house. In all of these alternatives, older persons can maintain a sense of independence and therefore more esteem in their own view, as well as in the eyes of others.

Those families who are willing and able to care for an older parent who needs some assistance could also be supported through societal programs to a much greater extent than at present. Programs which would enable a socially sanctioned respite from the care of a handicapped parent for a weekend or for a vacation might allow the family to gain a breather and to diffuse some of the resentment which is almost inevitable in such situations.[39] At the present time, most day-care programs do not offer such temporary care.

Another alternative living arrangement for elderly who cannot or do not wish to live alone is the foster home. Foster placement has in the past been primarily used for adults with psychiatric problems.[40] In 1978, an evaluation of some foster programs for the elderly where the foster family receives training and ongoing supervision was begun in several states. If foster care grows without tested standards, there is the danger that chicken coops might masquerade as foster homes and be worse alternatives than the institutionalization which they may delay.[41] With careful supervision, foster care could emerge as a viable form of early custodial care.

While alternatives to nursing homes exist, they are more often real alternatives only before placement; data show that people are rarely discharged from nursing homes to the community. Except for patients who are admitted following acute conditions, such as broken hips or surgery, there are few discharges except to hospitals and funeral homes; 85 percent of people who enter nursing homes die in them.[42] The old, unlike the speaker in Emily Dickinson's poem who says, "Because I could not stop for Death, He kindly stopped for me," are often literally forced to stop and wait for death once they enter a nursing home.[43] One reason for the lack of discharges is that, under the present reimbursement structure, nursing homes are paid more for bed-bound patients. To rehabilitate a resident to an ambulatory status insures lower payment.[44] In addition, the lack of sufficient community supports and the high incidence of health conditions which cannot be made better at the present time result in few discharges. The fact that community services are insufficient means that the same proportion of older people will remain inappropriately placed until environmental factors are modified, and more humane, rather than financially motivated, policy is implemented.

CONCLUSION

Only a minority of the elderly live in institutions such as nursing homes. There are certain factors which contribute to the likelihood that a person will enter a nursing home. Perhaps the most critical is environmental support, which, if absent, can shorten an older person's residence in the community. The importance of environmental supports, which include meals and intermediate care programs, has recently gained greater funding interest, partly because of the high cost of nursing home care.

Alternatives have been slow to develop perhaps because of the generally low status of the aged in our society. When productivity and consumption are key goals in the society, the elderly are seen as producing little and also consuming little. Consequently their value is relatively low.

In addition to their low status, the elderly, particularly those who are not employed or who are without spouses, have few roles to play. Because they do not fill positions of importance, their removal to nursing homes, once their health declines, has little societal impact.

The quality of nursing homes varies, as does any particular homes's appropriateness for a given resident. The determination of what quality care is must be identified and that standard enforced. At the same time, it is important to note that even in the best quality homes, oppressive features of institutions, as identified by Goffman, do exist. These features include the facts that: a barrier is placed between residents and the larger society by virtue of entry into the home; residents lose their prior identity; there is a need for conformity to rules which are the same for everyone; and indignities, however unintentional, are experienced at the hands of the more powerful staff.

Staff are also affected by the knowledge that they work in a nursing home. To the extent that they see their jobs as custodial or janitorial, are paid low wages, and feel that they deserve better, they may feel exploited and oppressed. The result may be that the residents are not being treated as well as they could be.

To answer the question posed in the introduction, the problems with nursing homes are not simply due to the profiteering of nursing home operators. While there is a sufficient documentation of this motive to know that it exists, it has been allowed to flourish because of the interest in profit and efficiency that characterizes our society. As part of this emphasis on profit and productivity, negative attitudes toward the less efficient and less able, including the handicapped aged, have developed. The modern nursing home profiteers have seen themselves as filling a need while they make money. The rest of society has seen nursing homes as a necessary, if somewhat undesirable, evil because of the low value of interaction with, commitment to, and responsibility for the elderly. The trend in the development of alternatives to nursing homes may indicate the beginning of a change in societal attitudes toward the elderly. In addition, the development of ombudsmen programs, which would provide for monitoring of nursing home practices by peers of the residents, may eventually increase the quality of life in those institutions.

In conclusion, it is oppressive to enter an institution which is regarded as the final move before the one to the funeral home. It is oppressive to live where one's choices about how to live are limited or nonexistent. It is oppressive to realize that there are few alternatives, especially if there is no close family or little money. All too often, the nursing home business has been able to exploit its position because of the rest of society's desire to avoid having to deal more personally with handicapped individuals of any age, but particularly the elderly.

Notes

1. Approximately 90 percent of nursing homes are proprietary (profit-making) according to Butler and Lewis (1977:244).
2. See Fisher (1978) for interesting historical information on aging.
3. See U.S. Senate Special Committee on Aging's report, "The Federal Role in Upgrading Nursing Homes" (1977:43).
4. For a discussion of the differences between longitudinal and cross-sectional estimates of the number of elderly in institutions see Kastenbaum and Candy (1973); Ingram and Barry (1977).
5. See Marjorie Fiske Lowenthal (1964).
6. See R. Wager (1972). The sample was made up of people applying for places in local authority welfare nursing homes. See also Eloise Rathbone-McCuan (1976) regarding the importance of environmental supports for the successful participation of the elderly in day care.
7. See Butler (1975).
8. Statistics presented in this section are taken from the U.S. Senate Special Committee on Aging's reports, "Every Tenth American" and "The Federal Role in Upgrading Nursing Homes" (1977: xix; 43, 47), and from Butler (1975).
9. See the U.S. Senate Special Committee on Aging's report, "The Federal Role in Upgrading Nursing Homes" (1977:43).
10. See Markson (1971).

11. See Kosberg (1973a).
12. See Judith Treas' (1977) article, "Family Support Systems for the Aged," for an analysis of social changes that lessen the elderly's opportunities for care by family.
13. See Goffman (1962) for a complete discussion of characteristics of an institution. The quote is from page viii.
14. For an excellent analysis of life in a nursing home see Jaber Gubrium's book: *Living and Dying at Murray Manor* (1976).
15. Personal communication.
16. Personal communication.
17. This poem, "A Crabbit Old Woman?", was given to one of us by a nursing home administrator. The poem included the fact that "it had been reported that this poem was found with the belongings of an elderly lady who died in a nursing home in Ireland."
18. See Langer and Rodin (1976).
19. See Schulz (1976).
20. See Maggie Kuhn (1976).
21. See the U.S. Senate Special Committee on Aging's report, "The Federal Role in Upgrading Nursing Homes" (1977: 45).
22. Stannard develops this idea (1973).
23. The social work profession has also had little attraction to the nursing home setting according to Kosberg (1973b). For documentation on the lack of interest in geriatric medicine by the medical profession, see the United States Special Committee on Aging's report, "The Federal Role in Upgrading Nursing Homes" (1977: 45).
24. See Kart and Manard (1976); Kahana (1973).
25. Personal communication.
26. Kesey (1962).
27. For a detailed exposé of the nursing home industry see Mendelson (1975:6).
28. See the U.S. Senate Special Committee on Aging's report, "The Federal Role in Upgrading Nursing Homes" (1977:47).
29. See U.S. Senate Special Committee on Aging's report, "The Federal Role in Upgrading Nursing Homes" (1977:43).
30. For a discussion of the Senate Committee on Aging's findings regarding kickbacks to nursing homes see *The New York Times,* Sunday, July 17, 1977, p. 34.
31. See U.S. Senate Special Committee on Aging's report, "The Federal Role in Upgrading Nursing Homes" (1977: 45–46).
32. Mendelson (1975) notes the illegal practice of some operators of misreporting the day of death in order to continue to receive third party payment.
33. See the U.S. Senate Special Committee on Aging's report, "The Federal Role in Upgrading Nursing Homes" (1977: 44).
34. Studies by Spitz and others, cited in McCandless (1967), describe cases of early death or emotional problems resulting from a lack of stimulation among infants who had been placed in orphanages.
35. See Blenkner *et al.* (1971).
36. Eva Kahana (1973) mentions that this idea was put forth by Cosin in 1958.
37. For an interesting discussion of the problems in cost-effective analysis see Doherty and Hicks (1975).
38. See the U.S. Senate Special Committee on Aging's report, "Health Costs and Problems in Medicaid and Medicare" (1977: 37).
39. See Johnson and Bursk (1977).
40. See Sherman and Newman (1977).
41. See Elaine Brody's comments on Sherman and Newman's paper (1977).
42. See Butler (1975).
43. See Emily Dickinson's poem in Bianchi and Hampson (1942:168).

44. See U.S. Senate Special Committee on Aging's report, "The Federal Role in Upgrading Nursing Homes" (1977: 48–49).

References

Bianchi, Martha Dickinson, and Alfred Leete Hampson (ed.), *Poems by Emily Dickinson*. Boston: Little, Brown, 1942.

Blenkner, Margaret, Martin Bloom, and Margaret Nielson, "A Research and Demonstration Project." *Social Casework* 52, 1971: 483–499.

Brody, Elaine, "Comments on Sherman/Newman Paper" *Gerontologist* 17(6), 1977: 520–522.

Butler, Robert N., *Why Survive? Being Old in America*. New York: Harper & Row, 1975.

Butler, Robert N., and Myrna I. Lewis, *Aging and Mental Health, 2nd ed.*, St. Louis: Mosby, 1977.

Doherty, Neville J. G., and Barbara C. Hicks, "The Use of Cost-Effectiveness Analysis in Geriatric Day Care." *Gerontologist* 15, 1975: 412–417.

Fisher, David Hackett, *Growing Old In America, Expanded Edition* New York: Oxford, 1978.

Goffman, Erving, *Asylums*. Chicago: Aldine, 1962.

Gubrium, Jaber, *Living and Dying at Murray Manor*. New York: St. Martin's, 1976.

Ingram, Donald K., and John R. Barry, "National Statistics on Deaths in Nursing Homes: Interpretations and Implications." *Gerontologist* 17, 1977: 303–308.

Johnson, Elizabeth S., and Barbara J. Bursk, "Relationships between the Elderly and Their Adult Children." *Gerontologist* 17, 1977: 90–96.

Kahana, Eva, "The Humane Treatment of Old People in Institutions." *Gerontologist* 13, 1973: 282–289.

Kart, Cary S., and Barbara B. Manard, "Quality of Care in Old Age Institutions." *Gerontologist* 16, 1976: 250–256.

Kastenbaum, Robert, and Sandra Candy, "The Four Percent Fallacy: A Methodological and Empirical Critique of Extended Care Facility Program Statistics." *International Journal of Aging and Human Development* 4, 1973: 15–21.

Kesey, Ken, *One Flew Over the Cuckoo's Nest*. New York: New American Library, 1962.

Kosberg, Jordan, "Differences in Proprietary Institutions Caring for Affluent and Nonaffluent Elderly." *Gerontologist* 13, 1973: 299–304 (a).

———,"The Nursing Home: A Social Work Paradox." *Social Work 18,* 1973: 104–10 (b).

Kuhn, Maggie, "Mobilization for Aging." *Prime Time* 5(4), 1976: 5–11.

Langer, Ellen J., and Judith Rodin, "The Effects of Choice and Enhanced Personal Responsibility for the Aged: A Field Experiment in an Institutional Setting." *Journal of Personality and Social Psychology* 34, 1976: 191–198.

Lowenthal, Marjorie, *Lives in Distress*. New York: Basic Books, 1964.

McCandless, Boyd R., *Children*. New York: Holt, Rinehart and Winston, 1967.

Markson, Elizabeth, "A Hiding Place to Die." *Transaction* 9, 1971: 48–54.

Mendelson, Mary, *Tender Loving Greed*. New York: Vintage, 1975.

Rathbone-McCuan, Eloise, "Geriatric Day Care: A Family Perspective." *Gerontologist* 16, 1976: 517–521.

Schulz, Richard, "Effects of Control and Predictability on the Physical and Psychological Well-Being of the Institutionalized Aged." *Journal of Personality and Social Psychology* 33, 1976: 563–573.

Sherman, Susan R., and Evelyn S. Newman, "Foster-Family Care for the Elderly in New York State." *Gerontologist* 17(6), 1977: 513–519.

Stannard, Charles, I., "Old Folks and Dirty Work: The Social Conditions for Patient Abuse in a Nursing Home." *Social Problems* 20, 1973: 329–342.

Treas, Judith, "Family Support Systems for the Aged." *Gerontologist* 17(6), 1977: 486–491.

United States Senate Special Committee on Aging, "Every Tenth American." In *Developments in Aging* Part I: 1976, p. xvii - xxvi. Washington, D.C.: United States Government Printing Office, 1977.

————,"The Federal Role in Upgrading Nursing Homes." In *Developments in Aging - Part I; 1976,* p. 43–52. Washington, D.C.: United States Government Printing Office, 1977.

————,"Health Costs and Problems in Medicaid and Medicare." In *Developments in Aging - Part I: 1976,* p. 23–42. Washington, D.C.: United States Government Printing Office, 1977.

Wager, R., *Care of the Elderly—An Exercise in Cost Benefit Analysis Commissioned by Essex County Council.* London: The Institute of Municipal Treasurers and Accountants, 1972.

CHAPTER **8**

Dying
And
Death*

Death is coming increasingly to be associated with old age. Since the turn of the century life expectancy at birth in the United States has increased from forty-seven years to seventy-three years. At the turn of the century more than half of those who died were under age fifty; today two thirds are over age sixty-five.[1] One of the major reasons that aging is stigmatized is its association with death. The effort to deny aging is unquestionably linked to the need to deny that death is approaching. The human, unlike other animals, is aware of death's inevitability; this result is a uniquely human source of oppression.

> The knowledge of death is reflective and conceptual, and animals are spared it. They live and they disappear with the same thoughtlessness: a few minutes of fear, a few seconds of anguish, and it is over. But to live a whole lifetime with the fate of death haunting one's dreams and even the most sun-filled days—that's something else.[2]

Our concern in this chapter is with various sources of oppression, exploitation, victimization, and discrimination associated with death and dying. We begin with a discussion of the efforts by hospital staff and family to keep knowledge of impending death from the patient, a practice which can be viewed as potentially oppressive and discriminatory. A consequence of this practice is the social isolation of the dying, which is one aspect of the more general phenomenon of "social death." In our attempt to account for why efforts are made to withhold information of impending

---

*Anne Munley, IHM, is a coauthor of this chapter.

death from a person, we will want to consider the relevance of the human fear of death and dying. We will want to ask how this fear contributes to the oppression of the aging as well as the dying. Dramatic evidence of the fear of death can be found in the first four of the five stages of psychological adaptation to impending death that Elisabeth Kubler-Ross outlines; however, even more important than her stage theory is the emphasis she has given to the need that many who are dying have to talk to others about death and other concerns related to dying. We will argue that, for many, this opportunity to face and come to terms with impending death can make the process of dying less oppressive.

The issue of euthanasia has been debated for many years. A case can be made that the denial of euthanasia sometimes contributes to the oppression of the dying, but the practice of euthanasia also has the potential for becoming a major source of oppression and victimization. While there has been a trend in recent years toward more liberal views and greater support for euthanasia, there has been another trend that offers a clear alternative to euthanasia; it is the hospice movement. This movement represents an effort to humanize the dying process by eliminating or at least reducing some of the most oppressive aspects of dying. The hospice is an institution in which the focus is on minimizing the physical pain and emotional stress associated with dying rather than on keeping the patient alive as long as possible.

The chapter concludes with a discussion of the exploitive practices of the funeral industry. The elderly, the lower classes, blacks, and widows are particularly vulnerable to the misrepresentations and high pressure sales strategies that take unfair advantage of the bereaved survivor's feelings of love, fear, and guilt.

AWARENESS OF DYING

One of the most common forms of discrimination against those who are dying in an institutional setting is the withholding of information concerning impending death. When a condition is not expected to be death-producing it is standard procedure to provide patients with accurate descriptions of what the disease is, as well as the prognosis. But when the patient's condition has deteriorated to the point that death is expected in a relatively short period of time, it is common to keep this information from the patient. This discrimination against dying patients has a number of consequences, some of which tend to make the final weeks or days more oppressive than they otherwise would need to be. One of the most careful studies to date of the management and control of information about a patient's terminal condition is reported in *Awareness of Dying,* a study by Barney Glaser and Anselm Strauss.

Of particular interest to Glaser and Strauss are the ways in which the management of information about the patient's condition affects patient and staff interaction. They organize their analysis in terms of four awareness contexts: (1) *closed awareness,* a context in which the staff are aware that the patient is dying, but the patient is not and does not even suspect it; (2) *suspected awareness,* a context in which the patient has come to suspect that the illness may be terminal and tries to verify this suspicion; (3) *mutual pretense awareness,* a context in which both the patient and staff are aware that each knows of the impending death, but they tacitly agree to interact as if the patient's condition were not terminal; and (4) *open awareness,* a context in which the patient's terminal condition is openly acknowledged by both the patient and the staff without any pretense.

Many physicians prefer to maintain a closed awareness context for as long as possible. In a variety of ways it suits their self-interest particularly well. In this context, the patient's expression of intense emotional feelings can be kept to a minimum. In all other awareness contexts, the patient's demands on the physician are likely to be greater. When the patient is informed of a terminal condition, there is the risk that the news will precipitate a highly emotional scene, an event which makes most physicians quite uncomfortable. If the bad news can be introduced more gradually and indirectly over a period of time, the physician may be spared the anguish of such scenes.

One reason physicians give for not being open about a terminal condition at the outset is that it places an oppressive psychological burden on the patient unnecessarily soon. In the initial stages of many illnesses the symptoms are minimal. For a period of months, or possibly years, the patient may be able to lead a near-normal existence, but if the patient is told that the illness is terminal, at least some of the burden of the "dying person" social role is unavoidable from that point on.

The burden of this new social role becomes very evident when the news of the persons's status gets out to friends and employers. Even though the person is quite able to continue working, many employers will not permit this. Why do employers discriminate against a worker who has been labelled a dying person? Some are concerned about the possibility of starting projects that will never see completion; some are concerned about a possibly prolonged period of reduced productivity as the disease progresses; and others are concerned about the impact such a person is likely to have on the morale and productivity of other workers. The "dying person" social role can have disasterous consequences for one's social life. Some previous friends do not want to be reminded of their own mortality; some have fears, often irrational, that they will catch the disease; and others feel extreme discomfort in the presence of a person who is known to be dying.

The family is often consulted by the physician about when and if to inform the patient of the terminal condition. It is not uncommon for the family to opt for not informing the patient. In some cases they too want to keep interactions with the patient from getting too intense. They may not feel comfortable interacting in an open awareness context. Some believe that interaction will be less demanding for all involved if the patient does not realize the illness is terminal.

As the disease progresses it becomes increasingly difficult to maintain a closed awareness context. The patient is likely to suspect that the condition is terminal. Once patients become suspicious and start trying to verify their suspicions, they begin to notice inconsistencies in the accounts given by different staff members. They become aware of evasiveness on the part of relatives and attendants. This evidence tends to make them even more suspicious.

Once the patient/staff interaction has shifted to one of suspected awareness, staff members must be very cautious if, as is often the case, they seek to prevent a shift to an open awareness context. The staff may find it necessary to create elaborate fabrications in an effort to explain away the inconsistencies with which the patient confronts them. Sometimes the effort to avoid a blatant lie by refusing to answer a question ends up indirectly providing the patient with the desired information. If a patient asks a nurse whether or not his condition is terminal and is told to refer such questions to his doctor, no direct answer has been given, but the evasion carries with it the implicit message that the illness is probably terminal.

Glaser and Strauss use the metaphor of a fencing match to describe the suspected awareness context. Patients keep taking the offensive in an effort to confirm suspicions while staff members attempt to keep them from this goal with appropriate defensive responses. A shift back into the closed awareness context represents a victory for the staff; a shift to an open awareness context represents a victory for the patient.

The shift to a suspected awareness context is not always the result of information accidentally conveyed to the patient. This information is sometimes introduced intentionally. The physician or a relative may decide that it is time to give the patient the opportunity to find out more about his or her condition, but instead of forcing the bad news upon the patient, some information is provided which is designed to raise suspicion. It is then left up to the patient to decide whether or not to pursue the issue. If pressed, the staff will then provide additional information, but at each step an effort is made to provide no more information than it appears the patient really wants.

After being informed that their condition is terminal, some patients prefer a shift to an open awareness context; others prefer a shift to a mutual pretense context. In this awareness context, the staff agrees to play

along with the patient's fiction that the condition is really not terminal. The staff may indulge the patient by engaging in extended conversations about future plans that both realize he or she will never live to realize.

> There was a long silence. Then the patient asked, "After I get home from the nursing home will you visit me?" I asked if she wanted me to. "Yes, Mary, you know we could go on long drives together. . . ." She had a faraway look in her eyes as if daydreaming about all the places she would visit and all the things we could do together. This continued for some time. Then I asked, "Do you think you will be able to drive your car again?" She looked at me, "Mary, I know I am daydreaming; I know I am going to die."[3]

After a period of mutual pretense a patient may prefer to shift to an open awareness context. Alternatively, she may want to maintain a mutual pretense context with some people, such as visiting relatives, while maintaining an open awareness context with others, such as a spouse or psychotherapist. The nursing staff often find it a relief to shift from a suspected awareness or mutual pretense context to an open awareness context. An open awareness context allows the patient the opportunity to have more control over how the remaining time is to be spent. Some will attempt to finish a pet project or pull together loose ends at work. Others will put a great deal of effort into making plans for their family's financial security. In an open awareness context, it is possible to offer support for dealing with the anxieties and fears that oppress many who are dying. Psychotherapy may be of great value to a person who is dying, but it is difficult to offer this form of support in other than an open awareness context.

From the preceding, it is clear that an open awareness context is likely to be much less oppressive than the suspected awareness and the mutual pretense contexts. These other contexts are oppressive, in part, because they contribute to the patient's social isolation. The aged are particularly vulnerable to this oppression because a high proportion of those who die are elderly. We all anticipate a need for a great deal of emotional support during our terminal illness and hope to be able to obtain this support from those who we have been close to throughout our lives. However, we are aware that those we are closest to may be unable or unwilling to meet our needs. This fear is not entirely unfounded. There is a tendency to withdraw from those who are dying. The outcome of such treatment is referred to as *social death*.

In his study of sociological aspects of dying in a large public hospital, David Sudnow noticed that nurses sometimes make an effort to close a patient's eyes just prior to the onset of death. This is usually done as part of preparing the body for the morgue, but it is much more difficult to execute after the person is actually dead. Sudnow uses the term "social death" to refer to this practice and others like it in which the patient is treated as a corpse while still alive.[4] Another example is the practice of asking the nearest relative to sign an autopsy form before the patient is dead. This is sometimes done if the staff anticipate any difficulty getting in touch with this person after the death.

The most dramatic of Sudnow's examples is that of the patient who entered the hospital with a perforation of a duodenal ulcer. The patient's wife was told that he was in critical condition and that his chances of survival were poor. At that point she stopped visiting her husband, but as it turned out, within a few weeks he had recovered and was discharged. Upon returning home he found that his wife had removed all his personal effects and clothing. On his bureau he found a letter she had written to a funeral home inquiring about rates. To top it all off, she had already found a new lover. This was more than he could take; he left the house and began to drink. The next day he was readmitted to the hospital with a severe heart condition.[5]

A patient in an irreversible coma may be treated as if biologically alive, but socially dead. For example, the staff may not hesitate to discuss the patient's impending death or what might show up in the autopsy, while at the bedside. Such a patient is in Erving Goffman's terms being treated as a "nonperson."[6]

Certain categories of patients are more likely to be treated as socially dead than others. This includes those who are considered by hospital staff to have less "social value," such as the senile, alcoholics, derelicts, those engaged in crime or violence, and those who have attempted suicide. Sudnow cites the case of a woman who was brought into the emergency room with a self-inflicted gunshot wound. While it was possible that she was still conscious, within hearing range one doctor is reported to have said, "I can't get my heart into saving her, so we might just as well have some fun out of it." Sudnow goes on to describe some of what happened in the operating room with this same patient:

> One of the operating surgeons performed a side operation, incising an area of skin surrounding the entry wound on the chest, to examine, he announced to colleagues, the structure of the tissue through which the bullet passed. He explicitly announced his project to be motivated by curiosity; one of the physicians spoke of the procedure as an "autopsy on a live patient," about which there was a little laughter.[7]

The concept of social death has been used in reference to the decrement in social value associated with growing old, and particularly with entry into a nursing home or geriatric hospital.[8] It also describes the fate of those who are avoided because they have contracted a dread terminal disease such as cancer. Many people feel squeamish about touching or kissing those who are dying and do their best to avoid doing so.

The most common injustice linked to what we have referred to as social death is oppression; the social isolation from family, friends, and caretakers is a major source of this oppression. Alternatively, we can point to the discrimination against the dying that is commonly associated with social death. A person with a terminal condition may choose to work as long as possible, but as we mentioned earlier, may find the employer unwilling to allow one so labelled to remain at work. This is only one of the more blatant forms of discrimination the dying may face.

It is not uncommon for those who have terminal conditions, particularly cancer, to be offered the opportunity to participate in experiments designed to test new and unproven techniques. For the patient, there is the hope, however remote, that this experiment may turn out to be a breakthrough. While a case can be made that such experiments are necessary if we are to make progress in developing better ways to cope with such diseases as cancer, it is also reasonable to consider the possibly oppressive consequences of the procedures involved. In some cases, the person is being used very much as an experimental animal, the ultimate form of social death. There is more research carried out in which there is virtually no chance of significantly lengthening the life of the patient, or of significantly improving the quality of the time which remains, than most medical researchers would have us believe. In view of this, it is reasonable to conclude that many who volunteer for and participate in medical experiments are vulnerable to victimization on the basis of their extremely precarious medical condition. Again we must note that it is older people who are most likely to be victimized because most deaths occur during the middle or late years.

The social isolation of the dying is in part due to the inability of those around them to confront and come to terms with their fear of death. In recent years, there has been a marked increase in the number of weekend workshops, seminars, and public lectures aimed at helping people come to terms with these fears. This is a hopeful sign; as more people confront and come to understand these fears, it may lead to more enlightened attitudes toward and treatment of those with terminal conditions.

FEAR OF DEATH AND DYING

Why is the fear of death so universal? We can approach this question by considering what would happen in the absence of this fear. Were it not for our fear of death, it is likely that we would be inclined to take unnecessary life-threatening risks.[9] This would lead to premature death which in turn would reduce opportunities to produce offspring. In short, it has clear survival value. Without this fear it is possible that the human animal would have become extinct some time ago. A sociobiologist might argue that the fear of death is in part instinctive. While it is possible that this fear may one day be traced to our genes, it is unlikely that socialization will ever be replaced as the most important determinant of our death-related fears.

This socialization begins in childhood and continues well into adulthood, much of it being indirect.[10] For example, one learns that the most serious crime a person can commit is murder. Doesn't this tell us something about the desirability of being dead? Similarly, when we look at the severity of the punishments meted out for various crimes, we find that the death penalty is reserved for only the most serious; this too suggests that it must be a grim fate.

Exposure to cultural beliefs about murder and the death penalty contributes to our fear of death; however, this is only one of many indirect sources of this socialization. Exposure to the efforts, priorities, and values of the medical profession is another important source. We learn that physicians are strongly committed to the preservation of life, even when the life being prolonged is oppressive to the patient. Consider the person in an irreversible coma who is maintained for years by modern medical technology even though there is no chance of ever regaining consciousness. A plea for euthanasia from a ninety-year-old patient suffering from a painful terminal cancer is typically ignored. If the profession is so strongly committed to the preservation of life under such miserable circumstances, this suggests that the alternative these people are being temporarily protected from must be ghastly.

For most people, the fear of death and the fear of dying are closely linked, but it is useful to distinguish between the two. Some claim that it is not so much death as it is the process of dying that they fear. When *Psychology Today* asked its readers what they found most distasteful about death, one of the most frequent responses was, "The process of dying might be painful."[11] One reason that the process of dying is feared is that it may involve a great deal of time spent contemplating the implications of impending death, such as the cessation of personal relationships and the ability to have experiences. Another fear is that the process will involve a loss of independence and autonomy; the terminal illness often involves a considerable amount of dependency on others. Some fear they will be abandoned or neglected at this time of need. However, the most frequently mentioned fear is that the process of dying will be painful.

In view of its prevalence, it is reasonable to ask whether the fear that one's terminal illness will be painful is justified or whether it tends to be greatly exaggerated. Is it common for the process of dying to involve a considerable amount of pain, or does this turn out to be a rare event? In attempting to answer this question, one of the first problems we encounter is that of reliably measuring the degree of pain a person is experiencing. We cannot assume that two people who face the same pain stimulus suffer the same amount. There have been cases reported of severely wounded soldiers in battlefield hospitals who refuse painkillers of any kind.[12] A number of studies have also found marked ethnic differences in tolerance for pain; for example, Northern Europeans tend to have a greater tolerance than do Southern Europeans.

Two people, both at an advanced stage of the same form of terminal cancer, may require very different levels of medication to bring the pain under control. Pain thresholds differ between individuals and vary for the same person from one situation to another. For this reason, it is very difficult to make definitive statements about how much pain is typically associated with the process of dying. Bearing in mind these and other related methodological limitations of the available pain studies, a reasonable estimate is that one person in eight suffers considerable pain in connection with a terminal illness.[13]

But physical pain is only one of several sources of physical distress associated with terminal illness. Nausea, vomiting, coughing, being hoarse, difficulty swallowing, extreme physical fatigue, difficulty breathing, and other physical symptoms often accompany a terminal illness. Some of these conditions are more difficult to control than physical pain. If we also take into consideration these additional forms of physical distress, a reasonable estimate is that one out of five suffer from physical symptoms in connection with a terminal illness. Note that we have said nothing of psychic stress and anxiety which would increase our estimates still further.

One might expect the elderly to suffer more in connection with their terminal illness than do the young and middle aged, but this turns out not to be so. In one study, 10 percent of those over age seventy experienced considerable pain in connection with their terminal illness. This can be contrasted with 23 percent of those age fifty to seventy and 45 percent of those under fifty.[14] The younger patients tend to have better general health. As a consequence, they frequently live to experience the more advanced and often more painful stages of the condition.

Equally important as the intensity of physical suffering is its duration. Another reason the process of dying is feared is that it sometimes involves a prolonged illness. One person in six is confined to bed for three months or more in connection with a terminal illness: two out of three have their activities severely restricted for three months or longer in connection with their terminal illness.[15] Based on the available evidence a reasonable estimate is that one adult in ten dies suddenly, in a matter of minutes, hours, or days. Another two out of ten are seriously ill for three months or longer. But most people, some seven out of ten, experience a terminal illness which lasts from a few days to three months. The widespread fear of a slow death, while somewhat exaggerated, is not entirely unfounded.

One might expect the elderly to be more fearful of death than those who are younger as they have fewer years remaining. But the empirical evidence does not support this conclusion. On the contrary, the aged tend to fear death less than do those who are younger.[16] Richard Kalish offers several possible explanations.[17] One is that the aged have had more exposure to death and dying. This experience gives them an opportunity to come to terms with the inevitability of their own death. Another explanation is that death is less likely to be seen as threatening to the life plans of the elderly. Family and career goals have typically been realized or set aside. Another factor is that many who are elderly feel they have lived their allotted time. They view themselves as, to some extent, already living on borrowed time. This is particularly true when a substantial proportion of former peers have died. In view of the preceding evidence, it should come as no surprise that the elderly are less likely than those who are younger to experience extreme anxiety during a terminal illness. One estimate is that one out of three who are over sixty show symptoms of extreme anxiety in contrast to two out of three for those who are under fifty.[18]

As we might expect, death fears and anxiety do seem to be influenced by one's religious beliefs. Several studies have found that those who are highly religious (measured in a variety of ways) report less fear of death than do the less religious.[19] Other investigators have found that agnostics and atheists are similar to the most religious in the extent to which death is feared. It is those in the middle, whom we might refer to as tepid believers, who show the greatest fear of death.[20] These findings are similar to those for the level of anxiety experienced during a terminal illness. The most religious and the least religious were found to show fewer symptoms of extreme anxiety than were those who professed religious belief but who were irregular in their church attendance.[21] We might expect the most religious to be confident that there is an afterlife and that it will be a positive experience. The least religious are likely to reject the idea of an afterlife and with it the possibility of any negative experience after death. Those who are unsure in their religious beliefs are most likely to have doubts as to whether there is an afterlife and, if there is, whether it will be a positive experience.

Why is the knowledge that life is finite a source of oppression to so many? One reason, no doubt, is the fear of the unknown. Despite the special knowledge some claim to have concerning the hereafter, many remain skeptical, or at least unsure about what to expect. As we have seen, some categories of people experience more anxiety than others as death approaches, but if we are to believe Kubler-Ross, it is a rare person who does not find knowledge of impending death oppressive, at least until working through the first four stages of psychological adaptation to this knowledge. However, it does seem that those who reach the fifth stage, which she refers to as "acceptance," appear to be much less oppressed than those who remain in the earlier stages.

PSYCHOLOGICAL ADAPTATION TO DYING

In her book *On Death and Dying,* Elisabeth Kubler-Ross presents a stage theory describing the course of psychological adaptation to knowledge of impending death.[22] The five stages are in order: (1) denial, (2) anger, (3) bargaining, (4) depression, and (5) acceptance. She does not argue that all dying patients traverse this entire set, but she does argue that this is the sequence most will follow if they don't become arrested in one of the stages along the way, or die too soon. The rate at which people move through this progression varies. There is generally some backsliding. A patient may show signs of acceptance one day and clear evidence of depression the next. It is even possible for the patient to show symptoms of more than one of these stages at the same time.

The first reaction (first stage) to receiving the bad news concerning a terminal condition is generally shock, quickly followed by *denial.* Some ask that laboratory tests be double-checked or redone; they suspect there may have been some mixup with another patient. Others request that additional physicians be called in as consultants. If this fails to yield the desired results, and it usually does, some will start frantically shopping around for a physician who will give a more favorable diagnosis and/or prognosis. If this too fails, some turn to quack healers and questionable remedies such as laetrile treatment.[23]

The next stage is *anger;* it is marked by a great deal of hostility and irritability. Those who attempt to make life more pleasant for the patient find themselves being rebuffed. The patient is acting out feelings of injustice. It seems entirely unfair that he must die while others, including his caretakers, continue to live normal lives.

The third stage involves *bargaining* which may be with God or the hospital staff. It is typically bargaining for more time. At later stages, in some diseases, it may be bargaining for relief from pain. Typical forms of bargaining are requests that the physician be sure to keep them alive until their daughter graduates from college or their first grandchild is born. Kubler-Ross cites the case of a former opera singer who wanted the opportunity to perform just once more prior to surgery which would make it impossible for her to sing. This stage is illustrated in the following example of a mother in the final stages of terminal cancer.

> She had made all sorts of promises if she could only live long enough to attend this marriage. The day preceding the wedding she left the hospital as an elegant lady. . . . She was "the happiest person in the whole world" and looked radiant. . . .
>
> I will never forget the moment when she returned to the hospital. She looked tired and somewhat exhausted and—before I could say hello—said, "Now don't forget I have another son."[24]

The fourth stage is *depression*. At this stage, the patient is overcome by a profound sense of loss. This depression may be due to a loss of self-esteem linked to an inability to fulfill former roles, such as those of parent or provider. This depression can also come from the contemplation of impending death and with it the loss of personal relationships, the ability to experience, and all that gives life meaning.

The last of the five stages is *acceptance*. At this stage, the patient has come to terms with impending death. This does not mean that he wants to die or feels happy about the prospect. Rather he has become resigned to its inevitability. This is a stage at which the struggle is over; it is a period almost void of feeling. The patient has typically lost all interest in what is going on in the outside world. Not everyone reaches this stage. Kubler-Ross argues that some will have to be helped through the earlier stages if they are to die in this stage.

The stage theory of Elisabeth Kubler-Ross has received a great deal of attention in recent years. The popular press has generally given the theory a favorable reception, but fellow professionals have been more critical. One criticism has been that the theory is often used *prescriptively* rather than purely *descriptively*.[25] That is, instead of being taken as a description of the stages that some or many patients are likely to traverse, it is taken as a set of stages through which all patients should traverse. Sometimes these expectations are communicated to the patient, who then feels responsible for not progressing. At other times, the caretakers feel that they are at fault. The danger of this prescriptive use of the theory is that the burden of not fulfilling staff expectations may be added to all the other oppressive aspects of dying.

While Kubler-Ross does not suggest that her theory be used prescriptively, it is clear that the final stage of acceptance is the preferred stage in which to die. In view of this, it is not surprising that the theory has been applied prescriptively. However, as Avery Weisman points out, what is an appropriate style of dying for one person may not be at all appropriate for another. It may be appropriate for one person to die in a stage which corresponds to what Kubler-Ross refers to as acceptance, but it might be much more consistent with the personality and preferred style of dying for some other person to die in a stage of anger.[26]

Another criticism of the theory is that it sometimes leads to ignoring important differences between patients. Staff members sometimes classify dying patients into one or another of Kubler-Ross's stages. Once the patient is so classified, the category can be used to account for his or her behavior. A patient's behavior, rather than being interpreted as an expression of individual need, may instead be discounted as evidence of a particular stage. This criticism is more an attack on the way in which some have used the theory than on the theory itself. Kubler-Ross would be one of the first to argue for the importance of being sensitive to variations among patients with respect to their individual needs. In fact, a strong case can be made that far more important than her stage theory has been her impact on those who care for the dying. Here, her major contribution has been to convince others of the importance of being sensitive to the dying patient's needs, particularly the need to talk to others about what he or she is experiencing, fears related to death, and concerns about significant others who will be left behind.

Dying patients are so vulnerable that even efforts to improve their lot may end up being yet another source of oppression. Few have been more sensitive to the psychological needs of dying patients than Kubler-Ross, and yet even her theory seems to have become a source of oppression to some who are dying. While it is clear that many more have been helped than have been hurt by the impact her work has had, still the fact that even a few have suffered underscores the vulnerability of those who are dying.

The euthanasia issue provides another illustration of this vulnerability. If we refuse the patient's request for euthanasia, we risk the oppression of a slow, painful death. But if we make it a policy to grant such requests, we risk the oppression that derives from the expectation of one's significant others that the time has come to request euthanasia. Do we legalize euthanasia or do we make more of an effort to improve the quality of life during those final days? How do we decide when it is in the patient's best interest to grant a request for euthanasia? Can a case be made that it is more appropriate to grant such a request when the patient is in the fifth of Kubler-Ross's stages (acceptance) than when the patient is in the fourth stage (depression)?

THE EUTHANASIA DEBATE

The term "euthanasia" is used to refer to the act or practice of painlessly putting to death, for reasons of mercy, persons suffering from an incurable condition or disease. Several years ago Dr. Herman Sander put a patient of his to death by injecting air into her veins; the procedure was quick and painless. She had been lingering near death for some time and was in considerable pain from an advanced stage of cancer. Dr. Sander's action was motivated by mercy; he saw no reason to prolong her suffering.[27] He was subsequently indicted for murder as a result of this action, but the jury found him "not guilty." This indictment and the final verdict illustrate our society's ambivalent attitude toward euthanasia. Such actions leave a person vulnerable to a charge of murder, but juries are very reluctant to find a defendent guilty even when the eivdence is quite compelling.

By the end of the nineteenth century, it was evident to the medical community that the high dosage levels of narcotics needed to control the pain associated with some terminal diseases tended to hasten the onset of death. The practice of giving ever-increasing dosages of narcotics to control pain and the consequent hastening of death is referred to as *indirect euthanasia.* The patient may die sooner than would otherwise have been the case, but it is only as an indirect consequence of the physician's primary objective, which is to bring pain under control.

Today, this practice is generally accepted in the medical community and by most major religions. This is part of the reason why euthanasia advocates seek to get the practice defined as a form of euthanasia and why euthanasia critics are unwilling to consider it a form of euthanasia. Plausible arguments can be made on both sides of the issue, but the argument against the practice being considered a form of euthanasia is somewhat stronger because it is rare that the physician intends to bring about death.

It is useful to make the distinction between *active euthanasia* and *passive euthanasia.*[28] If death is induced by some positive action, such as administering a lethal dose of a drug, the action is referred to as active euthanasia. If death is induced by the termination of some life-sustaining procedure or by the decision not to undertake a therapeutic procedure needed to prolong life, the action (or inaction) is referred to as passive euthanasia. A cancer patient may require extensive surgery to survive for a few additional months. If the decision is made not to undertake this surgery, the resulting death is an instance of passive euthanasia. Similarly, if the decision is made to turn off the heart-lung machine which is necessary to sustain the "life" of a person in an irreversible coma, the action is a form of passive euthanasia.

Proponents of euthanasia tend to minimize the distinction between active and passive euthanasia, but some critics of euthanasia feel that there is a fundamental distinction between the two. Among these critics are some doctors who practice passive euthanasia, but who are unwilling to refer to their action as a form of euthanasia. They prefer to refer to their actions as letting nature take its course. This allows them to practice what some would refer to as passive euthanasia and, at the same time, be firmly opposed to euthanasia.

Sometimes a person in the terminal stages of a painful illness requests a lethal dose of barbiturates. If a physician, spouse, or friend grants this request and the action brings about the person's death, it is considered *assisted suicide.* The question of interest to us is whether or not assisted suicide is a form of euthanasia. Proponents of euthanasia tend to minimize the distinction between assisted suicide and active euthanasia. They argue that there is very little difference between a physician's administering a lethal dose of barbiturates to a patient who has requested euthanasia and a physician's making the lethal dose available at the patient's bedside. However, critics of euthanasia tend to feel that there is an important distinction between assisted suicide and active euthanasia. Among these critics are some who advocate assisted suicide under appropriate circumstances, such as the final stage of a painful terminal illness, but who also consider themselves opponents of euthanasia under any circumstances.

In this context, mention is often made of those patients who request a lethal dose and then find they are unable to take the final step themselves. Critics take this as evidence that many who request euthanasia are not actually ready to die, but opponents argue that it is unreasonable to require people to take the final step themselves. It is less stressful to the patient if the action is carried out by another person without knowing the exact time that the fatal dose is administered.

It is generally assumed that one criterion for euthanasia is that the person be put to death to relieve *suffering*. However, there are situations in which it is appropriate to refer to the action as euthanasia even if the person put to death has not been suffering. Consider the patient who is in an irreversible coma. With the help of special (heroic) therapeutic measures, such as the use of heart-lung machines and intravenous feeding, the patient can sometimes be kept alive for months or even years. Some argue that it should be legal to allow such persons to die if, as is often the case, they cannot continue to live when their life-support systems are withdrawn (passive euthanasia). Others would advocate active euthanasia for those, such as Karen Quinlan, who continue to "live" even after the respirator has been disconnected. If the patient shows little or no brain activity, it is difficult to make the case that the action has been carried out to put an end to his suffering. In cases of irreversible coma, it is the relatives, not the patients, who are suffering.

Despite the arguments that can and have been made against the legalization of euthanasia, the general trend in the country has been toward a more liberal attitude on the issue. In 1947, Gallup put the following question to a national sample of Americans, "When a person has a disease that cannot be cured, do you think doctors should be allowed by law to end the patient's life by some painless means, if the patient and his family request it?" At that time, 37 percent of the respondents or slightly over a third of those questioned gave an affirmative response.[29] The same question was asked again in 1973. This time 53 percent or slightly over half of those polled gave an affirmative response.[30] Despite this trend, it is reasonable to conclude that it will be quite some time before euthanasia legislation becomes politically feasible. Public opinion results do not take into consideration the intensity of the attitudes of those who support or oppose euthanasia. It is quite possible that many who oppose euthanasia feel much more strongly about the issue than those who support it. In addition, there are a number of strong institutions, such as the American Medical Association and Catholic Church, backing those who oppose euthanasia. Euthanasia may never be legalized in this country, but if it is, it is quite possible that the courts will play a key role. The legalization of euthanasia may parallel the legalization of abortion in this respect.

Despite the present trend toward greater support for the legalization of euthanasia, it is quite possible that no such legislation will be enacted in the foreseeable future. One of the developments which could undercut the euthanasia movement is the hospice movement. Euthanasia advocates seek to assist those who would prefer death to futile suffering. By contrast, the objective of the hospice movement is to take whatever steps are necessary to keep the situation of the dying patient from becoming meaningless, degrading, and filled with unnecessary suffering.

THE HOSPICE ALTERNATIVE

In the late 1960s, a new kind of medical institution opened in London called St. Christopher's Hospice.[31] Hospitals are organized around the goals of curing illness and prolonging life; in contrast, the hospice is organized around the goal of making the process of dying as free from physical pain, anxiety, and depression as possible. Consistent with this difference in objectives, there is very little in the way of modern life-support technology at St. Christopher's; there is no heart-lung machine, no intensive care unit, and no resuscitation equipment.[32] If a patient develops pneumonia, as is not uncommon for those with terminal cancer, it would typically go untreated even though failure to treat this condition with antibiotics is likely to hasten the patient's death.[33]

While very little effort is made to prolong life, a great deal of effort is made to deal with pain; most of those who enter a hospice do so to deal with severe pain. At St. Christopher's, the staff is successful in bringing pain under control for most of their patients and in reducing it for the others. While caregivers generally do not administer medication directed toward the cure of illness, they use a variety of drugs to deal with the patient's pain, anxiety, and depression; the objective is to achieve these goals without ending up with spaced-out zombies. They are able to keep the patient alert and active until death is imminent by making use of heroin, which is very effective in dealing with depression and anxiety as well as pain. In most patients, heroin creates a pleasant euphoria without the side-effect of lethargy. Attendants make it a practice to provide medication before the patient has to ask for it; this contributes to a positive self-image by minimizing feelings of dependency on the drugs and those who supply them.[34]

The first objective for hospice personnel is to bring pain under control. After that has been done, they turn to other tasks, such as helping patients deal with impending death; hospice staff take the view that talk can be very therapeutic. If the patient wants to talk about fears of dying, the well-being of a spouse who will be left, and other such issues, there are always people available to listen and offer support. The goal is to provide a supportive environment and the assurance that there are people who care and who will offer support to the end. No effort is made to deny the reality of impending death; it is an issue to be faced and discussed openly. After this issue has been addressed, it is possible to deal with a variety of other issues which are also sources of concern to patients and their families, such as the economic adjustments the surviving spouse will have to make after the death of the patient.

Another of the major objectives at St. Christopher's, and many other hospices, is to bring the family together. It is common for the prolonged illness which has preceded admission to the hospice to have adversely affected the quality of interaction between the patient and his or her spouse. It is a source of stress, both to patients and their families, to part on unpleasant terms. It contributes to feelings of guilt among those who survive and to a feeling of abandonment for the person who is dying. One aspect of the effort to reunify the family is the provision of counseling for other family members.[35] This counseling and support continues to be available after the patient has died. An effort is made to make the family feel welcome and at ease while visiting the hospice; they can come whenever they want and stay as long as they want. They can take responsibility for feeding, washing, and caring for the patient in other ways. Participation in the care of a dying spouse is not without its therapeutic value; those who participate, tend to suffer less from feelings of guilt after the death.[36] Some continue as volunteer workers in the hospice long after the patient has died.

Cicely Saunders, the founder of St. Christopher's, like many other hospice advocates, has been an outspoken critic of proposals to legalize active euthanasia.

> When someone asks for euthanasia—defined not as desisting from active treatment, but as a killing act—we will find in almost every case that someone, or society as a whole, has failed that person. To suggest that such an act should be legalized is to offer a negative and dangerous answer to a problem which can be, and is being solved by better means.[37]

Undoubtedly among the reasons for this opposition is that it would reduce the pressure for such reforms as the introduction of hospices. One of the arguments for euthanasia is that it offers a merciful alternative to a slow, painful death in a dehumanizing environment. But hospice advocates are quick to point out that it is possible to control pain for almost everyone, and it is possible to create an environment for the patient far superior to that found in most hospitals. To legalize euthanasia is a cop-out. It is viewed as a cheap, expedient solution to the problem at the expense of the patient's best welfare. In a hospice, it would be possible for many, who might otherwise prefer the alternative of death, to enjoy their last days or weeks. Often this time can be spent in such worthwhile activities as coming to terms with one's impending death, assisting one's spouse in preparing for the adjustments that will be necessary, and in bringing together family members who have grown distant due to the strains of the illness.

THE FUNERAL INDUSTRY

In American society, care of the dead has been removed from the family and turned over to funeral experts with "rational" procedures for managing the events surrounding death. Embalming, restorative art, perpetual care contracts, obituaries, burial permits, death certificates, cemetery deeds, memorials, flowers, and eulogies are all elements of the cultural complex referred to by Jessica Mitford as the "American way of death."[38] America's institutional answer to the problem of disposing of the dead has not been without challenge. Critics of the funeral industry charge that the grief-stricken are exploited and demand that the bereaved be given options to obtain dignity, economy, and simplicity in funeral arrangements.

The traditional funeral ranks high with the older segment of the population. At all social class levels, the elderly spend more on funerals than do those who are younger.[39] They are more influenced by the style, cost, and color of the casket than are younger persons; and as age increases, the tendency to be pleased with cosmetic restoration of the body also increases.[40]

The poor and working class tend to have a more favorable attitude toward contemporary funeral customs than do the middle and upper classes. The desire by many of the elderly poor to have a decent funeral without putting a burden on relatives makes them particularly vulnerable to victimization by those who sell burial insurance at exorbitant rates, to say nothing of totally fraudulent policies. Blacks and poor whites tend to have a more positive view of the honesty of funeral directors than do middle class whites. One study found that blacks asserted by a two-to-one margin that they trusted their funeral director, while whites gave a two-to-one response that they distrusted their funeral director. Blacks expressed satisfaction with current funeral costs by a ratio of three to one, but for every satisfied white, there was one complainer.[41] The inverse relationship between social class and approval of contemporary funeral customs suggests that the people who can least afford to have expensive funerals are precisely those most inclined to desire them.

Before taking up the arguments of those who are critical of the funeral industry, let us consider the arguments made by those who speak on behalf of the industry. According to industry spokesmen, the high cost of dying is simply a reflection of the high cost of living. Funeral prices are just as subject to inflation as are the costs of any other goods or services. Funeral directors deserve recompense for the specialized services which they provide for the public. Care of the dead should not be placed in the context of pricing based on the economic principles of supply and demand. As for embalming, it is a vital aspect of funeral service; it is in the best interest of public health. By embalming the dead, funeral directors are, according to industry spokesmen, protecting the public from dangers of infection. Similarly healthy for survivors is the "memory picture" of the deceased made possible by embalming and restorative art. The memory picture is essential for successful adjustment to bereavement. Since so many people, the elderly in particular, die after lingering chronic illnesses, seeing a "loved one" in peaceful repose is a therapeutic means of coming to terms with death and of recognizing that the deceased has been released from suffering. The function of restorative art, beautiful caskets, and appealing surroundings is to provide a sharp contrast with painful memories and stark realities of death in a hospital environment.

Those who speak on behalf of the funeral industry also maintain that the specialized training of funeral directors makes them important resources to clients for whom confrontation with death is a new experience. Funeral directors are "sensitive professionals" skilled in helping clients through early stages of grief. Since death has become a phenomenon of the elderly, it no longer pervades American life. By providing set patterns of custom and ritual to the bereaved, funeral directors function as agents of socialization in the sense that they help survivors to respond "appropriately" to the death event.

Lasting memorials are public reminders of love and concern for the deceased. Memorialization of the dead is one recognized way of reacting "appropriately" to the loss of a "loved one." Monuments, mausoleums, cemeteries, crypts, bronze markers, statuary, and flowers are ways in which testimony can be given to the value of the life that has been lived. So too are sealer vaults, urns for "cremains," and caskets with a personalized touch, ways of commemorating a "loved one." The desire to memorialize the dead is a "natural" reaction to the irreversibility of death. One has only to walk through a memorial park or cemetery to recognize the extent to which many Americans have sought to erect permanent memorials to their dead. Forest Lawn Memorial Park in Southern California,[42] Mt. Auburn Cemetery in Cambridge, Massachusetts, and the above-ground sepulchers in New Orleans are three American examples of elaborate attempts to establish enduring memorials to the dead.

The other side of the argument is articulated most clearly by consumer advocates who have banded together to form memorial societies. Memorial societies are nonprofit organizations which seek to provide members with the opportunity to plan ahead for simple, dignified, and economical funeral arrangements.[43] Where do memorial societies stand in regard to these issues? Succinctly stated, the costs of funerals in America are exorbitant. Embalming is not necessary; laws about embalming, as well as health hazards resulting from not embalming, are misrepresented. The emphasis placed by funeral directors on the "memory picture" focuses too much attention on the body and fosters pompous materialism. The lives of the deceased should be commemorated, not their mortal remains. As for grief therapy, the time of death should be a leveling moment, binding together all that is human. An event of such intimacy should not be controlled by an impersonal "other" who uses learned techniques and merchandising skills to mitigate grief. Those who loved their dead while they were alive are best suited to determine the way in which to ritualize their loss and lend mutual support to one another. Finally, the best memorials are living memorials, such as organ donations or scholarships. Instead of "wasting money" on lavish funerals or marble monuments, memorial societies advocate death education alerting consumers to their right to choose simple burial, cremation, burial after viewing, cremation after viewing, or donation of their entire bodies to science.

As we mentioned earlier, those most likely to desire the "complete services" provided by the funeral industry are often the least able to afford them. This contention is reinforced by the present composition of memorial societies. Although they have tried to attract members from all social classes, the membership rolls of memorial societies are heavily weighted with the well-educated and persons of higher social status.

How has the American public responded to the pros and cons of American funeral practices? Since the 1963 publication of Jessica Mitford's *The American Way of Death,* media attention has been focused on the industry, and watchdog consumerism and investigative journalism have kept the controversy alive in the public forum. To the dismay of leaders of the industry, some of the strongest backers of a movement to simple funeral practices have been members of the clergy.[44] Many churches, in their efforts to emphasize the spiritual and communal dimensions of funeral rituals, have cut down on ostentatious display of expensive caskets during funerals by requiring that the casket be covered with a simple pall during the service. This is a blow to casket manufacturers whose ads boast of nineteen-gauge sealer caskets in "an exquisitely soft and feminine motif."

Requests by bereaved families that flowers not be sent have led to similar distress. The growing resistance to large expenditures on flowers is becoming so effective that a concerned flower industry is employing domino theory tactics in the ads which they run in funeral trade journals: "A Funeral without Flowers is a step toward NO Funeral Service!" The implication of this message is clear: "Look out, funeral directors; support us or you will be next!" Also of concern to the industry is a gradual increase in the use of cremation as a means of final disposition. However, the public reaction with the greatest potential clout is the proposed Federal Trade Commission rule to regulate practices in the funeral industry. If adopted, this trade regulation rule will be a major step toward protecting consumers in very vulnerable moments of grief. At the same time, its provisions do not preclude large expenditures based on informed choice, nor do they interfere with spiritual or social functions of funeral ritual.

It is striking that the report of the U.S. Bureau of Consumer Protection, upon which the proposed trade regulation rule is based, is replete with examples of manipulation of survivors' death feelings of love and fear. One might ponder the degree to which funeral costs are tied to attempts to express love for the deceased. One might also wonder to what extent the bereaved consumer is the victim of a role ambiguity experienced by funeral directors who are, in reality, both "service professionals" (however stigmatized) and businessmen, acting out of economic self-interest. One does not need to wonder, however, about the existence or magnitude of abuses in the funeral industry. It is the contention of the U.S. Bureau of Consumer Affairs that unfair and deceptive funeral practices are industry-wide and are in need of regulation.

Currently, the average expenditure for an adult funeral service, including final disposition costs, is approximately $2,000.[45] How much financial outlay does this amount to for the American public? Who benefits most from payments for funeral goods and services? From 1973 to 1977, the gross receipts of funeral homes and crematories climbed from an estimated $1.9 billion to nearly $3.5 billion, and they are projected to reach $7.3 billion by 1985 (U.S. Bureau of Consumer Protection, 1978). If outlays for related funeral items are included, the total figures rise dramatically. In 1974, for example, Americans paid $2 billion to funeral homes and crematories, $800 million for flowers, $735 million for cemetery expenses, $450 million for monuments and markers, and $305 million for burial vaults, bringing the nation's nation's funeral tab to$4.3 billion. Clearly, care and disposition of the dead in America is big busines. Figure 8–1 depicts the breakdown of the national funeral bill for 1974 and illustrates the composite nature of the death industry in the United States. Although funeral homes and crematories received the largest proportion of total expenditures (46.6%), the extent to which related industries profit from American funeral practices is evident.

What are some of the factors which push funeral costs high and keep them high and what might be done to reverse this trend? Fortunately, not all funeral directors engage in deceptive practices, but, unfortunately, the pattern of abuse is so widespread that it is recognized as a national problem. Abuses in the funeral industry consist of exploitative practices, resulting in waste and extravagance, misrepresentations, and use of salesmanship techniques and marketing strategies to take unfair advantage of the feelings of love and fear experienced by the bereaved.

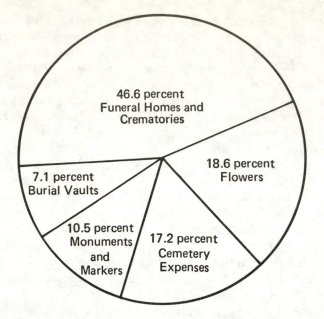

Figure 8–1 BREAKDOWN OF TOTAL FUNERAL-RELATED EXPENDITURES FOR 1974. SOURCE: ADAPTED FROM U.S. BUREAU OF CONSUMER PROTECTION (1975:3).

There are various ways in which the public is being exploited. At the time of bereavement, consumers often lack their usual bargaining power. If funeral directors are viewed as service professionals in the sense that "they know best," clients are especially susceptible to exploitation. Possession of the body gives the funeral director power over the bereaved. Few people are inclined to create a scene over expense at the time of death because it might appear that they are unwilling to show "proper" respect and love for their dead. Embalming without permission (even of Orthodox Jews), "tying in" sales (such as requiring a casket for immediate cremation when a suitable container would do), making a profit from cash advances paid in behalf of clients (for example, gratuities, flowers, and so on), and failing to pass on to the consumer the benefit of any rebates or discounts received on funeral items, all contribute to the high cost of funerals.

But playing more directly on death fears of survivors are a series of unethical misrepresentations. It is in this area that the public is most in need of education. The effect of misrepresenting legal requirements for embalming, health hazards of not embalming, requirements of religious customs, and the effectiveness of embalming, vaults, and sealer caskets is a limitation of the consumer's power of choice. Because embalming has been so widely accepted by the public, funeral directors tend to view it as a necessary "given" of funeral arrangements. In reality, state laws require it only if death is due to contagion or in cases where the body will be shipped by common carrier. The argument for embalming as a public health measure is similarly exaggerated. According to the United States Center for Disease Control, there is at present no evidence that embalming is a necessary means of disease prevention.

Misrepresentation of religious customs for financial gain is another deceptive practice. Catholics, for example, may be told that cremation is not permitted or the requirements of Orthodox Jewish services may be misrepresented or circumvented. (An example of outright violation of religious law is the use of metal screws under wooden dowels in caskets sold to Orthodox Jews, even though the family has been assured that the casket meets the religious requirement of all-wood construction and is charged accordingly.)

Survivors' fears about disfigurement of their dead are often related to a willingness to spend money for embalming, sealer caskets, and vaults. Actually, American embalming is not intended for long-term preservation. If embalming were done to preserve, the appearance of the skin would be tough and leathery. Instead, embalming is done for cosmetic reasons to create a lifelike "memory picture" for a few days.

The effectiveness of preservative qualities of airtight and watertight caskets and vaults is similarly misrepresented. There is no such thing as "enduring protection" from decomposition; nor is there guaranteed long-term preservation. Yet what do burial vault ads promise? The following advertisement from a funeral trade journal suggests the blatant emphasis being placed on creating an image of incorruptibility. Vaults of this company are tested by a mechanical device to measure their endurance after burial underground.

Testing is accomplished through a group of sensors within the burial vault attached by a single cable to an external digital readout instrument. This "burial vault tester" gives accurate readings of wall movement, temperature, and inside pressure. It also monitors whether there is moisture or any change in the relative humidity within the burial vault. The hitherto unavailable information thus obtained will provide valuable data on the engineering of current ———products for today's needs and those of the future.[46]

What future—one of eternal preservation? For what? This ad clearly forces one to confront the problem of using people's fears to make a profit.

Also a factor in high funeral costs are marketing techniques through which consumers can be led to spend more than they can afford on high priced merchandise. Casket selection is an occasion subject to various deceptive practices. The pitfalls of casket salesmanship are clearly described in the following excerpt from the report of the U.S. Bureau of Consumer Protection.

Selection room technique is designed to encourage the purchase of high priced merchandise, particularly caskets and to discourage selection of the low-priced. Discouragement can take the form of non-display of inexpensive caskets, failure to inform customers that a less expensive casket is available, deliberate limitation of colors, physical defacement or disparagement of the low price units, or variations on the bait-and-switch theme. It can also take the form of disparaging the customer's choices as being indicative of a lack of affection or respect for the deceased, a technique used for all aspects of the funeral transaction.[47]

Display of cheaper caskets in unattractive colors (for example, "silver taupe"—a cross between lavender and pink) has been one way of baiting consumers to switch to more expensive caskets in warm, attractive colors. Another bait-and-switch tactic is advertising a funeral for a low price and then undermining it in the consumer's eyes by referring to it as "a pauper's funeral." Use of terms such as "tin cans" or "boxes" for cheaper caskets and phrases such as "this is the last thing you can do for your mother" also exert pressure on clients to spend more money than they intended out of love and respect for their deceased.

An additional sales strategy used by some funeral directors is failure to display prices of funeral items. If consumers are confused about prices and options, they are more likely to buy things that they might not really want. One way in which this is done is through a system known as product tying. What occurs here is a package deal in which consumers pay for services and items which they may not use or select. Industry resistance to price advertising and to disclosing prices over the telephone also contribute to keeping consumers in the dark about funeral costs until they are in an emotionally stressful bereavement situation. These practices cut down the opportunity for comparison shopping, stifle competition, which might be to the advantage of the client, and force consumers to make decisions out of ignorance.

How would the proposed Federal Trade Commission regulation alleviate consumer difficulties with the funeral industry? In the words of its authors, the proposed rule

... is designed to provide the consumer with substantially more information on prices and choices, eliminate the devices used to obtain unfair leverage over the consumer, abolish the outright frauds and deceptions that have been structured into the industry, and free up the market so that the dealings between funeral director and customer will be more fair, and the growth of memorial societies and pre-need arrangements more possible.[48]

Specifically, the proposed rule prohibits: embalming without permission, unauthorized pick-up or release of corpses; requiring a casket for cremation; making profit on cash advances; failing to pass on to customers trade rebates or discounts; misrepresentations of the law, public health requirements, and religious customs; and unwarranted claims about the preservative capacity of embalming, caskets, or burial vaults. The rule seeks to curtail deceptive merchandising practices by requiring display of inexpensive items, the availability of less expensive items in desired colors, mandating full price disclosures over the telephone, and the use of itemized price lists with consumers during funeral transactions.

If effected, this regulation is likely to alter the "American way of death." Informed consumers may still opt for "complete funeral services," buy luxury items (even beautifully crafted showpiece pine boxes), build marble memorials to give public testimony to their dead, and spend thousands of dollars for gold urns for the cremated remains of pet parakeets, but they will be acting out of choice, not blindness.[49] The alternative of a simple burial will be available.

CONCLUSION

Much of the interaction between the terminal patient and hospital staff can be analyzed in terms of the struggle over the management and control of information concerning impending death. Glaser and Strauss analyze this interaction in terms of four awareness contexts: closed awareness, suspected awareness, mutual pretense, and open awareness. The general thrust of our argument has been that the effort to keep information concerning the approach of death from the patient tends to be a source of oppression. However, it would be a mistake to conclude that it is always less oppressive to be completely open with a patient; some patients would rather not be fully informed. There is some evidence that candor with patients who would prefer not to be too directly confronted with knowledge of death's imminence can be oppressive; this is particularly likely if the candor is not adequately followed up with the emotional support and counseling the patient needs to work through the grief reaction such information can bring on.[50] Dying is oppressive at any age, but the phenomenon is particularly oppressive to older persons, as most deaths occur with those who are middle-aged or elderly.

When a person is treated, in some respects, as already dead prior to the actual onset of death, we refer to the phenomenon as social death. One example of the discrimination associated with social death is the practice of moving the patient known to be dying off into an empty room, preferably at the end of the ward near the freight elevator used by the morgue attendant. A case can be made that some terminal patients who volunteer to be "guinea pigs" for medical experiments are being needlessly oppressed by the experience.

As an ever-increasing proportion of the population lives long enough to die of the chronic degenerative diseases associated with old age, euthanasia becomes an increasingly relevant issue. To many, the quick and painless death which would be involved seems an attractive alternative to a slow, painful death due to a disease such as cancer. No one advocates the legalization of all forms of euthanasia, but there are many who would like to see voluntary euthanasia legalized with an appropriate set of safeguards. These safeguards would be designed to protect patients against those with an interest in their estate or in the use of their organs for transplant purposes. These safeguards would also be designed to protect patients against those with an interest in cutting hospital costs by reducing efforts to prolong the lives of patients unable to afford expensive therapeutic procedures.

There are a number of long-term social trends which have contributed to a liberalization in attitudes towards euthanasia in recent years. These include the increase in the proportion of people who can expect to live long enough to die of the chronic degenerative diseases associated with old age, increasing concern about the quality of life, and the liberalization of attitudes on related social issues such as abortion. While most of these social trends should continue, there are also some new developments which could slow, and possibly halt, the growth in support for euthanasia. The most important of these is the evolution of the hospice, an institution with a commitment to making the end of life as free from pain, anxiety, and depression as possible. If it turns out to be possible to duplicate the success of St. Christopher's Hospice on a large scale, it is likely that the hospice movement will substantially undercut the perceived need and public support for the legalization of euthanasia.[51] The rapid expansion of the hospice movement in the United States during recent years would lead one to conclude that such a trend is underway. However, this same rapid expansion may eventually come to haunt the hospice movement. As one authority points out, "there may be commercial exploitation with hospices and problems with adequate standards and supervision."[52] Similarly, Robert Butler, Director of the National Institute on Aging, cautions that, "We don't want to go overboard and create death houses."[53]

In recent years, there have been strong objections to the profit-making dimensions of death in the United States. Exposés of exploitative funeral practices have pushed some Americans to question the appropriateness of elaborate efforts to disguise and euphemize the reality of death. A camaraderie of thought is emerging among investigative journalists, consumer advocates, members of memorial societies, and religious, as well as secular, humanitarians in their expression of desires for simplicity, personalism, and dignity in funeral arrangements. Still, among Americans—who have a marginal standard of living—the old, the disadvantaged, the persons of low socioeconomic status—the inclination for "the complete services" of funeral directors remains firmly entrenched. It is perhaps these Americans who stand to gain the most from proposed regulation of the industry.

Notes

1. In 1900, only 41 percent of the population were expected to live to age sixty-five; today, 74 percent are expected to do so and the median age at death is now seventy-six years (National Council on the Aging, 1978:103–105).
2. Becker (1973:27).
3. Glaser and Strauss (1965:75–76).
4. Sudnow (1967:75–76).
5. Sudnow (1967:77).
6. Goffman (1959:151–52).
7. Sudnow (1967:108).
8. Kastenbaum (1977:31–33).
9. This does not rule out the possibility that some persons, such as Evel Knievel, seek out life-threatening situations in part as a mechanism for coping with their fear of death.
10. Children learn about death from many sources. Some experience the death of a grand-parent, and they all see dead animals. The hideous appearance of decaying animals may contribute to a fear of death, but the fear of separation from parents is clearly the major component of the child's fear.
11. Shneidman (1974:214).
12. Beecher (1956).
13. Hinton (1972:72).
14. Hinton (1965).
15. Hinton (1972:69).
16. Feifel and Branscomb (1973); Kalish and Reynolds (1976).
17. Kalish (1976).
18. Hinton (1972:85).
19. Feifel and Branscomb (1973); Templer (1972).
20. Kalish (1963).
21. Hinton (1972:84–85).
22. Kubler-Ross (1969).
23. For a description of several of the quack remedies people turn to see Ducovny (1969:74–89). Just because a remedy is unorthodox does not mean that it is without value. In recent years a number of promising but unorthodox alternatives have evolved as part of the holistic health movement. We cannot, as yet, entirely rule out the possible efficacy of laetrile (Chowka, 1978); also of interest is the work being done by the Simontons which "combines traditional medical management of cancer with the intense personal involve-ment of patients in exploring the psychological factors that affect the growth of their malignancies" (Roggenbuck, 1978:32).
24. Kubler-Ross (1969:83).
25. For a very useful summary of the arguments which have been made by the critics of Kubler-Ross's stage theory, see Kastenbaum (1977:209–13).
26. Weisman (1972:20).
27. Heifetz and Mangel (1975:107–108).
28. Russell (1975).
29. Gallup (1972:656).
30. Gallup Opinion Index (1973).
31. The first hospice to open in the United States was Hillhaven Hospice in Tucson, Arizona. As of this writing, there are less than a dozen hospice facilities operating in the United States, but more than 100 others are in various stages of discussion and development. In the present discussion we focus on St. Christopher's because it is the model on which many of the United States hospices are based. Some of the principles of the hospice are now being tried in units within standard hospitals, such as St. Luke Hospital in New York City, and also in hospitals for the terminally ill, such as Calvary Hospital also of New York City (Craven and Wald, 1975; Kastenbaum, 1977).

32. Heifetz and Mangel (1975:146–159).
33. As should be evident from the preceding discussion, indirect euthanasia and passive euthanasia are common at St. Christopher's and would be common in any hospice.
34. Saunders (1976:519).
35. Saunders (1976:520).
36. Hinton (1972).
37. Cicely Saunders, "Questionable Dogma." *World Medicine,* September 20, 1978.
38. Mitford (1963).
39. Pine and Phillips (1970).
40. Khleif (1976).
41. Salomone (1968).
42. Forest Lawn was the inspiration for *The Loved One,* Evelyn Waugh's well-known satire of American funeral practices.
43. At present, there are memorial societies in over 170 cities in the United States and Canada; total membership is in excess of 500,000 people.
44. Fulton (1971).
45. The standard adult funeral service package includes the following: removal of the remains to the funeral home; preservation, restoration, and dressing of remains; use of funeral home facilities and equipment for viewing and the funeral services; arranging for obituary notices, church services, burial permits, and transcripts of death certificates; arranging and care of flowers, use of hearse; arranging for veteran, Social Security, fraternal, labor union, and/or life insurance burial benefits; arranging for pallbearers; and the services of the funeral director and staff. (U.S. Bureau of Consumer Protection, 1975).
46. See page 5 of the March, 1978, issue of *The Director.*
47. U.S. Bureau of Consumer Protection (1975:49).
48. U.S. Bureau of Consumer Protection (1975:5).
49. Morgan (1968).
50. Natalie Spingarn argues that in a misguided effort to be more honest and humane, some physicians are asking patients to make decisions they are not qualified to make. She points out that this candor risks destroying the patient's sense of hope. There are many who argue that this hope is an important aid in the patient's fight for life. (See Natalie Davis Spingarn, "Are Doctors Killing Us with Too Much Candor?" *Boston Sunday Globe,* August 20, 1978.)
51. The hospice is still an experimental concept. As Robert Kastenbaum (1977:230) points out, ". . . It seems premature to judge that the movement as a whole has demonstrated an ability to meet the needs of all kinds of people facing chronic illness and death." It may prove very difficult to create the hospice atmosphere in large secular institutions, which lack the charismatic leadership of a person like Cicely Saunders.
52. Kenneth L. Woodward et al., "Living With Dying." *Newsweek,* May 1, 1978.
53. Ibid.

References

Becker, Ernest, *The Denial of Death.* New York: Free Press, 1973.

Beecher, Henry K., "Relationship of Significance of Wound to Pain Experienced." *Journal of the American Medical Association* 161, 1956:1609–1613.

Chowka, Peter B., "Laetrile at Sloan-Kettering, Part I." *New Age* 4, (July, 1978): 40 ff.

Craven, Joan, and Florence S. Wald, "Hospice Care for Dying Patients." *American Journal of Nursing* 75, 1975:1816–1822.

Ducovny, Amram, *The Billion $ Swindle: Frauds against the Elderly.* New York: Fleet Press, 1969.

Feifel, Herman, and Allan B. Branscomb, "Who's Afraid of Death." *Journal of Abnormal Psychology* 81, 1973: 282–288.

Fulton, Robert, "The Funeral and The Funeral Director: A Contemporary Analysis." In Howard C. Roether (ed.), *Successful Funeral Service Practice,* pp. 216–235. Englewood Cliffs, N.J.: Prentice-Hall, 1971.

Gallup, George R., *The Gallup Poll: Public Opinion 1935–1971.* New York: Random House, 1972.

Gallup Opinion Index, "Majority of Americans Now Say Doctors Should Be Able to Practice Euthanasia." *Gallup Opinion Index* 98, 1973: 35–37.

Glaser, Barney G., and Anselm L. Strauss, *Awareness of Dying.* Chicago: Aldine, 1965.

Goffman, Erving, *The Presentation of Self in Everyday Life.* Garden City, N.Y.: Anchor Books, 1959.

Heifetz, Milton D., and Charles Mangel, *The Right To Die.* New York: Berkeley, 1975.

Hinton, John M., "Distress in the Dying." In John N. Agate (ed.), *Medicine in Old Age.* London: Pitman, 1965.

———., *Dying.* 2nd ed. Baltimore: Penguin, 1972.

Kalish, Richard A., "An Approach to the Study of Death Attitudes." *American Behavioral Scientist* 6, 1963: 68–80.

———., "Death and Dying in a Social Context." In Robert H. Binstock, and Ethel Shanas (ed.), *Handbook of Aging and the Social Sciences,* pp. 483–507. New York: Van Nostrand, 1976.

Kalish, Richard A., and David K. Reynolds, *Death and Ethnicity: A Psychocultural Study.* Los Angeles: University of Southern California Press, 1976.

Kastenbaum, Robert J., *Death, Society, and Human Experience.* St. Louis: Mosby, 1977.

Khleif, Baheej, "The Sociology of the Mortuary: Religion, Sex, Age and Kinship Variables." In Vanderlyn R. Pine et al. (ed.), *Acute Grief and the Funeral,* pp. 55–92. Springfield, Ill.: Charles C Thomas, 1976.

Kubler-Ross, Elisabeth, *On Death and Dying.* New York: Macmillan, 1969.

Mitford, Jessica, *The American Way of Death.* New York: Simon & Schuster, 1963.

Morgan, Al, "The Bier Barons." *Sociological Symposium* 1, 1968: 28–35.

National Council on the Aging, *Fact Book on Aging: A Profile of America's Older Population.* Washington, D.C.: The National Council on the Aging, 1978.

Pine, Vanderlyn R., and Derek Phillips, "The Cost of Dying: A Sociological Analysis of Funeral Expenditure." Social Problems 17, 1970: 405–417.

Roggenbuck, Peggy Elman, "The Good News about Cancer." *New Age* 3 (May 1978):32 ff.

Russell, O. Ruth, *Freedom to Die: Moral and Legal Aspects of Euthanasia.* New York: Dell, 1975

Salomone, Jerome J., "An Empirical Report on Some Controversial American Funeral Practices." *Sociological Symposium* 1, 1968: 47–56.

Saunders, Cicely, "St. Christopher's Hospice." In Edwin S. Shneidman (ed.) *Death. Current Perspectives,* pp. 516–523. Palo Alto: Mayfield Publishing Co, 1976

Shneidman, Edwin S., *Deaths of Man.* Baltimore: Penguin, 1974.

Sudnow, David, *Passing On: The Social Organization of Dying.* Englewood Cliffs: Prentice-Hall, 1967.

Temper, Donald I., "Death Anxiety in Religiously Very Involved Persons." *Psychological Reports* 31, 1972: 361–362.

U.S. Bureau of Consumer Protection, *Funeral Industry Practices: Proposed Trade Regulation Rule and Staff Memorandum.* Washington, D.C.: U.S. Government Printing Office, 1975.

———., *Funeral Industry Practices: Final Staff Report to the Federal Trade Commission and Proposed Trade Regulation Rule.* Washington, D.C.: U.S. Government Printing Office, 1978.

Weisman, Avery, *On Dying and Denying.* New York: Behavioral Publications, 1972.

9

The
Other
Victims
Of Aging*

Up to this point, our emphasis has been on the ways in which the aging and the aged are exploited, victimized, discriminated against, and oppressed. There is, however, another side to this unfortunate reality. The focus in this chapter is on examining data which suggest that there are also ways in which the aged directly or indirectly contribute to the exploitation and oppression of others.

This balancing shift in our analysis does not alter the evidence already provided regarding the injustice experienced by older adults. Relative to other age groups, they are the primary victims of aging. To use the language of the theatre, they are the actors at front and center stage. But it must not be forgotten that the aged are not alone on that stage. Their children, neighbors, friends, work companions, and others are more than bit players; they are the significant others with whom the aged interact. The changing fortunes of older adults have meaningful consequences for the not so old and vice versa. The aged may be the primary victims of aging, but inevitably other age groups are in the "fallout" zone. The process of aging not only redefines the situations of older persons, it also redefines the situations of others with regard to them. It is these changing definitions of the situation that can oppress the nonaged as well as the aged.

To note this reciprocal relationship and to focus here on the oppression of the nonaged should not be read as an indictment of the aged. We are not blaming victims. We are indicating that aging is often indiscriminate in "making" victims. There are victims, other than older adults, whose

*John D. Donovan is a coauthor of this chapter.

problems are sometimes the products of aging and of the ways in which the aged react to their newly defined situations. Too often these other victims of old age are perceived only as causative agents of the problems of the elderly.

PERSPECTIVES: HISTORICAL AND DEMOGRAPHIC

In 1900, there were 3 million people in the United States who were age sixty-five and older. They represented 4 percent of the population. In mid-1975, there were 22.4 million older people or slightly more than 10 percent of the population.[1] In the late 1970s, middle-aged adults in the United States had increased possibilities of having at least one elderly parent. The middle years have increasingly found adults expected to be responsive to their children and to their parents; in earlier times, the middle-agers were more likely to be the oldest generation.

The uniqueness of the position of today's middle-aged population relative to the generation of their parents has more than demographic interest. The key fact is that older adults may not know from their own experience either the problems or the benefits which their longevity has added to the life situations of their middle-age sons and daughters. They experienced and lived through the stages of middle life, but during that phase most of them were not involved with the concerns of aged parents. Today's middle-aged adults may be at least partially burdened by the fact that their parents, through no fault of their own, did not experience what many middle-agers now live with—responsibilities simultaneously to the young and to the old.

This historical and demographic difference has additional meaning. Increased longevity means that for a longer period of time than ever before more people are in the roles of mother and father, grandmother and grandfather. This also means that more other people are for longer periods of time in the roles of sons and daughters, grandsons and granddaughters. The parent age eighty has been father or mother for fifty-five to sixty years. The middle-aged person has been son or daughter for that same fifty to sixty years. And at that age, they have been husband and father or wife and mother for thirty to thirty-five years. The implications of this prolongation of familial roles are varied, of course, but a distinctive point is that the longevity of individuals is paralleled by the longevity of kinship roles.

THE FAMILIES OF THE AGED

Changes in society over time have not lessened the importance of family relations in the lives of the elderly, especially in times of illness, difficulty or crisis, or on ceremonial occasions.[2] Perhaps more surprising is a finding by Ethel Shanas and her colleagues that 84 percent of older people living in the United States, England, and Denmark had at least one child living within 30 miles of them.[3] For the elderly in American society, affectional and supportive functions of the family emerge as crucial integrative mechanisms.[4] In fact, emotional support by adult children may have replaced day-to-day physical assistance for the elderly member in many families.[5] Daughters have been found to be involved in the day-to-day details of their parents' lives.[6] Sons, traditionally, have provided direct financial help when economic assistance has been needed. The strength of this support from sons and daughters becomes apparent when one looks at older adults who do not have it. Those elderly who have no family or close relationships tend to be overrepresented in the caseloads of social agencies.[7]

In a recent review of research concerning aging families, the conclusion was reached that these family relationships are the last social stronghold to which the elderly adhere[8] While the continuing involvement of the elderly with their families is regarded positively by society, the process of aging can be stressful not only for the person who is growing older but also for that person's family. Adult children are often aware of the tensions in their relationships with parents. They frequently perceive the tensions as something over which they have no control and which will only be changed by death.[9]

At the present time, there is little support for adult children of aged parents. The same ethic which considers the privacy of the family with young children as something to be guarded, results in little knowledge by outsiders of the qualitative workings of extended families which include the older grandparent and even great-grandparent generations. Adult children (even the term is incongruous) are often caught in the difficult situation of caring for an elderly parent and caring for their own children and even grandchildren. The caring, in the form of emotional and physical support, continues even if the generations do not share the same household. Because of the very real needs of the elderly for this support, their children's needs have been regarded as more expendable.

Unfortunately, the responsibility for elderly parents can be difficult for some adult children to handle. In addition to the need in some cases to provide physical care, the emotional responsibility can be even more formidable. Some older parents feel hurt and make others feel guilty if they are not included in every family affair, even if they are included most of the time.[10] Other older parents angrily refuse advice even when it is offered with the best of intentions. The adult child must sometimes tread a fine line between the role of adult, as a helper, chauffeur, and confidant, and the role of child, to whom the parent says, "mother knows best," and "don't tell me what to do."

For the increasing number of middle-aged women who are entering or reentering the labor force, the responsibility of day-to-day parental care or support can be even more difficult. These women may be attempting to offer supportive services to parents while, at the same time, holding down full-time jobs.[11] Being overburdened with demands made by their jobs, their spouses, their children, and even grandchildren, they may be less able to deal with the demands made by their parents. The difficulties for the middle-aged generation posed by the increasing dependence, affectional or physical, of the older generation can be significant. The financial, emotional, or other expenditures of the adult children can be more than occasional. As previously noted, many members of both the middle-aged and the older generations have had no role models on which to pattern their interactive behavior with each other. One result can be expectations and demands which are difficult to meet.

THE EXPRESSIVENESS OF INTERGENERATIONAL RELATIONSHIPS

Evidence and intuition suggest, not surprisingly, that adult children desire emotional support from their parents.[12] Older parents who are not very supportive emotionally of their children are likely to have been similarly unsupportive at earlier stages.[13] The children also would have been less involved in helping their parents at earlier stages. In addition, when children are young, they idolize their parents no matter how unsupportive they are: "I want to be just like you, Mommy." As the children go through puberty and young adulthood, they are more interested in being supported by their peers: "But Mom, everyone is doing it." However, once the children assume more responsibility toward their parents, they are likely to want reciprocity in the form of appreciation and recognition. The older parents' personality styles may not allow such behavior, with the result that the adult children may feel oppressed by their interactions with their older parents: "I break my back for her and all she does is criticize me." While the "problems" between parents and children may be life-long, they may be exacerbated by the difficulties that some parents and children face as they grow old together.

The fact that many older parents have less income, more chronic health problems, more friends who have died or moved away, and fewer choices regarding places to live suggests that they may have fewer assets with which to balance the greater resources of their middle-aged children.[14] When their personalities are incompatible with those of their children, the imbalance may be further heightened. However, at the same time, adult children may continue to look to their parents for the emotional support which they may or may not perceive that they received at earlier ages. In other words, in spite of the few aces in their hands, the parents still have a trump card. Adult children can still be controlled, consciously or unconsciously, through the withholding of emotional support, as well as through guilt mechanisms.

When they feel they are more crucial to their parents' well-being, when their parents are more dependent on them, the adult children may feel more oppressed and frustrated by a lack of positive emotional response from their parents.

In one situation, children who assume the responsibility for a parent may not have regarded themselves as the favorite child. They may take on the added burden in an attempt to gain their parent's favor. They are sometimes disappointed. Mother may say, "If only your brother lived closer, my life would be better." From their perspective, the older parents may not understand the resentment of their middle-aged children—the parents perceive themselves as behaving as they always have, which may be the problem.

In addition to the tensions that are sometimes exacerbated between parents and children as the parents grow old, the parent's aging can also create tensions between children. Again, a lack of good role models in our rapidly changing society and sometimes a lack of empathy by others who are in positions to be helpful may contribute to less than pleasant family relations. The sibling who lives closest to the parent may be expected by everyone to be the person most involved with that parent. That sibling may resent brothers and sisters for not being more helpful. These resentments may be intensified if the parent has always preferred another child.[15]

An older person who has to care for a handicapped spouse or an adult child who attends to an older parent can also be victims of a societal attitude which sometimes is less than supportive of their actions. An example of this type of nonsupport was evidenced in a day-care center for the elderly. An older man who needed some supervision following cancer surgery regularly attended the day center. There were some staff members who felt that his wife, who was a healthy older woman, should not be "dumping" him at the center. Her need for personal space was regarded as frivolous even though her ability to have some independence may have allowed her to continue to keep her husband at home in the evenings and on weekends.

If they see their children less than they would like, older people may blame the fact that they are old. In fact, that may be part of the problem. Another part may be the parents' personalities and lack of support for their children. These latter aspects were documented in Ann Lander's column.[16] Although the data are not the result of a scientifically effected research study, serious issues that receive great response after appearing in widely read publications are useful as indicators of some of the public's concerns. The letter which appeared in Ann Landers, follows:

Dear Ann Landers:

I just read the letter from the woman who suggested, as "The Perfect Gift" for a mother-in-law, a whole day alone with her son ...
That letter blew my mind. Please tell me, Ann, how can I get my husband to spend a day with his mother when I can't even get him to telephone her? ... The facts are these: My husband does not have very good feelings about his mother. She is a complainer, a nag, and a bore. She is an expert at laying on guilt. (You always seem too busy for me. Why don't you call? Why don't you include me?) ...

Our name is legion

(Ann's Reply)

Thank you for expressing you gut feelings. It was distressing for me to receive thousands of letters from daughters-in-law who said the same thing. What in the world is happening to families anyway? I wish I had some easy answers, but alas—I have none.

Unfortunately, the difficulties between mothers and daughters, mothers and sons, or fathers and their children do not dissipate as the family ages. In fact, the tensions are likely to increase if more demands are placed on the younger generation. These demands for physical care, living space, and for financial help can result in institutionalization sooner than other wise might be expected for the parent where intergenerational relationships have already been strained.[17]
The lack of opportunity for older people to have their needs met by anyone other than their families is, at least partly, the result of the older person's lack of involvement in two life areas which facilitate integration with the wider community: the labor force and child rearing. Society encourages, sometimes mandates, retirement, and biology necessitates withdrawal from child rearing. As a result, older people are forced to rely more and more on their families for both aid and social interaction. In addition, the lack of adequate societal resources for older people who need help to remain in the community, not only affects their lives but makes the lives of those who have traditionally been expected to offer that care, the daughters, more difficult. By the same token, as gerontologists and others try to improve the lives of the institutionalized elderly by pointing out the problems with institutions, families who must institutionalize a relative may feel even worse about such a decision than otherwise.
In summary, the oppression of old age in our society often is personally

realized for the first time when a parent grows old. As adult children feel guilty for not doing more, they may actually do less in an attempt to avoid unpleasant encounters and/or more guilt. A great deal of the responsibility for this unfortunate situation lies with societal attitudes toward aging and the aged, attitudes which can directly affect not only the life quality of the elderly but also that of the adult children.

ECONOMIC AND POLITICAL ASPECTS

Although the economic status of the elderly may not be as good as everyone would like, Social Security payments, the backbone of that status, have increased significantly in the past decade.[18] The program is essentially a transfer program in which current contributions by the employed finance current benefits to the aged, disabled, dependent children, and spouses. The proportion of employee income that is used to pay for the program's benefits has risen steadily. It is clear that without basic revisions in the financing of the program, those younger workers who are currently supporting those who are retired will receive less of a return themselves when they grow old. The declining birth rate and the growing proportion of older people have created this precarious situation.

The small number of people sixty-five and over who are wealthy are as eligible as anyone else for Social Security payments, provided that they contributed the required number of years to the program.[19] Wealthy individuals who have large assets are entitled to Social Security benefits even though they may not need the money from that source. In addition, Social Security benefits paid to the wealthy (and anyone else) are not taxable since the taxes were paid at the time the income was earned.

The ethic that everyone sixty-five and over is entitled to benefits as a "Senior Citizen," whether the benefits are Social Security or fare discounts on bus rides, may have been fostered to encourage participation by those needy individuals who would have shunned such programs if they were considered to be "welfare." Unfortunately, the discounts and benefits available to *all* those sixty-five and over may result in higher costs to other age groups. The elderly and their advocates encourage the view that old people are a heterogeneous, not a homogeneous, group. Such a view tends to humanize the elderly. However, some highly visible programs, such as Social Security, transportation discounts, and Medicare encourage the opposite view—that all people sixty-five and over, regardless of individual characteristics, deserve special monetary and other benefits. Other age groups may feel that the elderly want to have their cake and eat it too.

A further analysis of the Social Security system and related government programs, such as Medicare, suggests that a case can be made that the aged get more from these programs than they have, in an actuarial sense, paid in. Is this fair? Is it unfair to some of those in the labor force who are in much worse shape economically than some of the aged who are recipients? Older people who are eligible for Medicare are much better off than the temporary or part-time worker, often female, who has the responsibility of providing health care for herself and family. Health insurance at a reasonable cost is often unavailable to such workers. An individual who requires family health insurance coverage and who does not have access to group medical coverage can be forced to pay a substantial percent of income each month for a good inclusive insurance plan. Premiums of seventy dollars to one hundred dollars per month are not unusual for good nongroup coverage. The health costs of the aged may be a substantial factor in the high premiums that others are forced to pay for adequate health insurance.

In one very basic sense, the argument that the aged are exploited in our society is linked to the conclusion that the aged are not getting their fair share of what our society produces. The realization that resources are finite necessitates allocating them among all needy groups in society. In response to those who say the elderly are not getting enough, some might ask how to determine how much would be enough?[20] Ivan Illich, a social critic, suggests that regarding health care, the elderly are "insatiable."[21] We can also raise other questions, such as what are some of the problems we might run into in any effort to obtain the "fair" distribution which critics of the present distribution advocate. When we give to the aged, it must come from someone. Is it possible that under most existing transfer proposals, it would come in large measure from other segments of the population which also include needy persons? If greater taxes were placed on working individuals to support the older population more adequately, might there be serious disincentive effects on worker productivity? The aged might end up getting a larger share of a smaller pie. The question of whether they would then be better or worse off remains.

A related issue that is often discussed when the economics of aging are considered is whether or not the aged are a significant political force. Is there truth to political scientist and gerontologist Robert Binstock's argument that there is no aging vote in the sense that there is a labor vote?[22] Or do the aged have a disproportionate influence on the political process in this country? Does it make any difference that the older age categories are disporportionately represented among judges, senators, and congressional representatives? Is there any age-related political bias in government policy which can be attributed to the seniority system, particularly in Congress? As the median age of the population continues to increase, will there be a shift toward more conservative policies?

There is some evidence that each generation is more liberal overall than its predecessor.[23] Rather than a change with age toward conservatism, there is a certain stability. The cohort born in 1925 is likely to have always been less liberal overall than the cohort born in 1950. However, as the median age of the population advances, it can be expected that there will be a trend toward conservatism, not because people become more conservative as they age, but because there will be more people who are more conservative than those following them. An interesting report of a political movement of older people in Arizona suggests some potential ramifications of the rise in the median age. It offers evidence of, at least, a limited way in which older people can become an effective political force.[24]

The "Adults Only Movement" in Arizona was successful in directly influencing the passage of legislation to legalize exclusively adult-only communities in that state. Is it fair to families with children to deny them the opportunity to live where they choose? Why should adults with children support programs for the elderly, when it appears that some of the elderly would not support their freedom to live where they choose?

When older people talk about their desires to live within a fairly homogeneous milieu, whether age-integrated or not, it sounds very positive. But are they really expressing their desire to keep everyone who is not like themselves, white or black, rich or poor, Italian or Chinese, and so on away from them? There is evidence, which we have already discussed in the previous chapter on crime, that the high degree of fear of crime which is expressed by many of the elderly may really be a fear of changing social conditions.[25] Among white elderly this may mean a fear of having blacks, even older blacks from whom they have little to fear on a personal level, move into their neighborhoods. There are data which suggest that elderly whites are bothered by the movement of elderly blacks into their neighborhoods.[26]

CONCLUSION

If we are to humanize the elderly, if we are to see them with their individual characteristics, then we must expect to find that some of those characteristics are less desirable than others. If we have no trouble believing that other age groups contain both nice and not so nice people, both prejudiced and unprejudiced people, then the fact that the elderly have a similar mix should not be surprising. Stereotypes, whether they are positive or negative, are only that. The real picture is always more complex and sometimes much more interesting.

Whether they have nice or not so nice personalities, the aged, typically, suffer a substantial reduction in income after retirement relative to their preretirement income. The average retirement income is about 50 percent of preretirement income.[27] In addition, for many of those who have been retired several years, there is an increasing gap as the overall standard of living continues to rise. In such a situation, it should not surprise us to find that people do what they can to reduce this gap. Since the option of reducing the gap through labor force participation usually does not exist, either because of discrimination against hiring older people or health problems which preclude a return to employment, efforts to obtain favors, money, and the like from other sources, including discount programs and their children, become one of the few viable strategies. Although there are older people who exploit and oppress others by such demands, we can also ask, is it fair to blame them when there are virtually no alternatives?

A more equitable solution, particularly for those who feel oppressed and exploited by the aged, is for the burden to be shared more evenly by the more affluent members of society. The families of the needy elderly, some of whom may be needy themselves, should not have to bear the brunt of practices which result in the elderly's need to be demanding. Where the personality of the elderly person is the problem, children may need to learn to do their best and not to feel guilty that they cannot be all things to their parents, anymore than parents, of any age, can be all things to their children.

On balance, it appears that the aged are more often discriminated against, oppressed, victimized, and exploited by those who have control over economic and other resources than they are the perpetrators of the injustice. Regarding the issues of crime, living environments (especially nursing homes), health care, work, and retirement, the elderly poor are more likely to experience difficulties beyond what might occur simply because of age-induced changes in physiology.

Older people who have low, but what they consider to be adequate, incomes in retirement, are forced to live with the possibility that they may face destitution if they require specialized care in older age. Some families of older people also face the prospect of economic hardship should one of their parents require individual and extensive care particularly if public assistance is undesirable or unavailable—community–based care programs are often reimbursable only for Medicaid recipients. Those older people who have low incomes above the much lower Medicaid eligibility standards may find that their only recourse when some help with community living is required is to seek help from their families. Another alternative is to enter a nursing home, where assets will quickly be devoured with consequent eligibility for Medicaid assistance.

White women have, as a result of their longer life expectancy—a fact more often regarded positively than negatively—more opportunities to become poor, regardless of their earlier situations. Advocates of the traditional social structure who encouraged, even demanded, the economic dependence of women on men have enhanced the possibilities for financially-based problems in the female's later years. Outliving their husbands, these women must become independent at a time when the primary avenues for independence, a career or a husband, are no longer viable options. Those minority group members who survive into advanced age continue to be worse off, regarding finances, than other subgroups. They might, more appropriately, be referred to as survictims than survivors.

The traditional, sexual attractiveness criteria—youthful beauty for women and some form of power for men—practically insures the inability of aging people, particularly aging women, to meet those standards. Identity as male or female, identity which is fostered from birth, is gradually considered unimportant by members of society as a person ages. For some of the aging, the adaptation to these changing values and standards may be difficult to accept with grace and without resentment. Rather than the aging and the aged being viewed as victims, some may regard them as malcontents.

The knowledge that death is inevitable is probably oppressive for everyone at some time in their lives. Traditional medical practices which have fostered the isolation of the dying patient from others may have contributed to increasing the oppression associated with the actual death experience. Since the majority of people in the United States who die are over sixty-five years of age, the aging and the aged have greater possibilities for incurring injustices associated with the dying experience. Furthermore, cultural traditions which establish the need for expensive funerals can be burdensome for the survivors of the deceased, particularly when their own financial situations are less than perfect. The psychological vulnerability of people in times of great grief allows them to be exploited by unscrupulous members of the funeral industry.

Even if economic conditions were improved for the aged, even if a quality continuum of health care became a right and not a privilege, even if standards of attractiveness were less uni-dimensional for each sex, and even if attitudes toward aging were improved, old age would probably not be anyone's preferred state. However, it might be less of a cause for anxiety and fear than it can be at present.

The recapturing of youth, with its fantasy of endless possibilities, will never be a reality. However, the prospects of an older age with alternatives which exist within the security of the knowledge that adequate, quality help is available when needed is a real possibility. Some steps toward this goal have started in the past few years. The challenge for all of us as we grow old is to maintain the momentum that has begun.

Notes

1. See the United States Senate Special Committee on Aging's report, "Every Tenth American" (1977).
2. See Sussman and Burchinal (1962).
3. See Shanas, Townsend, Wedderburn, Friis, Milhøj, and Stehouwer (1968).
4. See Puner (1974).

5. See Sussman and Burchinal (1962).
6. See Townsend (1957) and Lopata (1973). Lopata notes the special importance of the widowed mother/adult daughter relationship.
7. See Puner (1974).
8. See Troll (1971) for an excellent review of research concerning aging families; see also Sussman (1976).
9. See Johnson (1978).
10. Many of these types of issues were brought out in a workshop for adult children which one of us directed.
11. See Treas (1977).
12. See Johnson (1979).
13. The continuity of personality in old age would lead one to this conclusion. See Neugarten, Havinghurst, and Tobin (1968).
14. See Dowd (1975) and Johnson (1978).
15. See Grollman and Grollman (1978) for a very readable informative book designed for adult children. Other books include Silverstone and Hyman (1976) and Otten and Shelley (1976).
16. This particular Ann Landers column appeared in the *The Boston Evening Globe* on Wednesday, October 12, 1977, p. 55.
17. See Brody (1966).
18. See Schulz (1976).
19. See Schulz (1976:24). He reports that a Social Security Administration survey found that in 1967, 13 percent of elderly couples and 5 percent of elderly unrelated individuals had financial assets of $20,000 or more.
20. Herb Shore (1977) writes about the needs of older Americans.
21. See Illich (1977).
22. See Binstock (1972).
23. See Glenn (1974).
24. See Anderson and Anderson (1978).
25. See Furstenberg (1971).
26. See Sterne, Phillips, and Rabushka (1974).
27. See Atchley (1976).

References

Anderson, William A., and Norma D. Anderson, "The Politics of Age Exclusion." *Gerontologist* 18(1), 1978:6–12.

Atchley, Robert C., *The Social Forces of Later Life, 2nd ed.* Belmont, Calif.: Wadsworth, 1976.

Binstock, Robert H., "Interest Group Liberalism and the Politics of Aging." *Gerontologist* 12, 1972: 265–280.

Brody, Elaine, "The Aging Family." *Gerontologist* 6, 1966: 201–206.

Dowd, James, J., "Aging as Exchange: A Preface to Theory." *Journal of Gerontology* 30, 1975: 584–594.

Furstenberg, Frank J., "Public Reaction to Crime in the Streets." *American Scholar* 51, 1971: 601–610.

Glenn, Norval D., "Age and Conservatism." In Frederick R. Eisele (ed.), *Political Consequences of Aging*, p. 176–186. Philadelphia: American Academy of Political and Social Science, 1974

Grollman, Earl A., and Sharon Hya Grollman, *Caring for Your Aged Parents.* Boston· *Beacon Press,* 1978.

Illich, Ivan, *Medical Nemesis.* New York: Bantam, 1977.

Johnson, Elizabeth S., " 'Good' Relationships between Older Mothers and Their Daughters: A Causal Model." *Gerontologist* 18(3), 1978: 301–306.

Johnson, Elizabeth S. "Role Expectations and Role Realities of Older Mothers and Their Daughters." Unpublished paper. Kingston, R.I.: U.R.I. Program in Gerontology, 1979.

Lopata, Helen Z., *Widowhood in an American City.* Cambridge, Mass.: Schenkman, 1973.

Neugarten, Bernice L., Robert J. Havighurst, and Sheldon S. Tobin, "Personality and Patterns of Aging." In Bernice L. Neugarten (ed.), *Middle Age and Aging,* p. 173–177. Chicago: University of Chicago Press, 1968.

Otten, Jane, and Florence D. Shelley, *When Your Parents Grow Old.* New York: Signet, 1976.

Puner, Martin, *To the Good Long Life: What We Know about Growing Old.* New York: Universe Books, 1974.

Schulz, James J., *The Economics of Aging.* Belmont, Calif.: Wadsworth, 1976.

Shanas, Ethel, Peter Townsend, Dorothy Wedderburn, Henning Friis, Poul Milhøj, and Jan Stehouwer, *Old People in Three Industrial Societies.* New York: Atherton, 1968.

Shore, Herbert A., "A Plea from the Older Individual." In Richard A. Kalish (ed.) *The Later Years,* p. 11–14. Monterey, Calif.: Brooks/Cole, 1977.

Silverstone, Barbara, and Helen K. Hyman, *You and Your Aging Parent.* New York: Pantheon, 1976.

Sterne, Richard S., James E. Phillips, and Alvin Rabushka, *The Urban Elderly Poor.* Lexington, Mass.: Heath, 1974.

Sussman, Marvin B., "The Family Life of Old People." In E. Shanas and R. Binstock (ed.) *Handbook of Aging and the Social Sciences,* pp. 218–243. New York: Van Nostrand, 1976.

Sussman, Marvin B., and Lee Burchinal, "Kin Family Network: Unheralded Structure in Current Conceptualizations of Family Functioning." *Marriage and Family Living* 24, 1962: 231–240.

Townsend, Peter, *The Family Life of Old People.* Routledge and Kegan, Paul. London, 1957.

Treas, Judith, "Family Support Systems for the Aged: Some Social and Demographic Considerations." *Gerontologist* 17, 1977: 486–491.

Troll, Lilian E., "The Family of Later Life: A Decade Review." *Marriage and Family Living* 33, 1971: 263–290.

NAME INDEX

SUBJECT INDEX